Language and Literacy

for the

New Millennium

MIC LIBRARY
WITHDRAWN FROM STOCK

EDITORS:
Gerry Shiel
Ursula Ní Dhálaigh
Eithne Kennedy

READING ASSOCIATION OF IRELAND

Published by
Reading Association of Ireland
c/o Educational Research Centre
St Patrick's College
Drumcondra, Dublin 9

© Reading Association of Ireland, 2000

ISBN:0-9526511-2-2

Editors: Gerry Shiel, Ursula Ní Dhálaigh, Eithne Kennedy
Design: Mark Loughran, Identikit
Cover Design: Mark Loughran, Identikit
Origination: Hilary Walshe

Printed in the Republic of Ireland by e-print, Dublin

CONTENTS

PREFACE v

SECTION 1: ORAL LANGUAGE

Language in the Revised Primary School Curriculum 3
Anne McGough

Irish as a Second Language in the Gaeltacht: Bringing Theory to
the Practice 15
Maire Mhic Mhathúna and Frances Uí Chinnéide

Oral Language Development in the Early Years at School 30
Liz Dunphy

SECTION 2: READING

Morality as an Ideology in Children's Fiction – Celebrating
Children's Literature in Ireland 43
Frank Flannagan and Áine Cregan

Multiple Curricula Approach for Developing Reading
Comprehension with Low-Achieving Readers 59
Timothy Blair

Folk and Fairy Tales in Sanctioned Reading Schemes in Primary
Schools: A Review 67
Mary Shine Thompson

Language Play and Vocabulary Development in the Primary
School 87
George Hunt

Perspectives on Learning Support Policy and Practice in Irish
Schools: The Urgency of a Whole-School Initiative 108
Antóin Ó Dubhghaill

Alder, Froebel and Reading Pedagogy: A Spirituality of Children's
Literacy 122
David Carey and Séan Griffin

Reading in Romanian Schools: New Directions 151
Adela-Luminita Rogojinaru

SECTION 3: WRITING

Undergraduate Academic Writing: An Analysis of Errors and
Weaknesses in Syntax, Lexis, Style and Structure. 167
Anne O'Keeffe

Developing Self-Esteem Through Writing Activities: A Unit of Work
for Pupils with Learning Difficulties at Senior Primary Level. . . 187
Finian O'Shea

Write Out of This World – The Process and the Product 195
Mary Meaney

Writing in the Revised English Language Curriculum for Primary
Schools: Are Teachers Ready? 212
Fidelma Healy-Eames

SECTION 4: ASSESSMENT

Measuring Reading in the New Millennium: The Pennsylvania
Reading Assessment 231
Jeanne S. Cranks

Assessing Children's Oral Language 243
Gerry Shiel

PREFACE

Much has happened since the Reading Association of Ireland published its last volume, *Developing Language and Literacy: The Role of the Teacher,* in 1998. A revised *English Language Primary School Curriculum* has been launched and all primary teachers have received some inservice training in the implementation of this curriculum. A new English Leaving Certificate Syllabus has been implemented in second-level schools. The White Paper on Adult Education, *Learning for Life*, has been published. And the National Reading Initiative has been launched with the objective of raising the awareness of the general public regarding the importance of reading.

The current volume, *Language and Literacy for the New Millennium*, is a compilation of papers delivered at recent conferences and seminars of the Reading Association of Ireland. In addition to reflecting on some of the changes that have occurred recently, the papers point to the way forward in four related areas – oral language, reading, writing and assessment of literacy.

An important feature of the revised primary curricula for English and Irish is the strong emphasis on the development of oral language. This emphasis is reflected in the current volume where no fewer than three articles deal with the development of listening and spekaing skills. In her article, 'Language in the Revised Primary School Curriculum', Anne McGough emphasises the importance engaging children in 'the kind of talk which goes beyond everyday communications in the classroom', in order to provide them with 'maximum cognitive challenge' from an early stage. In addition to focusing on acquisition of language as a system, she stresses the important role of language in developing pupils' thinking skills, and in promoting emotional and imaginative development. In her article on 'Oral Language Development in the Early Years at School', Liz Dunphy suggests a number of strategies for engaging pupils in oral language work, and illustrates how pair work can be used to engage children in exploring story. Strategies such as pair work are relevant to the implementation of the revised *English Language Primary School Curriculum* and the revised curricula in other subjects as well. The article, 'Irish as a Second Language: Bringing Theory to Practice', by Máire Mhic Mhathúna and Frances Uí Chinnéide, describes a programme offered by the Dublin Institute of Technology to language assistants (tutors) working with children in Gaeltacht schools for whom Irish is a second language. The comprehensive nature of the course that was offered, and the impact it had on the work of the language assistants, have implications for improving oral language instruction in a range of settings where children encounter difficulties.

The articles in the second section of the volume deal with the teaching of reading, though several are also relevant to oral language and writing. Three articles deal with issues relating to literature for children. In 'Morality as an Ideology in Children's Fiction – Celebrating Children's Literature in Ireland', Frank Flannagan and Áine Cregan reflect on the role of story in children's development and examine, in particular, how children's moral development can be shaped by what they read. In a related article, 'Folk and Fairly Tales in Sanctioned Reading Schemes in Primary Schools', Mary Shine Thompson describes the different types of story that may be found in sanctioned English reading schemes, and argues that some stories may not impart the Christian standards implied in curriculum documents and official statements. David Carey and Seán Griffin, in their article, 'Adler , Froebel and Reading Pedagogy: A Spirituality of Children's Literacy', apply a philosophy of spirituality espoused by Adler and Froebel to the training of teachers and to the development of children's understanding of stories – an understanding that goes beyond basic comprehension, yet can be nourished by sensitive teachers.

Two articles deal with the teaching of basic elements of the reading process. George Hunt, in 'Language Play and Vocabulary Development in the Primary School', presents ten strategies for developing children's knowledge of word meanings. A feature of the strategies is their generative nature – after children learn a strategy, they can apply it to acquiring new words in different contexts or extending their understanding of words already encountered. Throughout the article, George stresses the need to develop an 'attitude of curiosity towards words' in children and to encourage 'spontaneous play with language'. In 'A Multiple Curricula Approach for Developing Comprehension with Low-Achieving Readers', Timothy Blair stresses the need for teachers to allocate time to the development of reading comprehension, and the need to teach children how to engage in various comprehension processes including interpretative comprehension, critical comprehension, strategic comprehension and content subject comprehension.

Timothy emphasises the importance of the dialogue that occurs between teacher and pupils during comprehension development.

Antóin Ó Dubhghaill's article, 'Perspectives on Learning Support Policy and Practice in Irish Schools: The Urgency of a Whole-School Initiative' points to serious difficulties with the provision of learning support (formerly 'remedial education') in primary and post-primary schools. While some progress has been made at primary level in addressing these difficulties with the recent publication of new *Learning-Support Guidelines* by the Department of Education and Science, attention now needs to be given to the effective implementation of the *Guidelines*. In addition, there is a need to address the difficulties that arise in implementing learning support programmes in post-primary schools. Antóin's proposal for a whole-school approach to addressing learning difficulties is equally relevant at both primary and post-primary levels, though schools may need assistance in implementing such an approach. In her article, 'Reading in Romanian Schools: New Directions', Adela-Lumina Rogojinaru also deals with the issues of pedagogical and organisational change. While the gist of her article is largely positive, she identifies potential impediments to progress including the inclusion of children's literature as merely an optional element of the language curriculum at primary and post-primary levels. In common with several of the Irish authors in this volume, Adela dwells on the importance of empowering teachers to implement change through the provision of appropriate inservice training.

Two of the four articles on writing deal primarily with instructional issues. In 'Developing Self-esteem through Writing Activities: A Unit of Work for Pupils with Learning Difficulties at the Senior Primary Level', Finian O'Shea illustrates how children's writing can be developed by providing a range of writing activities that focus on various aspects of children's own lives. The activities are consistent with the thinking underlying the teaching of writing in the *English Language Primary School Curriculum*, and allow for in-depth interaction between teacher and pupils, and between pupils themselves. Among the formats that are suggested are writing logs, diaries and letters. In her article, 'Write Out of This World – The Process and the Product', Mary Meaney describes a writing programme she implemented in a combined second-third class, and shows how the publication of a book based on the programme resulted in high levels of motivation among pupils, and a high level of writing quality. The article illustrates how the programme again capitalised on pupils' own interests and feelings.

The remaining articles on writing deal with the quality of undergraduate academic writing, and with the teaching of writing in schools. In 'Undergraduate Academic Writing: An Analysis of Errors and Weaknesses and Syntax, Lexis, Style and Structure', Anne O'Keeffe examines the errors made by undergraduate students as they engage in writing non-fiction texts. While some of the errors are quite humorous, others are quite basic, and raise issues about the teaching of writing in primary and post-primary schools, and the strategies schools may need to implement to facilitate pupils' ability to meet the demands of academic writing in third-level institutions and in real life contexts. In 'Writing in the Revised English Language Curriculum for Primary Schoos: Are Teachers Ready?', Fidelma Healy-Eames raises concerns about the readiness of teachers to embrace the process-based approach to writing that is embedded in the revised curriculum. While teachers in her study were in favour of meaning-based approaches to teaching writing that capitalised on links between oral language and writing, they experienced difficulties in implementing such approaches in their classrooms. At the conclusion of the article, Healy-Eames provides four recommendations that are relevant in the context of implementing the writing element of the revised *English Language Primary School Curriculum*, and in the context of more general efforts to improve the quantity and quality of children's writing.

The final two articles in this volume deal with assessment. The first, 'Measuring Reading in the New Millennium: The Pennsylvania Reading Assessment' by Jeanne Cranks, is interesting from several perspectives. First, in the context of the forthcoming publication of the report on *The 1998 National Assessment of English Reading*, it is interesting to observe how Pennsylvania implements a standards-based approach to state-level assessment that specifies 'what a student should know and be able to do at a specified grade level'. While the framework underpinning the Pennsylvania reading assessment is quite similar to that used in our own national assessment of reading in fifth class, the purposes of the assessment are somewhat different. Second, in the context of concerns about the quality of children's writing, the work being undertaken in Pennsylvania suggests that a writing assessment might be implemented in parallel with our national reading assessment, without undue difficulty.

The second article dealing with assessment, 'Assessing Children's Oral Language' by Gerry Shiel, outlines the difficulties that arise in assessing the performance of pupils in oral language and provides suggestions for assessing language competence in the context of everyday classroom activities. The suggestions, which are in line with the approach to assessment put forward in the revised English Language Primary School Curriculum, enable teachers to observe critical features of pupils' development in speaking and listening, and to maintain records of performance over time. The suggestions for engaging pupils in assessing their own oral language development may be of particular interest to teachers of pupils in the senior primary classes.

We wish to thank the authors who contributed to this volume for their patience and understanding during the editing process. We are grateful to Thomas Kellaghan, Director of the Educational Research Centre, for his support, and to Hilary Walshe, also of the Centre, for her work in typesetting this document and incorporating the many edits. We wish to acknowledge the help of Bernadette McHugh and her colleagues at the National Reading Initiative. Finally, we wish to express our appreciation to our colleagues on the Executive Committee of the Reading Association of Ireland for their support and encouragement.

Gerry Shiel
Ursula Ní Dhálaigh
Eithne Kennedy
September 2000

Funding for this publication was provided by the In-career Development Unit, which is co-funded by the Department of Education and Science and the European Social Fund, and by the National Development Plan 2000-2006, through Department of Education and Science and the National Reading Initiative.

SECTION 1

Oral Language

Language in the Revised Primary School Curriculum*

. . . .

Anne McGough
Special Education Dept.
St. Patrick's College, Dublin

It is a significant advance in Irish primary education that the spoken word has now been recognised as a legitimate area for teaching and learning in our schools. All of us are aware of the commitment of schools to the written aspects of language. In particular, we are acutely conscious of the time and energy devoted to bringing children to literacy. Teachers are expected to teach children to read and there is no question as to the relevance and legitimacy of the task. Indeed, the ability to bring children to literacy is probably one of the defining characteristics of the teaching role.

However, we have only recently come to consider and to attempt to define our role in developing children's oral language competence. It seems that until now in mainstream education, in planning and delivering curricula, we have taken for granted that the spoken word would be in place. We have assumed that curricula and teaching need not be concerned with developing oral language and we have defined the teaching role mainly in terms of the written aspects of language.

*Based on a keynote address delivered at the Spring Seminar of the Reading Association of Ireland, Dublin, March 20, 1999

It seems to me that these assumptions have had serious consequences for our conduct as educators. Firstly and most obviously, we simply have not focused on developing children's oral language competence in the way that we should have done. Lacking this focus, we have neglected related forms of knowing which are given expression through oral language. So, we have not exploited the roles of play and drama in learning, and we have not given sufficient attention to poetry, song and story throughout the curriculum. Perhaps the lack of focus on oral language as a symbolic system has also contributed to the low priority given to other forms of representation as in the visual arts, music and dance.

The absence of a language curriculum has also contributed to our slow growth in awareness and understanding of the role of language in learning. A further consequence has been that teachers have not been given the opportunities to develop the knowledge and expertise necessary to assess children's levels of difficulties in relation to oral language competence. Obviously, in circumstances where we are not habitually assessing needs, planning and teaching programmes and evaluating progress for children whose language is in the normal range of development, we do not then have a barometer against which to measure children's difficulties.

The teachers who have most experience of language and communication are those who work with children who have learning difficulties and disabilities. Of course many of these teachers work in special situations and have little access to their mainstream colleagues. Within mainstream settings, remedial teachers will have expertise in oral language teaching and learning but until now, without a specific focus on language learning in the mainstream curriculum, mainstream teachers may not have harnessed this expertise for their general teaching, perhaps taking the view that language teaching is required only when there is a difficulty with language learning.

Happily we are now in the process of changing this perception and shifting our focus to a recognition of the need for a language curriculum for all children. In this context I would like to discuss the content of the language curriculum as it is presented to us in the revised *English Language Primary School Curriculum* (Ireland, 1999a, 1999b) and in so doing I will attempt to identify its pedagogic principles and the kinds of practice it will require.

The Role of Language in Learning

In discussing content, we need to consider the dual or twofold nature of language. That is, language is both a system to be acquired and a resource, or tool which promotes and supports other crucial areas of learning so that, in learning language, children are also learning through language. The language curriculum needs to acknowledge both of these aspects of language and teachers need to be knowledgeable in relation to both. Firstly, let us consider the notion of language as a system to be acquired.

Learning language as a system. Language is a meaning system. It carries with it knowledge and understanding of the culture and society into which the child is born. So, a major objective of schooling must be mastery of the language of the culture, as without this, children are denied further access to that culture and they are denied command of the instrument which will give them power and influence in determining their own roles within that culture and society. A more specific way of making this argument is to look at the relationship between language competence and school achievement. School achievement continues to be one of the major factors in determining an individual's chances for advancement within a society (Hannan & Ó Riain, 1993; NESC, 1997). School failure has been identified as the most obvious personal characteristic of those who are described as being disadvantaged within a society (Kellaghan et al., 1995; Bryant & Ramey, 1987; Schweinhart et al., 1993). Children's knowledge of language, their understanding of its communicative function, and their orientation towards particular kinds of language use are major determinants of their abilities to achieve in school (Tough, 1977). School learning requires children to receive, to create and to communicate meanings in ever richer, more complex and more diverse ways. This is apparent in the levels of language competence required to master the knowledge content of the curriculum and also in the ways in which children are required to display that knowledge almost always in terms of written or spoken language. Where differences occur between children's oral language performances on school learning tasks, these differences are related to children's levels of competence in using language to support and to promote complex levels of thinking as in considering propositions, creating imaginary situations, solving problems, reasoning and making judgements (Tough, 1977). Obviously these behaviours are crucial to school learning and they are promoted or inhibited to the extent that children can exploit the potential of language in developing them. So, my point again is that mastery of the language system must be a major objective of schooling.

Language as a resource for learning. Equally, as I have said, we must develop children's use of language as a resource for learning. Here a principal concern is the relationship between language and cognitive development or language and the life of the mind. This relationship turns on the way in which language contributes to and influences our abilities to formulate, clarify and communicate ideas and on the role of language in the development of memory and perception. Equally, language contributes to the imaginative life of the mind. The relationship between language and cognition is also apparent in the learning behaviours I have outlined above. A second consideration is the role of language in interpreting and articulating children's personal, social and emotional experience. And of course, at a more specific level, we are concerned with the relationship between language and literacy.

So, language teaching is a critical concern. Schools must teach children the language of their culture while simultaneously teaching them to use that language to help to achieve their potential within that culture. Language is the fundamental means by which children come to know themselves and their relationship with the world, by which they acquire a body of knowledge, become critical thinkers, and develop imaginative and creative minds. During the primary school years, concern for oral language development should be at the heart of every teaching / learning encounter.

Language and Curriculum

Having presented a brief rationale for a language curriculum, I would like to relate some of these perspectives to the language curriculum as presented to us in the revised *English Language Primary School Curriculum*. Here the body of content is presented as four strands, or four areas of learning:
(i)   Receptiveness to language
(ii)   Competence and confidence in using language
(iii) Developing cognitive abilities through language
(iv) Emotional and imaginative development through language.
It seems possible to consider the first two of these strands as relating to language as a system to be acquired, while the second two relate to the role of language in the key areas of cognition, emotion and imagination. These are to be developed through language, so language is to be a resource. Of course, in describing the dual nature of language as system and resource, I am simply using an academic construct by way of identifying the nature of the learning involved. I am not suggesting that children learn language in a sequence of two stages, first acquiring it and then using it as a tool. Rather, as we know, both aspects of the learning proceed in tandem. Language and language use serve each other in a kind of benign circle, so that, having language, children use it to do things or to get things done and, in using it, they expand and develop their knowledge of it.

Keeping these strands in mind, I would like now to look in some detail at the relationship between system and resource. How do we enable children to become receptive to language and what do children have to know in order to achieve competence and confidence in using language? To begin, it may be helpful to describe the elements of the language system and to identify them as they are expressed in terms of learning outcomes in the curriculum document.

Elements of language. From a psycholinguistics perspective, the elements of language are described as phonology, grammar, semantics and pragmatics. *Phonology* is described as the sound system of a language. It includes the ways in which individual sounds within words combine to make the sound of the word. It also refers to intonation patterns in a language and how and where we lay stress and emphasis in articulating sentences. *Grammar* has to do with the structure of our sentences and includes word order, ways of combining sentences, and rules relating to use and formation of tense. *Semantics* refers to the meaning content of our talk, literally the words and phrases we choose to carry through the meaning we wish to convey. *Pragmatics* refers to the ways in which we use language as social beings, changing our topic, our tone, the whole nature of our conversation according as the context demands. So, we are required to speak differently in different situations.

Once again language is presented here in terms of these separate elements as a means only of recognising the areas of learning involved. In reality, children acquire them in an integrated way, so that in any one utterance we can see how words carrying semantic meaning are combined in grammatical structures and used for specific purposes in particular situations. Indeed this integration of content, form and use is recognised in the design of the curriculum strands. For example, in the learning outcomes for infants in the Receptiveness to Language strand, one requirement is that the child should be enabled to listen to a story or description and respond to it. Here, at a receptive level, the child is experiencing language use in the form of recall of story, the semantic content is carried through in the particular words and phrases appropriate to that story and the teacher employs the specific tense and sentence structures to match the semantic content.

A quibble with this particular learning outcome is that the requirement to respond is a rather vague one. It would be very much in order and should be expected under the second strand, Competence and Confidence in using Language, to expect the level of response to include: the child will be enabled – (i) to recall the story in correct sequence, naming the characters and using the appropriate nouns and adjectives; and (ii) to speculate about their feelings and propose a different outcome. Under the fourth strand, Emotional and Imaginative development, children in the infant classes are expected to create and tell stories but again there is no indication of the level of complexity required.

These statements of learning outcomes fall short in terms of the need for maximum challenge in relation to language content, form and use in the early years of primary schooling. Many teachers are already seeking and getting more complex levels of response from their infant classes. It is to be hoped that a process of revision will address the possibility that we have underestimated the strengths and the needs of early learners and the relevance and importance of an early years language curriculum.

One of the most critical determinants of children's abilities to create and communicate meaning will be their habitual use of vocabulary and their facility in combining what needs to be a rich store of words in sentences which convey not simple, everyday messages but complex meanings reflecting school learning. The child's store of words is a reasonable barometer of that child's pool of meaning and that pool needs to be deep and rich. In the revised edition of his book of essays entitled *Language and Silence*, George Steiner (1985) says that civilisation and society as we know them are the product of interactions between word and world. His view is that all of human meaning derives from language. We capture, construct and plan meaning in words. In Steiner's expression, 'our history is made of the past tense, spoken or written. Our utopias lie in the future of the verb' (p.12).

Of course knowledge and use of words is inextricably linked to cognitive development. By naming objects, the child is classifying the components of the physical world, extracting principles, imposing structure. For the young child learning language, words are mapped on to experiences naming them and capturing them for reference against other words, conjuring yet other experiences. This is the beginning of a process through which the child moves to the point where the word itself represents the experience and the child achieves increasing levels of independence from the immediate felt experience of the concrete world. So, as Bruner (1975) puts it, in learning language, the child is simultaneously delineating concepts and growing in awareness of the representational function of language.

Language competence. Jerome Bruner is one of the theorists who has taught us most about the role of language in thinking In a paper entitled *Language as an Instrument of Thought* (1975), he identifies three kinds of language competence – linguistic, communicative and analytic. These have relevance to the curriculum strand entitled Competence and Confidence in Using Language. In discussing linguistic competence, Bruner (1983) agrees with Noam Chomsky that as human beings we do have an innate capacity to acquire speech, that is, to achieve linguistic competence. Indeed in all cases where development follows normal patterns, children do achieve speech. However, we know that communicative and analytic competence are closely connected to adult/child interaction and that the quality of that interaction will influence the nature of these competencies. The curriculum makes good provision for these levels of language learning at the senior end of the school. Learning outcomes relating to communicative and analytic competence are included throughout all four strands for the senior classes.

The role of the teacher. Teachers will have a crucial role to play in developing communicative and analytic competencies and will have to do this by structuring small group contexts where teachers and children can engage in the kind of talk which goes beyond the everyday communications of the classroom. Analytic competence requires children to think about propositions, employing strategies of mind to explain behaviour, describe a problem, suggest solutions or predict outcomes. Bruner suggests that it is this kind of learning behaviour which eventually determines children's educational fate. The foundations for this kind of competence are laid in essential ways from the earliest stages of language development. So, it is essential that the language curriculum in the primary school presents maximum cognitive challenge to children and that this challenge begins in the infant classes.

Language and cognitive development. From that perspective, concerns arise again in relation to the statements of learning outcomes for language and cognition for the early years, that is, for the infant and first and second classes. Again in this area of content the statements underestimate children's abilities, allowing them to underachieve. Equally, they deny the need to engage children in the specific forms of language use which will initiate them into particular patterns of learning behaviour, helping them to develop the particular styles of thinking and talking necessary to the kinds of learning required at senior level; the kinds of learning outlined above. In the strand on Developing Cognitive Abilities through Language, the most challenging demand for the infant years is that children should be enabled to discuss different, possible solutions to simple problems. Not until the first and second classes are they expected to report, to explain, to enquire, to persuade and not until the third and fourth classes are they expected to discuss cause and effects in relation to processes and events and predict possible outcomes.

We know about the importance of thinking styles from the work of Vygotsky and from those who have interpreted him for us including Joan Tough, Jerome Bruner, Gorden Wells. Children develop their thinking styles through particular kinds of talk – talk which includes setting up hypotheses, and verbalising doubt. In this form of language use, possibilities are tried out, ideas are attended to, evidence is introduced and tentative decisions are reached. Learning proceeds in what Joan Tough (1977) describes as the 'hypothetical' or 'exploratory' mode. This style of teacher/child interaction is a kind of 'thinking out loud', an external dialogue.

When teacher and child engage in effective talk, the child's learning is not just confined to the subject matter in hand. This kind of dialogue is a rehearsal for later patterns of thinking, that is, for the internal, unsupported dialogue with the self; the 'analytic competence' which Bruner identifies. The need for some adjustment is evident here also. It is to be hoped that revisions will bring higher levels of expectation in relation to competence and performance in the junior language curriculum. From experience of the Early Start programme, where teachers are working with three- to four-year olds, we know that by the end of the year children are asked to and do engage in quite complex language uses such as describing a problem and suggesting possible solutions, describing a process, predicting outcomes, making and justifying hypotheses, and using language to create and to sustain imaginary play situations.

Finally I would like to offer some perspectives on the relationship between language and emotional and imaginative development. Here language has a truly representational function. In creating and sustaining imaginary contexts as in play, and drama, in responding to poetry, in creating or in entering into a story, children are using language to create and to interpret meaning in ideas and images. So, for example, in using neutral, non-specific objects such as building blocks or lego or lengths of colourful cloth, or simply a row of chairs, children create and inhabit imaginary contexts where the play/ drama/ story is driven by ideas rather than objects. The children are engaged both intellectually and emotionally and the meaning is carried through principally by the power of the spoken word.

It is indeed exciting to see this expressed recognition of the emotional life and of the life of the imagination. It is wholly appropriate I think that both of these areas should be presented and treated as closely related aspects of human development. Margaret Meek (1993) describes imagination as a fusion of the intellectual and the emotional; a meeting of head and heart where all of children's imaginative acts are 'shot through' with emotion.

Winnicott's (1971) view of imaginative acts such as play and drama is that they present a context for highly creative living, allowing for the exploration and assimilation of experiences which contribute to the development of mind and to the child's initiation into the common pool of humanity.

I think it is also true to say that story or narrative is also at the heart of this area of learning. Barbara Hardy (1977) has described narrative as a primary act of mind – the principal way in which our minds work in making sense of the world. Story is certainly central to the world of childhood and so finds its rightful place at the heart of the language curriculum. Ultimately, story is the basis of play and drama too.

James Britton (cited in Pradl, 1982) describes language as beginning in 'delight'. I think it is true to say that all of the areas of delight – play, drama, story, rhyme, verse, poetry and song – are included in this area of the curriculum and the statements of learning outcomes indicate the levels of engagement required.

Finally, to end where I began, it is indeed an exciting development to have an oral language curriculum. It will make a crucially important contribution to our children's development and as in James Britton's perspective, hopefully, it will also bring delight.

REFERENCES

Bruner, J.S. (1983). *Child's talk: Learning to use language.* Oxford: Oxford University Press.

Bruner, J.S. (1975). Language as an instrument of thought. In C.B. Cazden (Ed.). *Language in early childhood education.* Washing D.C.: NAEYC.

Bryant, D.E., & Ramey, C.T. (1987). An analysis of the effectiveness of early intervention programmes for environmentally at-risk children. In M.J. Guralnick & F.C. Bennett (Eds.). *Effectiveness of early intervention.* Orlando, FL: Academic Press.

Hannan, D.F., and Ó Riain, S. (1993). *Pathways to adulthood in Ireland: Causes and consequences of success and failure in transitions among Irish youth.* Dublin: Economic and Social Research Institute.

Hardy, B. (1977). Narrative as a primary act of mind. In M. Meek, (Ed.). *The coolweb.* London: Heinemann.

Ireland. (1999a). *English language primary school curriculum – Content statement.* Dublin: Stationery Office.

Ireland. (1999b). *English language primary school curriculum – Teacher guidelines.* Dublin: Stationery Office.

Kelleghan, T., Weir, S., Ó hUallacháin, S., and Morgan, M. (1995). *Educational disadvantage in Ireland with particular reference to its identification.* Dublin: Educational Research Centre/Combat Poverty Agency.

Meek, M. (1993). *On being literate.* London: The Bodley Head.

National Economic and Social Forum. [NESC]. (1997). *Early school leavers and youth unemployment: Forum Report No. 11.* Dublin: Stationery Office.

Pradl, G. M. (1982). (Ed.). *Prospect and retrospect: Selected essays of James Britton.* London: Heinemann.

Schweinhart, L.J., Barnes, H.V., & Weikart, D.P. (1993). *Significant benefits: The High Scope/Perry pre-school project through age 27.* Ypsilanti, MI: High Scope Press.

Steiner, G. (1985). *Language and silence.* London: Faber.

Tough, J. (1977). *The development of meaning.* London: Unwin Education Books.

Wells, G. (1985). *Language development in the pre-school years: Language at home and at school.* Cambridge: Cambridge University Press.

Winnicott, D.W. (1971). *Playing and reality.* London: Tavistock Publications.

Irish as a Second Language in the Gaeltacht: Bringing Theory to the Practice*

. . . .

Máire Mhic Mhathúna
Dublin Institute of Technology

Frances Uí Chinnéide
Scoil Dhún Chaoin, Dún Chaoin, Co. Chiarraí

Due to changing demographic and linguistic patterns in the Corca Dhuibhne Gaeltacht area, Irish is no longer the first language of all children entering Gaeltacht primary schools. In order to enable the children to benefit from their education and to maintain Irish as the language of the school, Oidhreacht Chorca Dhuibhne employed a number of local women as Language Assistants in the infant and junior classes of the primary schools on a pilot basis in 1993. This was extended to all Corca Dhuibhne Gaeltacht schools in 1995. Although the Language Assistants were guided by the classroom teachers, it quickly became apparent that training in this field was required. Oidhreacht Chorca Dhuibhne approached the Dublin Institute of Technology (DIT) to design, teach and accredit a short course for the Language Assistants. This paper describes the background and process of this innovative scheme and evaluates the delivery of the course from the perspective of both students and organisers of the course.

*Paper presented at the 23rd Annual Conference of the Reading Association of Ireland, Limerick, September 17-19, 1998.

Introduction

In keeping with its theme of Irish as a Second Language in the Gaeltacht, this paper is presented in both Irish and English. The first part deals in English with the background and organisation of a course for Language Assistants in Corca Dhuibhne Gaeltacht schools and the second part describes in Irish the personal experience of Frances Uí Chinnéide, one of the Language Assistants.

The Language Assistants, who are all native speakers of Irish, work with the children for about an hour a day. They work in co-operation with the classroom teacher, who is, in all cases, teaching multi-grade classes.

The decline in the number of native speakers of Irish in the country as a whole to the current level of 2% (Ó Riagáin and Ó Gliasáin, 1994) is mirrored in the corresponding decline in the Corca Dhuibhne Gaeltacht (Ó Riagáin, 1992), and as such can be seen to follow the general trend in the pattern of language use in Ireland (Ó Murchú, 1985). This change can be traced back to the mid-sixteenth century, with the plantations of the land of the Irish chieftains by English-speaking settlers. Gradually public life, in the spheres of politics, law, business, religion and education began to be dominated by English-speakers and this change was compounded by the tragedy of the Great Famine. This consolidated the image of the Irish language as being associated with poverty and deprivation. By the end of the 19th century, English had become the dominant language of Ireland, with only certain areas, Gaeltachtaí, retaining Irish as a community language.

On the other hand, the Revival Movement of the late 19th and early 20th century saw a growth of interest in the Irish language as a symbol of national identity and cultural distinctiveness. This movement influenced the formation of State policy regarding the conservation and promotion of the Irish language, mainly in the education sphere. Present State policy also supports Irish as an entry requirement for certain posts, gives a range of Gaeltacht subsidies and supports Irish language broadcasting. This is in line with widespread public support for the teaching of Irish in schools and for a range of measures including Gaeltacht grants, services through Irish and broadcasting (Ó Riagáin and Ó Gliasáin, 1994). The State does not, however, ensure that those who wish to conduct official business through Irish have a guaranteed opportunity to do so. Ironically, at a time of increasing demand for all-Irish schooling outside the Gaeltacht (116 Gaelscoileanna were operating in 1997/8), problems are being experienced at a significant level in Gaeltacht primary schools and the declining number of native speakers, *cainteoirí dúchais,* does give cause for concern.

Due to the rising level of prosperity in the country, there have been changes in the composition of the population in many rural areas, including the Gaeltacht. In the case of the Corca Dhuibhne Gaeltacht schools, this has led to non-Irish-speaking children entering the school system. Many local emigrants have returned, often with young children of school-going age, who were raised through English in England, the United States and Australia.

Prosperity has also led to a search by some families for an alternative life-style, away from the pressures of city life. This includes both Irish families and people of other nationalities moving to a beautiful part of the country. Many Irish families in the cities felt that they too would have a better quality of life through participation in the rural re-settlement scheme and were happy to move to this area. However, the largest group of non-Irish speaking children come from local families who feel that their children will have a better future if they are brought up bilingually or through English only 'as they can learn Irish in school.'

Due to these demographic and linguistic factors in the Corca Dhuibhne Gaeltacht area, it became clear that steps would have to be taken to maintain Irish as the language of the classroom and school-yard and it was decided that extra support in learning Irish for children entering school, in the form of Language Assistants, would be a suitable way forward. The author of the second half of this paper, Frances Uí Chinnéide, was the first Language Assistant to be involved with the scheme.

Although the Language Assistants were guided by the classroom teachers, it quickly became apparent that training in this field was required. Oidhreacht Chorca Dhuibhne approached the Dublin Institute of Technology (DIT), whose Early Childhood Care and Education course includes Second Language Acquisition by young children, to design, teach and accredit a short course for the Language Assistants.

Course Preparation

DIT were very pleased to be involved in the project and welcomed the challenge of designing a new course for this particular purpose. The first step involved bringing together a team of experts who would plan and teach the course. These included two psychologists, one of whom specialises in Early Childhood Care and Education and the other in Adult Education, a specialist in Language Acquisition in Early Childhood, who was very familiar with the Gaeltacht area, a specialist in teaching Irish in the primary school curriculum and the Development Officer from Oidhreacht Chorca Dhuibhne who gave the impetus to the scheme in the first place.

A preparatory visit was made to Kerry by a member of the Course Team to meet the Language Assistants and to ascertain their needs for the course. In order to come as close as possible to a course situation, the visit included two lectures, on Child Development and Second Language Acquisition. The discussion during and after the lectures showed that the Language Assistants had a good appreciation of the issues that arise in Second Language Learning, such as motivation and the role of the First Language. Many of the students expressed an interest in understanding Child Development and children's ways of thinking. They also wished to acquire a range of teaching skills, suitable for various age-groups and stages of development, and wanted to develop Child Management skills.

The Language Assistants also stressed the need for a substantial course that would be accredited and were very happy with the short course accreditation provided by DIT. This is a Certificate in Continuing Professional Development, which is awarded to those who successfully complete a course with a minimum of 90 hours duration and which also attracts European Credit Transfer System (ECTS) credits.

Course Aims

The aims of the course were to provide the students with a basic understanding of
- how children think and learn
- how they learn a second language
- the primary school curriculum
- a repertoire of teaching skills
- an intellectual basis for their interest in the Irish language and culture.

Structure of Course

The course was structured on the above aims and on the philosophy of dealing with the Whole Child (Hendrick, 1992). We were very conscious that the purpose of the course was to train Language Assistants, but that it was important to keep the social, emotional, cognitive and physical needs of the child in mind. We also advocated a play-based curriculum as being in tune with the learning style of young children (Moyles, 1989, Whitebread, 1996). This approach happily coincided with current understanding of the importance of meaningful contexts for children learning language (Ellis, 1994, Tabors & Snow, 1994). A module of Teaching Practice was also included as this was to be an applied course and it was considered necessary for the participants to have practical experience of teaching Irish as a Second Language to young children.

A draft outline of the course was prepared, which, after several modifications, emerged as follows:

Psychology of the Child. Duration: 20 hours
- Introduction to child development
- How children think and learn
- Are there stages of development?
- Basic principles of learning
- Language, learning and making sense
- Role of the adult in facilitating learning
- Parents and education

Classroom Pedagogy. Duration: 20 hours
- Curriculum of Primary School
- Oracy, reading and writing
- Teaching of Irish in primary school
- Irish rhymes, songs, stories, books for children
- Language games
- Use of puppets and drama in promoting learning
- Use of video, television in promoting learning
- Communication with children, parents and teachers

Learning a Second Language. Duration: 20 hours
- Acquisition of first language
- Acquisition of second language
- Input and interaction
- Context and errors
- Bilingualism and learning
- Bilingualism and education in Ireland
- Bilingualism in the international context
- Language and identity

Irish Language and Heritage: Duration 15 hours

- History of the Irish language
- Literature in Irish, past and present
- Irish in the present
- Accuracy in the Irish language
- Dialect of Corca Dhuibhne
- Local folklore for children
- Archaeology of the Dingle Peninsula: Field trip
- Flora of the locality: Field trip

Teaching Practice: 30 hours

Experience of working in a Gaeltacht primary school or naíonra, under the guidance of the classroom teacher or naíonra advisor.

Admission Requirements

All those who were working as Language Assistants or in a naíonra were invited to attend the course. No prior educational qualifications were set. Advertisements were also placed in local papers and broadcast on Raidió na Gaeltachta, inviting applications from other interested people. Ten of the total of 23 participants were Language Assistants, ten were working in naíonraí and three were interested in becoming Language Assistants. A nominal charge was made for the course.

Lectures

Lectures were held for three hours every Friday evening in Dingle Education Centre and for another three hours on alternate Saturday mornings, between November 1997 and April 1998. About half of the lectures were delivered by DIT staff and the remainder were given by guest lecturers from Colleges of Education. Local teachers also participated in giving two workshop sessions, where lesson planning and delivery could be discussed in detail. We were fortunate that many Irish-speaking lecturers had the required expertise and subject knowledge. This allowed 80% of the lectures to be given in Irish, 10% in English and the remaining 10% bilingually in Scots Gaelic and English.

Assessment Procedures

Assessment for adults is always difficult as it is such a sensitive area, particularly for those returning to study. However, in an accredited course, standards must be maintained and every effort was made to devise an appropriate, yet rigorous system of assessment. It was decided to use three types of assessment, based on DIT models:

1. School/Naíonra Journal, which would be both a planning-tool and, it was hoped, an aid to reflection on the content of the lectures and on the students' progress as practitioners (Holly and McLoughlin, 1989). A detailed handout was provided and two submission dates were set.
2. Report on Teaching Practice from the Classroom Teacher or Naíonra Advisor. The nature of this report was explained to the teachers at a meeting held at the beginning of the course and students were also given copies of the report form for reference.
3. Tutorial Visit from a lecturer involved in the course. This took the form of an observation of the student working directly with the children and a discussion was held afterwards to highlight the successful strategies and to offer help with any problems. It also enabled the lecturers to meet the school principals, teachers and children and to appreciate the classroom situation.

Student Evaluation of the Course

An evaluation form was given to the students at the end of the course, seeking their opinions on many aspects of the course.

All of the students expressed a high level of satisfaction with the range of subjects and were very happy with the standard of lectures. They did, however, say that they would have liked some more practical lectures on playing board games with the children, using puppets, making posters, organising nature walks, etc. They would have liked some information on Child Health and on First Aid and more sessions with the local teachers.

They found the tutorial visits helpful, but some admitted to being quite nervous — 'Cuireann sé brú áirithe ort.' [It puts a certain amount of pressure on you.] Another student said that although she was very nervous before the visit, she felt much more confident about her work following the discussion. The visits were made by appointment, but some students would have preferred a surprise visit.

The students were happy with the contact between the school and the course, the meeting with teachers, the Teacher's Report and the Tutorial visit.

The written work, the School Journal, was found by many students to be difficult, as they said they had been out of contact with this type of work for many years — 'Bhí deacracht agam leis seo mar ní raibh taithí agam ar a leithéid a scríobh.' [I found this difficult as I had no experience of writing such work.] Other students emphasised the importance of the journal as a learning-tool. 'Bhí sé go maith mar chaitheas suí síos agus mo mheabhair a bhailiú.' [It was good because I had to sit down and think.] 'Tá sé go deas do dhearcadh féin a chur ar an méid a chuala tú ins na léachtaí.' [It is very good to give your own opinion on the content of the lectures.] Two submission dates were set, early December and the end of February. Many participants said they would have preferred shorter intervals between submissions. Several said that it was beneficial to have a record of the work they had done and that it was good to look back on. Some said they would have preferred more help with the written work and with note-taking from lectures.

Most students were happy with the timing and frequency of lectures, but felt that the course was a little too long and that the three hours per night was long also. As course organisers, we were constrained by the fact that many lecturers were travelling long distances and we were trying to make the best use of their time as well as facilitate the students.

The students also praised the organisation of the course very highly. In spite of having ten different lecturers over 25 sessions, there were no hitches, no no-shows and almost 100% attendance from the students. The Development Officer from Oidhreacht Chorca Dhuibhne was responsible for this high level of organisation. She had also arranged with the Librarian in Dingle Library for a stock of our recommended texts to be acquired and made available to the students in the Education Centre every week. This made an important contribution to the effectiveness of the course.

Most students were satisfied with the books recommended, but some were found to be too academic. However, they welcomed the range and the challenge involved. We have agreed to make a further list of suitable books available to Dingle Library.

Discussion

Despite the favourable evaluation of the course, there were, nonetheless, a number of constraints and problems that arose. These were mainly to do with the fact that this was an outreach course, being run from Dublin, 230 miles away from Dingle.

Tutoring, in particular, is one aspect of the course that we would have liked to expand. Two visits to the students during the course would have been ideal, one early, one late, with more time for detailed discussion afterwards about their particular work situation. More individual tutoring would also have been worthwhile, both to get to know the students earlier and to offer suggestions and help.

As the Language Assistants work in co-operation with their classroom teachers, more contact with the teachers would have been welcomed by all. Classroom Assistants are a new development in Irish education and the change has implications for both the assistant and the teacher. As well as a teaching role, the teachers are now being asked to play a management role in this relationship and the respective roles and responsibilities need to be examined. This issue is also highlighted by Hutchings in her discussion of special teacher assistants in England (Hutchings, 1997). She states that 'teachers need to have the opportunity to think creatively about the potential benefits of working with the support of special teacher assistants and to develop guidelines for collaborative ways of working.' As the Language Assistants scheme in Corca Dhuibhne has been granted funding for the next three years, it would seem prudent to consider some medium-term collaborative planning on how best to use this resource.

Overall, however, the course was deemed by all to have been a great success. This was due in no small measure to the enthusiasm of the students and to the commitment and dedication of the lecturers and administrators involved, both at local and at DIT level. The availability of the Dingle Education Centre and of the recommended books from Dingle Library made the organisation much easier and allowed us to concentrate on the more complex issues of content and timetabling. Everyone involved realised the importance of the course to the progress of the Language Assistants and was happy to give their best to this important development in education and in the promotion of Irish in this Gaeltacht region.

The next section describes Frances Uí Chinnéide's experience of being a Language Assistant in a Gaeltacht primary school and gives her evaluation of the course.

Cúntóir Teanga

Is timpeall an ama seo, Meán Fómhair 1992, a thosnaíos mar chúntóir teanga i mbunscoil Gaeltachta i gCorca Dhuibhne. Bhí seisear leanbh nua ag tosnú ar scoil an téarma sin agus níorbh í an Ghaeluinn a ngnáth-teanga. Dóibh sin, bhí triúr go raibh tuiscint acu ar an dteanga ach ní raibh aon chleachtadh ná taithí ag an dtriúr eile. Bhí eolas ag na múinteoirí ar an gcóras sa Bhreatain Bheag agus le cabhair airgeadais ó Eagraíocht na Scoileanna Gaeltachta, beartaíodh duine éigin ón bparóiste a fhostú sa scoil chun cabhrú leis an ngrúpa leanbh seo gnáth-chumarsáid na scoile a thuiscint chomh tapaidh agus ab fhéidir. Bhí buachaill beag Gearmánach tosnaithe ag freastal ar an scoil an bhliain roimhe sin, ach ní raibh mórán deacaireachtaí acu leis toisc nach raibh ann ach duine amháin agus d'fhoghlaim sé Gaeluinn gan mórán moille. Nuair a chruann ar an gcailligh, caitheann sí rith!

Cuireadh ceist orm fé phost an chúntóra agus ag féachaint siar air anois, bhí an-mhisneach agus coráiste agam agus thugas fé. In 1979, bhí baint agam le bunú naíonra sa pharóiste agus sa naíonra san bhí sé de nós againn go gcaithfeadh gach máthair maidean sa choicíos ann ag cabhrú leis an stiúrthóir. Bhí taithí éigin agam mar sin a bheith ag obair le leanaí don aois 3 - 5 bliana. Ag an am san, bhí Gaeluinn ag gach leanbh a bhí ag freastal ar an naíonra, fiú iad siúd nach ón ndúthaigh na tuismitheoirí. Mar sin ní raibh cleachtadh agam ar shealbhú an dara teanga. Dheineas suas m'aigne gurbh iad na cluichí, na gníomhaíochtaí agus na leabhartha a bhí oiriúnach don naíonra a bheadh mar bhunábhar cleachtan agam.

Diaidh ar ndiaidh, fuaireas amach cad iad na cluichí agus na hábhair cheachta ab éifeachtaí. Ní raibh na leabhair as Gaeilge comh tarraingteach ag an am san. Ach toisc nach raibh na leanaí ábalta léamh, bhaineas úsáid as leabhair Béarla. Ag amanta i rith na bliana sin, cheapas go mbeadh an toradh céanna agam ach na cait a bheith liom, ach ní raibh eolas agam ar 'an Tréimhse Tostach' an uair úd. D'fhreagair duine mé lá amháin, dúirt sé 'Sea' is bhíos ar neamh, is lá eile dúirt buachaill beag 'Sin réilthín.' Thóg sé tamall maith sara raibh aon toradh ar fónamh le feiscint.

I rith na bliana sin, nuair a chuala múinteoirí eile na leithinise fén scéim sa scoil, chuireadar in iúl go raibh gá leis ins na scoileanna acu féin. Mar sin an dara bliain, cuireadh cúntóirí teanga i naoi scoil sa leithinis. Thug Eagraíocht na Scoileanna Gaeltachta le chéile sinn in Ionad na Múinteoirí sa Daingean ó am go chéile; fiú amháin nuair nach raibh cainteoirí againn, bhí toradh maith ar an bplé agus ar an gcaidreamh eadrainn. Ní rabhas amuigh sa bhfásach a thuilleadh agus ba faoiseamh ceart a chlos go raibh leanaí crosta ag daoine eile leis. Thugamar isteach na cluichí agus na leabhartha a bhí á úsáid againn agus bhí mórán le foghlaim againn óna chéile.

Toisc nach raibh sa scoil agamsa ach dhá sheomra ranga, bhíos ó thús ag obair ins an seomra céanna leis an múinteoir. Tá buntáistí agus míbhuntáistí ag baint leis seo. Bímid i gcónaí suite chun boird agus ní féidir linn mórán gleoigh a dhéanamh. Mar sin, ní bhíonn cluichí le liathróid ná le huisce riamh againn; fós, b'fhéidir, ó thaobh iompar na leanbh, gur fearr é.

Tá cuid mhaith cluichí cártaí agus bréagáin eile bailithe anois agam. Tá cuid acu seo agam ó bhí mo chlann féin óg. An rud is luachmhaire dom ná nach raibh Lego an tí tugaithe uaim agam. Bíonn fonn ar gach leanbh sa tseomra páirt a ghlacadh linn inár scléip gach Céadaoin. Ba nós leis an múinteoir scoláire nó dhó a chruthaigh go maith an mhaidean sin a scaoileadh chugainn don 20 neomaint sin. Ciallaíonn san nach raibh aon drochmheas riamh ar na leanaí a bhí i mo ghrúpa ach a mhalairt, ba rud speisialta é.

Is féidir mórán a mhúineadh le cluiche cártaí speisialta. Is féidir comhaireamh a chleachtadh, 1, 2, 3 chárta a dháileadh: 'domsa, duitse, dó-san, di-sin.' Dathanna agus an foclóir a bhaineann leis na pictiúir imeartha. Arú inné, bhí an-áthas orm mo scoláire nua a chlos ag rá 'I have a péire.' Is buntáiste mór é an uimhir bheag atá agam an bhliain seo — ceathrar. Tá tuiscint ag gach duine agus bíonn 75% den gcumarsáid as Gaeluinn. Ní labhraimse aon Bhéarla. Tá fonn ar na leanaí atá á dtógaint le Béarla focail nua a fhoghlaim agus tuigim an seans atá liom. Is féidir leanbh diúltach a bheith agat leis, fiú amháin agus gan é a bheith ach 4 mbliana d'aois.

Thug an cúrsa ar a raibh trí dhuine is fiche againn ag freastal an-mhisneach dúinn. Nuair a thuigeann tú gur páirt nádúrtha do shealbhú teanga focal amháin as Gaeluinn a úsáid in abairt Béarla, ní theipeann do mhisneach. Thug sé tuiscint dúinn ar thábhacht cumarsáide idir leanaí iad féin agus b'fhéidir míniú ar chruacheist: má bhíonn ceathrar leanbh le Gaeluinn ag caint agus go dtagann leanbh le Béarla amháin isteach sa chomhluadar, cad 'na thaobh go dtosnóidh gach éinne ag caint Béarla? Tugadh samplaí dúinn do lámhobair chruthaitheach go mbainfimid úsáid as go minic. Tá a fhios againn go bhfuil beartanna áirithe nach féidir le leanaí a dhéanamh go dtí go mbíonn aos áirithe sroiste acu. Má bhíonn orainn caint le tuismitheoirí, beidh a fhios againn conas a gclann a phlé leo.

Cuireadh ár n-intinní ag obair arís mar bhí aistí le scríobh againn, staidéar le déanamh ar fhilíocht agus béaloideas agus leabhartha crua casta le léamh againn. Bhí cruth nua le cur ar ár ndeireadh seachtaine. Le linn an ama seo, chuireamar aithne ar mhná cumasacha tuisceanacha go raibh spéis acu in ár ndeacaireachtaí. Bhíodh briseadh caifé againn agus bhíodh plé againn eadrainn féin ar na tuairimí nua seo ar fad agus cé mar a chuirfimís ag obair iad inár suíomh oibre féin.

Dé hAoine seo 'mhithe tharainn a bronnadh na teastaisí orainn agus is sinn a bhí mórtasach. De bharr ár gcuid oibre a bhí na teastais seo á mbronnadh orainn.

Tá an-mholadh ag dul do Mháire Uí Shíthigh, Oifigeach Forbartha Oidhreacht Chorca Dhuibhne agus tá an-chreidiúint ag dul di as an bpointe seo a bheith sroiste againn, an scéim leathnaithe amach go dtí 11 bunscoil agus anois céim eile fós, na meánscoileanna ag lorg cúntóirí. Tá éirithe léi airgeadú a fháil don scéim ón Roinn Ealaíon, Oidhreachta, Gaeltachta agus Oileán ar feadh trí mbliana romhainn amach. Bhí fís aici agus lean sí é. Go dtí go bhfuair sí éisteacht ó Institiúid Teicneolaíochta Bhaile Átha Cliath agus an tacaíocht don gcúrsa ní raibh cás láidir aici do Ranna Rialtais. Gan a foighne siúd, ní bheinnse anseo inniu!

REFERENCES

Ellis, R. (1994). *The study of second language acquisition.* Oxford: Oxford University Press.

Hendrick, J. (1992). *The whole child.* New York: Times Mirror/ Mosby.

Holly, M.L. & McLoughin, C.S. (1989). Professional development and journal writing. In M.L. Holly & C.S. McLoughin (Eds), *Perspectives on teacher professional development.* London: Falmer Press.

Hutchings, M. (1997). The impact of a specialist teacher assistant training programme on the development of classroom assistants. *Early Years, 18,* 35-39.

Moyles, J. (1989). *Just playing? The role and status of play in early childhood education.* Milton Keynes: Open University Press.

Ó Murchú, M. (1985). *The Irish language.* Dublin: Department of Foreign Affairs and Bord na Gaeilge.

Ó Riagáin, P. (1992). *Language maintenance and language shift as strategies of social reproduction.* Dublin: Institiúid Teangeolaíochta Éireann.

Ó Riagáin, P. & Ó Gliasáin, M. (1994). *National survey on languages 1993.* Dublin: Institiúid Teangeolaíochta Éireann.

Tabors, P.O. & Snow, C. E. (1994). English as a second language in preschool programmes. In F. Genesee (Ed.), *Educating second language children* (pp. 103-125). Cambridge: Cambridge University Press.

Whitebread, D. (1996). *Teaching and learning in the early years.* London: Routledge.

Oral Language Development in the Early Years at School[*]

....

Liz Dunphy
Education Department
St. Patrick's College, Dublin

Talk is a tool that aids the development of intellectual growth and is therefore a vital process in learning (Wells, 1986; Wood, 1988). Ideas regarding the potential of children's talk as a tool for their learning, and as a window on their thinking have been developed over a number of decades. Recently, educationalists have been exploring and verifying the ideas of Vygotsky and other theorists regarding the close relationship between language and thought. The draft revised *English Language Primary School Curriculum* (National Council for Curriculum and Assessment, 1997a, 1997b) places oral language very much at the centre of the teaching and learning process. To talk is to express what is in the mind. We make our thoughts clear and accessible when we speak. Likewise, through talk we form and fashion our thoughts and we 'know' what we mean. Listening carefully and respectfully to children's ideas and thoughts, through their talk, and responding appropriately is now considered an essential skill for effective, responsive teaching of young children (Tharp & Gallimore, 1988).

*Based on a presentation at the Spring Seminar of the Reading Association of Ireland, Dublin, March 20th, 1999

The Kinds of Talk that Are Relevant for Learning

As adults we use talk for many different purposes and in many different settings. We have developed different ways of using oral language as a tool. We use it to explain and describe; justify and evaluate; compare and argue; organise and analyse; communicate and clarify; persuade and narrate; question and interpret. The range of purposes is wide, as wide as the range of thinking processes we employ. The ability to use oral language in all the different ways, i.e. to think in these ways, is a fundamental aim of the curriculum we offer young children. Language used in these ways promotes the development of higher-order thinking skills: analysis, interpretation, prediction and synthesis. If this aim is to be achieved, then children must have opportunities to use these processes in their learning.

Strategies to Promote Talk in Classrooms

In the draft revised *English Language Primary School Curriculum* (NCCA, 1997a, 1997b), English is seen as having three equally important elements: oral language, reading and writing. Traditionally, infant teachers have recognised the importance of oral language development for young children (INTO, 1995). Workable strategies to promote this development have, in practice, proved challenging. Teachers have used, to varying degrees, strategies such as

- Whole class discussion
- Newstime
- Story

Whole class discussion. It could be argued that whole class discussion as it has been implemented, is of limited value in language development with young children. A number of factors contribute to this, not least of which are difficulties imposed by large classes of young children, who are only just beginning to learn the conventions of school. The ability to wait one's turn to speak and to listen attentively to others are mature behaviours that take time to develop. It is suggested that the imposition of these conventions on young children as soon as they enter school can result in many children being denied the opportunity to express themselves orally. Some choose not to talk at all in these circumstances. This is clearly indicated by the work of Willes (1983) and Wells (1986).

Those who do actually talk without complying with the rules of the classroom, may find that what they say is disregarded and that attention is drawn to their transgression. The practice of *bidding* for attention (Willes, 1983) and the teacher's reaction to failure to comply with this practice – 'But you didn't put up your hand!'– must appear very strange to the young child on first entering school. Indeed, it seems to take some children a long time to come to terms with what it means. Think of the child who puts a hand up, but keeps it up throughout the time s/he is talking, as if somehow, the raised hand is a necessary accompaniment to talking to teacher.

Newstime. A strategy used by many teachers to promote oral language development in young children is the daily *Newstime* during which children are encouraged to share current interests and events with their peers and teacher. Again, difficulties similar to those mentioned above, emerge. It is suggested that teachers are well aware of the inappropriateness of having young children sit in silence for lengthy periods, passively waiting for the opportunity to express, perhaps, one sentence. They know that the child is possibly capable, and indeed eager, to say lots more. However the circumstances in which the talk is taking place do not always allow this. In truth, the teacher is the only one having the opportunity to lead the discussion, change the subject, react and interact with the speaker, ask questions and hypothesise. Indeed, s/he has every opportunity to use oral language in the ways we wish to enable children to use it.

Storytime. The reading of a story is a central strategy which teachers use to promote language development. Generally, the teacher reads the story, questions the children to check recall of details, and may ask children to retell the story in sequence. Although seen as a way to promote language development, reading stories to and with children is often viewed as a low-status activity to be used at the end of the school day when children are tired, or perhaps as a reward for having worked hard at some high-status activity.

Undoubtedly whole class discussion, newstime and storytime can offer opportunities for children to develop oral competency. However, with some new emphases and a clear understanding on the part of the teacher, and some slight adjustments to procedural details, these occasions can become very much more powerful in relation to their potential for oral language development.

Providing Children with Real Opportunities to Talk at School

The culture of many classrooms has been such that it was generally believed that if children were *talking* then they could not be *working* – a culture in which the teacher with the silent children was the one believed to be in control of his/her class. Discussion and talk quickly gave way to formal work even with very young children. There is evidence from Britain that this culture can be changed to accommodate the central place that oral language plays in children's learning (Norman, 1992). It is expected that the revised *English Language Primary School Curriculum* will provide the impetus for change in Irish classrooms.

The challenge to teachers is to ensure that children have *real opportunities* in which they can use this language to learn right *across the curriculum.* This means we must move away from the idea that we can develop children's use of language by timetabling a period of the day during which we do 'Oral Language'. Rather, what is envisaged is that oral language will be part of every aspect of the curriculum and that, in planning, the teacher makes explicit his/her intentions for the *ways* in which children will be encouraged to use language to promote their thinking and learning.

Talking in pairs. The challenge facing teachers in early years classrooms is how to maximise the potential for children to share experiences through talk, and use talk as a means of learning. Student-to-student dialogue is the foundation on which co-operative learning is based and is, as such, a critical way of organising learning experiences for young children (Berk and Winsler, 1995).

It is suggested that the use of *Pair Work* right across the curriculum is an effective and efficient way of promoting discussion, i.e., student-to-student dialogue between children. This strategy involves children talking in pairs for very short periods of time on topics of immediate interest. The children engage in active listening and talking. Meanwhile, the teacher may move around the room facilitating, joining in, instigating and supporting the talk. At pertinent points the teacher may stop the talk to draw together some points, to focus children's attention on common themes, or to highlight a particular point. Pairs may be random, or assigned, or indeed chosen by the children themselves. Some children may benefit from talking to a friend initially, but later grow in confidence from the experience, and work with a child whom they may not know so well.

This strategy may be extended to Newstime when children might exchange news in pairs and then perhaps report on their discussion to a larger group or to the whole class. The teacher may choose to organise this, using key questions to focus the discussion e.g. 'Did anyone make a journey?' The discussion will engage children more effectively if they can see and hear each other clearly. This can be achieved by seating the children in a circle arrangement.

Extending pairs across the curriculum: Stories. The act of reading a story to children has been described as a shared, imaginative process that involves the inseparable features of language, thought and feelings (Meek, 1991, p.91). In discussing a story, the teacher and children negotiate the meaning of the story. The teacher can use this occasion to promote the planned uses of complex forms of language and ways of thinking that will promote children's learning. Furthermore, this thinking can be expressed through children talking with each other in pairs, in addition to talking with the teacher. The conversation is, however, carefully guided to ensure that children have the opportunity to use their talk to speculate and imagine. The story offers the shared experience or the context in which the teacher will seek to encourage children's talk in ways that will promote their thinking.

To illustrate, let us examine this activity which is central to teachers' efforts to connect with young children and thereby, to establish talking points with them and to engage their interests. Reading stories to and with children offers the teacher tremendous potential to use talk to promote thinking skills. Story comprises both text and *illustrations.* These can be used together or separately to guide learning through talk. Children's growth in language usage and in thinking will be influenced by the extent to which they are guided and encouraged to speculate, describe, hypothesise and compare. The teacher's awareness of the importance of talk will mean that s/he will plan carefully the questions that children will discuss. This discussion will, of course, incorporate the spontaneous reactions of children to the text and illustrations presented. The framing of the tasks around the cognitive activities of analysis, interpretation, prediction and synthesis is central to the development of children's ability to think and act in these ways.

Exploring text and pictures through talk. In the next section, it is proposed to illustrate the potential of the story, both text and illustrations, for the development of children's thinking in different curricular areas. It is hoped to show that it is possible to plan for young children learning and teaching opportunities that are rich in potential to develop their thinking skills.

Exploring a Story: *My Great Grandpa*

My Great Grandpa (Waddell and Mansell, 1991) is the story of a little girl and her Great Grandpa who have a very special relationship. It provides a very good context in which to introduce talk related to concepts of generations, agedness and familial responsibilities. Furthermore, such discussion can easily accommodate the stated learning objectives of the early years curriculum in history. This integration of learning and confidence regarding the importance of these experiences for young children's learning is the essence of quality language work during the early years at school.

The young girl's relationship to the old man can be represented on *a family tree*. Through discussion, Great Grandpa can be described as a father and at the same time a Grandpa and a Great Grandpa. Children, through talk, can explore and clarify the relationships for themselves and each other. The concept of familial responsibility can be discussed and children can analyse the changing states of dependency within the family.

Through careful planning, questions such as 'In what ways does Great Grandpa need help?' may be discussed in pairs and then a list might be compiled. The children can then, with help from the teacher, compare this with ways in which older members of the family help younger children. This can be personalised by having children, in pairs, describe help given and received by members of their family. Grandparents and great-grandparents can be described and perhaps children could be encouraged to discuss similarities and differences between their experiences.

According to the text, Great Grandpa knows things that no one else knows. 'What kind of things?' Children may speculate and compare ideas about this and use their talk to reconstruct a past for this man who has lived for a long time.

Children can speculate as to why Great Grandpa's house was allowed to fall into a state of disrepair. By carefully examining the *illustrations* they can compare the house *then* and *now*. Evidence can be examined using questions such as: 'How do you know this house is empty?' 'What has changed and what has stayed the same?' 'I wonder what happened?' and 'Where is Grandma, I wonder?' These are questions that may lead children to speculate on the events that could have led to the present situation. They can justify their interpretations with evidence from the story or by arguing their point with each other in pairs.

Developing Perspective

Children may argue the case for Great Grandpa using a wheelchair sometimes. They can empathise and state how he might *feel* at various points in the story. They can do this by talking in pairs, addressing questions that they or the teacher have raised. By examining the expression on Great Grandpa's face as he sits musing in his chair, children can speculate about his thoughts and empathise with his situation. 'What do you think he is thinking about?' or 'Pretend you are Great Grandpa. Tell us what you are thinking about as you sit in the park in your wheelchair.'

Telling a story from another perspective is an important skill for an historian and the child can experience thinking and talking in this way by telling the story as if s/he were Great Grandpa.

In pairs they can take on roles, and experiment with being someone else. While these discussions are taking place children are *acting like historians* using the skills of the historian, and through their use of *particular forms of language* they are also *thinking like historians.* The ability to view events from another perspective is an important skill in developing historical understandings, as is the examination of evidence.

The discussion of the various *similes and analogies* in the text can be used by the teacher to appraise the child's understanding of how language used in specific ways can help to convey meaning. Children's satisfaction, or indeed dissatisfaction, with these as a way of describing can help the teacher to assess the level of understanding of these forms of language and indeed the ability to use such forms.

Children can evaluate statements such as 'He says I'm as smart as a button, but a button isn't much' for themselves. By reflecting on the children's thoughts, their arguments and their justifications, the teacher has a window into their understanding of this sophisticated way of using language.

Why does the little girl not like being called a little mouse, and why her preference for a lion? 'But I'm not a mouse, I'm a lion!' And then, 'He says we are peas from a pod. I say I'm a runner bean!' Willingness to use these forms of language, and the ability to provide examples, are useful to the teacher as an indication of understanding, and as a signpost to areas of language use that might be addressed in a planned way.

Conclusion

In summary, teachers will need to plan across the curriculum for opportunities in which children will engage in *real* discussion, using language in a range of different ways. It is essential that useful strategies be found to give children the opportunity to both speak and listen in meaningful contexts. It is necessary that the culture of schools change to accommodate talk, and that there is widespread acknowledgement of the premise that children learn to talk by talking. Young children at school need opportunities to acquire, practise, and polish their oral language skills and their use of language to promote learning.

The opportunity to present ideas in speech to a peer, to a group or perhaps to the teacher is a powerful way for the young child at school to develop ideas. The activities of hearing and reflecting on other people's ideas and perspectives and the discussion of these are essential in facilitating learning.

REFERENCES

Berk, L. E. and Winsler, A. (1995). *Scaffolding children's learning: Vygotsky and early childhood education,* Washington D.C.: National Association for the Education of Young Children.

Irish National Teachers' Organization. [INTO]. (1995). *Early childhood education: Issues and concerns.* Dublin: Author.

Meek, M. (1991). *On being literate,* London: The Bodley Press.

National Council for Curriculum and Assessment. [NCCA]. (1997a). *English language primary school curriculum – Content statement. Draft.* Dublin: Author.

National Council for Curriculum and Assessment. [NCCA]. (1997b). *English language primary school curriculum – Teacher guidelines. Draft.* Dublin: Author.

Norman, K. (1992). *Thinking voices: The work of the National Oracy Project.* London: Hodder and Stoughton.

Tharp, R.G., & Gallimore, R. (1988). *Rousing minds to life: Teaching, learning and schooling in social context.* New York: Cambridge University Press.

Waddell, M. and Mansell, D. (1990). *My Great Grandpa.* UK: Walker.

Wells, G. (1986). *The meaning makers: Children learning language and using language to learn.* Portsmouth, NH: Hodder and Stoughton.

Willes, M. (1983). *Children into pupils.* London: Routledge & Kegan Paul.

Wood, D. (1988). *How children think and learn,* Oxford: Blackwell

SECTION 2

Reading

Morality as an Ideology in Children's Fiction - Celebrating Children's Literature in Ireland*

. . . .

Frank Flannagan and Áine Cregan
Mary Immaculate College/University of Limerick
Limerick

This paper explores some of the positive effects, particularly in relation to morality as ideology, of children's experience of literature and begins to investigate how the recent blossoming of Irish literature for children may contribute to the moral development of the child.

Literature and Education

Educators of young children constantly ponder the question of the purpose of education. Herbert Spencer, in common with many others, summed up the fundamental purpose of education when he wrote that 'Education has for its object the formation of character'. It is unlikely that many will dissent from the idea that people send their children to school – and that teachers teach them there – not only to learn academic competencies but to learn to be good. We want our children to grow up not just 'good scholars' but good

*Paper presented at the 23rd Annual Conference of the Reading Association of Ireland, Limerick, September 17-19, 1998.

people; the latter is arguably our principal educational aim. In general we wish our children to grow up to be compassionate rather than vicious, generous rather than mean, forgiving rather than spiteful, co-operative rather than selfish.

But, as W.H. Auden reminds us, 'goodness is easier to recognize than define'. In order to transcend the narrow confines of a self-centred existence and truly believe that we can make a significant contribution to life (which is the essence of human goodness), a person needs to be satisfied with him/herself and with what he/she is doing. It is perennially true, as Bettelheim (1978) believes, that 'the most important and also the most difficult task in raising a child is helping him to find meaning in life' (p. 3).

Among those influences which best promote the child's ability to find meaning in life is literature. Bettelheim identifies

> parents and others who take care of the child; second in importance is our cultural heritage, when transmitted to the child in the right manner. When children are young, it is literature that carries such information best (p. 4).

Stories and example, rather than maxims and prescriptions, are the principal means whereby we form the next generation.

Story has been acknowledged from time immemorial and in all cultures as the most powerful agency in forming the moral attitudes of children. Stories promote and embody the most cherished values and virtues of each human culture. The highest objectives in literature and in education are the same: to be good, to live morally, and to acknowledge what is true (Inglis, 1981). 'People slip without realising it from talking about children's books to talking about educational philosophy' (Hollindale, 1988, p. 4) for they have the same essential purpose, the formation of the next generation.

Stories have a moral effect on readers and listeners: the more immature and inexperienced the listener/reader, the greater the potential effect of the story on their moral and intellectual development. The qualities of good stories and literature generally mirror the qualities of good people: they model the values we need for the development of our ethical lives. What we call 'good literature' reflects a world view and an attitude to life which embodies the same qualities which we value in people whom we would esteem and trust and learn from: truth, consistency, courage, sympathy. In addition 'good literature' enables us to adopt the appropriate response to its meaning and significance. In Fred Inglis' words 'when we say of fine prose that it is vivid, we mean just that: it recreates the life of the event at the same time as it gives us a way of accommodating its meaning' (Inglis, 1981).

Martin Waddell's *Can't You Sleep, Little Bear?* can be read as a metaphor for story: in story the adult takes the child by the hand and leads him/her out into the world. Stories enable and empower the child to confront whatever is critical for him/her at a particular time – fear, anxiety, confusion, frustration, wonder, curiosity, uncertainty, immaturity.

So stories are not trivial or dispensable or peripheral; they are not marginal features of our lives. They are of such vital human importance that children without stories are profoundly impoverished; they lack the means to locate themselves in time, space, society and culture. Who we are is part of an ongoing story; to understand ourselves we need to be able to understand – and to contribute to – that story. Stories enable us to locate ourselves, morally and emotionally, in relation to things which happen to us, and to structure our experience so that it becomes comprehensible; to develop our sense of self: who we are is a function of the part we play in events – no matter how trivial on the cosmic or global stage, our stories are the source and measure of our importance.

The importance of story in the life and education of the child is not a novel idea. Plato realised that stories were of such importance in the early formation of children that they must be strictly controlled. In the *Republic* he identified two components of the intervention:

(O)ur first business is to supervise the production of stories and choose only those we think suitable, and reject the rest. We shall persuade mothers and nurses to tell our chosen stories to our children and so mould their minds and characters.

It has become fashionable in recent times to be sceptical, if not wholly dismissive, regarding Plato's larger political vision, yet we cannot ignore the fundamental importance for any society of the formation of its children in accordance with its own ideals and principles. Plato realised that an educational programme requires the manipulation of available material in pursuit of a specifically moral programme. The educational programme is not just a negative programme of censorship: Plato is unapologetically advocating a programme of formation, if not indoctrination. His moral programme is quite explicit: 'It is . . . of the utmost importance that the first stories (children) hear shall aim at producing the right moral effect'.

As well as excluding what might create undesirable impressions in the minds of the young, Plato also advocates a more positive, creative approach.[1]

The didactic programme advocated by Plato and the recognition of the serious social and moral purpose can be found at all points in the intervening 2,000 years. Any consideration of adult intervention in the learning experiences of children is incomplete unless it reflects the two sides to the story, so to speak: the negative *exclusionary* side which we call censorship, and a more positive, creative, *intrusionary* side aimed at character formation, moral development, and the passing on of the prevailing or aspirational cultural and moral ideology.

Qualities/Characteristics of Good Literature

Of course not everything purportedly written for children attains these social or ideological objectives. Bettelheim dismissed 'much of the literature intended to develop the child's mind and personality'. His dissatisfaction is not as overtly censorious or politically motivated as Plato's. Bettelheim condemns such literature because it 'fails to stimulate and nurture those resources (the child) needs most in order to cope with his difficult inner problems'. According to Bettelheim stories should not only entertain and arouse the child's curiosity but crucially enrich the life of the child. The story or the book

> must stimulate his imagination; help him to develop his intellect and clarify his emotions; be attuned to his anxieties and aspirations; give full recognition to his difficulties, while at the same time suggesting solutions to the problems which perturb him. In short, it must at one and the same time relate to all aspects of his personality – and this without ever belittling but, on the contrary, giving full credence to the seriousness of the child's predicaments, while simultaneously promoting confidence in himself and in his future. (Bettelheim, 1978, 4-5)

No mean ideal.

Perhaps the best way to highlight those qualities which constitute good literature for children is to compare and contrast literature for children and literature for adults. Adult narratives introduce us to the fragmented complexity of life: buried in this complexity the moral fundamentals, the classic, mythic binary opposites – courage/cowardice, loyalty/betrayal, light/darkness, generosity/viciousness, love/hate, oppression/freedom, justice/ injustice – are difficult to discern. The complexity of the adult novels often seems to obscure rather than illumine these elemental opposites which are no more than metaphors for the most fundamental, primeval conflict between good and evil.

Good children's books on the other hand, without denying life's complexities, provide a salutary reminder that beneath the complexity of adult life the fundamental (though not simple) issues persist and must be addressed. They provide a fresh, uncomplicated and naive moral vision as a counterbalance to the apparent disorder of adult ethical experience.[2] They embody a world view which we need reminding of from time to time: a belief that the world is, despite cruelty, greed, materialism, suffering and injustice, a good place to be; that there is a moral order, a moral pattern, which we transgress at our cost.

Mackie (1990) identifies another significant difference between literature for children and literature for adults. He tells us that in imaginative literature

> what may be good in human life is concretely represented, both directly and by contrast with what is not good . . . (It) is sufficient for (the authors of imaginative literature) if they show real possibilities of life in some detail, rather than romanticised impossibilities – or, if these are shown, that they are labelled as what they are – leaving the reader to draw his own moral conclusions. (p. 169)

This depiction of the world is radically different from accounts written for children. Children cannot be left to draw their own moral conclusions because they are not yet in a moral position to do so; they have neither the moral experience, the moral insight nor the moral capacity. Being shown the appropriate moral responses is a necessary part of their moral education. This didactic feature of children's literature is fully recognised by those who take children, as well as literature, seriously. Fisher (1964) insisted that

> Some thread must be held out to the young reader as he wanders in the maze of volumes of today and yesterday. Some advice must be offered to him, if only because his reading is so much more thorough, so much more definite in its impact, than the reading of an adult. (p. 9)

She goes on to remind us that no story can be written without a moral 'though it may not take the sermon form familiar to the child of the last century' (p. 17). The writer for children is, among other things, 'an interpreter of life, especially of contemporary life, and in this sense the child expects that writer to inform him, to make categorical statements to him which he is not old enough to make for himself.'

Vehemently supporting this point of view, Gooderham (1993) writes that

> although the moral tale and overt moralising are rightly a thing of the past, in books for children of all ages the moral dimension continues to be of importance and should not be neglected . . . children's experiences of reading their first books provide for them as significant an early learning experience in the moral as in any other domain of human knowledge and feeling. (p. 115)

For an author to succeed in advancing a young reader's moral development, Gooderham suggests three imperatives: a conservative imperative; a progressive imperative; and an imperative derived from the politics and economics of book-buying. His recommendation is that

> if texts are to touch young children morally, they must, like fairy tales, acknowledge our first retributive and prudential morality: a conservative imperative. Equally, however, if they are to encourage development to more mature moral judgement, they must be appropriately structured to facilitate this development: a progressive imperative. (p. 121)

To these he adds an imperative derived from the politics and economics of book-buying: account has to be taken of 'the gatekeepers of young children's reading', the adults who select and buy reading material for children and who have a strong interest in inducting the young into their own moral world.[3]

Stephens (1992) endorses the Platonic tradition by contending that generally the purpose of those who write for children is to foster positive perceptions of socio-cultural values favoured by authors and other adults involved in bringing the book and the child together. Children's fiction 'belongs firmly within the domain of cultural practices which exist for the purpose of socialising their target audiences'. This use of story 'as an agent of socialisation is a conscious and deliberate process'. Drawing heavily on Hollindale's exploration of ideology in text, Stephens goes on to say that this process ranges from the didactic extremes of 'bibliotherapy', books purporting to help children to confront and deal with particular problems in their lives, to books with no overt didactic intent. The implicit presence in a text of the writer's unexamined and often unconscious assumptions is possibly more powerful in effect, for such assumptions embody values which are widely taken for granted in the society that produces and consumes the text. These ideological positions, though implicit, are invested with legitimacy through the implication that things are simply 'so'. Finally Stephens argues that many books for children are in fact ideological in both ways, since a conscious attempt to bring about change in attitude will inevitably and unavoidably be grounded in a great many contingent presuppositions about the individual and society.

So stories are irreducibly moral: they attempt to represent experience so that the reader or listener is drawn to accept the world represented by the author. The truth of a story is not in the accuracy of its descriptions of actualities but in its 'rightness' in structuring and giving form and shape to feelings, convictions, fears and hopes regarding the experiences it relates and, insofar as it is relevant, to our own life experience.

Authors of books for children, fiction or non-fiction, teach. Since children have neither the experience nor the guile to make their own moral or literary judgements, the author must at one and the same time reflect reality and act as a guide through it. For the child, the experience of reading fiction, whatever its quality, is a new experience, not only of reading but of the reality reflected in the story. The perceptions, the judgements, the values, the explanations and the reassurances of the writer are often the first encounter with alternative realities and outlooks that the child will have had.

Context for Development of Children's Literature in Ireland

Returning to Stephens' argument that many books for children involve a conscious attempt to bring about changes in attitude and are inevitably and unavoidably grounded in a great many contingent presuppositions about the individual in society, grounding children's fiction in an Irish society for Irish children is a phenomenon which existed only intermittently prior to the early 1980's.[4] Before that Irish children's reading came essentially from the same shelf as that of their English counterparts.

In the decade of the 1980's however, the founding of the Children's Press publishing house, the upsurge in interest in the market for young readers shown by other publishers, notably O'Brien, Poolbeg and Wolfhound, support from the Arts Council of Ireland, along with a growing appreciation of the importance of children's literature, saw what Jeremy Addis describes as at first a trickle, then a flow, and now a veritable flood of fine books for every age between toddler and teenager, adding a vital dimension to what is by any standards a cultural phenomenon – a phenomenal increase in both writing and publishing for children in Ireland.

The dynamic renaissance in children's literature in Ireland has undoubtedly emphasised the 'Irishness' of the literature. According to O'Sullivan 'the declared intention of the Children's Press from the outset was to produce Irish Books for Irish Children' (p. 8). However, O'Sullivan rightly recognises that 'the national emphasis in children's literature in Ireland coincides with major changes in long-held notions of Irish identity' (p. 8). This reality is colourfully expressed by Declan Kiberd:

If the notion of Ireland seemed to have become problematic, that was only because the seamless garment once wrapped like a green flag around Caitlín Ní Houlihán had given way to a quilt of many patches and colours, all beautiful, all distinct, yet all connected too. No one element should subordinate or assimilate the others: Irish or English, rural or urban, Gaelic or Anglo, each has its part in the pattern. (Quoted in O'Sullivan, 1997, p. 9)

In terms of children's literature, Dunbar asserts that 'earlier obsessions with forging an identity have given way to a much more general acceptance that identity can manifest itself in a multiplicity of ways,' although, in relation to children's literature, he feels that 'we are caught between the need to hold on and the desire to let go, or the need to let go and the desire to hold on' (Dunbar, 1997, p. 318). That the new wave of contemporary Irish Children's Literature manifestly sets out in Stephens' words 'to foster positive perceptions of socio-cultural values' and to promote and embody our current contemporary view of what matters, i.e. our cherished values and virtues, there can be no doubt.

Serious writers of historical, fantasy, and realistic fiction for children must attempt to structure and explain the painful experience of life for the child and balance it against the joys, all of which are an inescapable part of childhood. Children cannot articulate their own experience of the lived world adequately. They require an adult who has the imagination, the sensitivity, the recollection, and the sympathy to structure this experience for them and to make it accessible without alienating children from it. Good writers structure, explain and evaluate the experience of childhood and empower the child to come to terms with it. They 'enable the child to live a full life as a child'.[5] This is not only a laudable educational priority but a vital necessity for any fiction which presumes to the title of 'literature for children'.

There are no general rules for children's stories. As soon as we attempt to formulate one we find counter-examples crowding in from all sides. One thing, however, is certain: all children should get from their reading at some time an acknowledgement of their own everyday experience, the 'common places' which make up the basic fabric of their lives. These common places are the weave and woof without which integrated or superimposed patterns of meaning cannot make sense.

Take, for example, Lively's *The Ghost of Thomas Kempe.* Without the detailed evocation of James' ordinary relationships – with his sister, his parents, his would-be friend Simon, his teacher Mrs. Verrity, even his dog – the book would have degenerated into just another scary story sufficient for a momentary shiver down the spine but incapable of insight. Without the quotidian details to anchor them in a recognisable and reassuring reality, James' experiences with the mischievous apothecary – the eponymous Thomas Kempe – would have become trivial and incredible.

There is a two-way relationship at work here between the text and the reader: the reader can identify with the familiar familial location and so bear the weight of James' lonely battle to rid himself of Thomas Kempe's unquiet spirit. At the same time, the common places point up the reader's own experiences and give them new significance and stature in an affective context with which the reader can identify. Even James' parents' inability to hear what he wants to tell them, rather than what they want to hear (or expect to hear), is part of the daily experience of the child at home and in school.

Literature in the Curriculum

Given the similarity of objectives in life, in education, and in literature, and given the power of story to form moral attitudes and promote values and virtues, and given the capacity of literature to teach and to provide a mirror on reality, allied with the phenomenal growth in availability of Irish Literature of high quality, it must surely be a logical conclusion that children's literature would play a central and prominent role in the educational experience of the child. We would venture to suggest on the contrary, however, that we participate in an education system which is at least preoccupied with, if not perhaps at times overwhelmed by, the practical difficulties of teaching children how to read and with the achievement of performance objectives – a concept of reading which is quantifiable in empirical terms. Though understandable, it is probably also unforgivable that our focus is almost exclusively on the fact of children reading and considerably less attention is given to the quality of what children read, the range of their reading, their responses to what they read and the value of the experience of good literature for the child. According to Bettelheim, the acquisition of the mechanical skills of reading is of scant value when what one has learned to read adds nothing of importance to one's life. Reece (1990) suggests that in recent years research has shown that the offering of a wide range of books to children by an enthusiastic book-loving adult is the single most important factor in creating a desire to read and to read diversely. Fisher (1980) reminds us that 'Children are not natural literary critics. They acquire standards and preferences as an incidental to enjoyment and one would not wish it otherwise. But they will acquire no standards at all unless they are encouraged by a great variety of fiction, offering them many different and unexpected settings and points of view' (p. 112).

But this will not come about in most cases without significant adult intervention in selection, provision, and encouragement. Left to their own resources many, if not most, children will be content to develop a taste for a particular formula and pursue that to boredom. When that boredom occurs it is 'reading' that the child faults, not the narrowness of his or her choices.

It is imperative, therefore, that teachers, in addition to giving due consideration to the development of skills-acquisition in relation to reading, focus also on exposing children and helping them to work through the very best of their own Irish Literature (an experience denied to generations of their ancestors) along with the best the rest of the world has to offer.

In this respect it is most heartening to note that in the proposed NCCA curricular reforms in relation to reading at primary level, the following aspiration is expressed:

The curriculum also gives particular consideration to children's reading needs after they have achieved some mastery of reading skills. The reading scheme needs to be supplemented with other material. The class reader on its own will not cater adequately for the child's reading needs. These will only be fulfilled through the experience of engaging with a wide and varied range of text and this will only be achieved through the use of well-stocked and regularly supplemented school and class libraries (NCCA, 1997, p. 23).

It now remains to be seen whether these aspirations can be translated into practice in primary school classrooms around the country, given adequate in-service education for teachers, adequate resourcing for classrooms, and adequate parental support for the concept of a wide and enriching experience of literature for our children.

Ultimately, we must remember that reading is an empowering capability. It is not possible, despite all that has gone before, to predetermine what will be read, how it will be interpreted, what effect it will have, how it will be evaluated, or even at what emotional or moral level response will occur. To make people readers is to make them free. With freedom comes risk. The most we can hope for is that what they read will itself play its part in the moral and critical formation which will equip them to become positive participants in literature as well as in life.

REFERENCES

Addis, J. (1996). Children's publishing in Ireland. In V. Coghlan & C. Keenan (Eds.), *The big guide to Irish children's books* (pp. 14-19). Dublin: The Irish Children's Book Trust.

Bettelheim, B. (1978). *The uses of enchantment: The meaning and importance of fairy tales*. New York: Vintage Books.

Department of Education. (1971). *Curaclam na Bunscoile* (Vol. 1). Dublin: Stationery Office.

Dunbar, R. (1996a). Children's literature: The contemporary Irish dimension. *Kingston Hill Papers in Education.* Kingston-Upon-Thames, Surrey: Kingston University.

Dunbar, R. (1996b). Fantasy. In V. Coghlan & C. Keenan (Eds.), *The big guide to Irish children's books* (pp. 40-49). Dublin: The Irish Children's Book Trust.

Dunbar, R. (1997). Rare, pure and never simple: The world of children's literature. *The Lion and The Unicorn, 21, 3,* 309-321.

Fisher, A. (1964). *Intent upon reading.* Brockhampton.

Fisher, A. (1980). The reader, the critic, and the recalcitrant author. *The New Era: Jornal of the World Education Fellowship, 61,* 3.

Flanagan, F. M., (1996). Children's literature in Ireland: the historical background. *Kingston Hill Papers in Education.* Kingston-Upon-Thames, Surrey: Kingston University.

Gooderham, D. (1993). Still catching them young? The moral dimension in young children's books. *Children's Literature in Education, 24, 2,* 115-122.

Hickey, T., quoted in O'Sullivan, E. (1997). Ireland and the world of children's books. *Children's Books in Ireland, 16,* p. 6.

Hollindale, E. (1988). Ideology and the children's book. *Signal, 55,* p.4.

Inglis, F. (1981). *The promise of happiness: Value and meaning in children's fiction,* Cambridge: Cambridge University Press

Kiberd, D., quoted in O'Sullivan, E. (1997). Ireland and the world of children's books. *Children's Books in Ireland, 17,* p.9.

Mackie, J.L., (1990) *Ethics: Inventing right and wrong.* Penguin Books.

Morris, E. (1996). Realistic fiction. In V. Coghlan & C. Keenan (Eds.), *The Big guide to Irish children's books* (pp. 94-103). Dublin: The Irish Children's Book Trust.

National Council for Curriculum and Assessment [NCCA]. (1997). *Curriculum for primary schools: English language.* Dublin: Author.

O'Sullivan, E. (1997). Ireland and the world of children's books. *Children's Books in Ireland, 16,* 6-7.

Reddin, K. (1946). Children's books in Ireland: Were we all brought up behind a half-door? *Irish Library Bulletin, 7.*

Reece, L. & Rosenstock, G. (Eds.). *Irish guide to children's books, Decade 1980-1990.* Dublin: Irish Children's Book Foundation, 1990.

Scott, M. (1997). By imagination we live: Some thoughts on Irish children's fantasy. *The Lion and the Unicorn, 21(3),* 322-329.

Stephens, J. (1992). *Language and ideology in children's fiction.* London: Longman.

ENDNOTES

1. Aristotle in *The Politics* did not disagree. 'The officials known as the Trainers of Children ought to pay attention to deciding what kinds of stories and legends children . . . are to hear; for all that kind of thing should be preparation for their future occupations.' Again, it is not the intention to endorse Aristotle's social vision but to acknowledge the influence of childhood experience on any subsequent adult undertaking.

2. Martin Waddell tells us that 'An immature audience means a difference of approach. It means writing with a window of hope left at the end. For the very young the window is wide open.' (Reece & Rosenstock 1990, p. 164)

3. An example and story operating at all these various levels is John Burningham's *Mr Gumpy's Outing*. 'For young readers the story provides significant moral purchase – you break the rules so the boat capsizes and the notion that if you are going to enjoy your treat in the boat you must come to terms with the boatman and with the other passengers. Both of these levels of understanding are comprehended within the larger context. The patterned narrative, the gentle and impressionistic illustrations and perhaps most significantly the use of symbols like journey, fall and reinstatement, wise old man, and common meal serve to open up a larger context of aesthetic, moral and spiritual value' (Gooderham 1993, p.121).

4. It is important to acknowledge that Irish children's literature has a history dating back some 250 years although over that period, as Robert Dunbar says, the concept of 'Writing for children may occasionally require some wily manipulation and interpretation' (Dunbar, 1996a, p.43). Some great writers of children's literature in Ireland have included e.g. Oscar Wilde, Pádraig Pearse, An Seabhac, An tAthair Peadar Ó Laoghaire, James Stephens, Pádraic Colum, Patricia Lynch, Eilís Dillon, Walter Macken. The scope of this paper necessitates a focus on contemporary Irish Children's Literature, but it is important to recognise and acknowledge the existence and contribution of its predecessors. See Flanagan, F.M., 'Children's Literature in Ireland: the Historical Background', paper presented to the first European seminar on Children's Literature, Douai, France,

February, 1996. Published in Kingston Hill Papers in Education, (Kingston University, n.d.)

5. *Curaclam na Bunscoile* (Department of Education, 1971).

A Multiple Curricula Approach for Developing Reading Comprehension with Low-Achieving Readers*

. . . .

Timothy R. Blair
University of Central Florida, U.S.A.

The overall goal of reading instruction is the development of active readers who can both comprehend printed language and strategically monitor and regulate their own reading performance. Simply put, reading is comprehension. Pronouncing words is certainly a significant part of reading, but pronouncing words without meaning isn't reading. Central to reading comprehension is a student's prior knowledge and past experiences. In essence, a student constructs meaning from the text by integrating both information in the text and their own prior knowledge and experiences. Reading teachers in the last fifteen years have increasingly come to view reading as an active, constructive and strategic process based on what students already know (Heilman, Blair and Rupley, 1998).

*Paper presented at the 23rd Annual Conference of the Reading Association of Ireland, Limerick, September 16-18, 1998.

Also, in this same period, reading teachers have been exposed to a new wave of research on the explicit teaching of reading comprehension skills and strategies. Emanating from Durkin's classic study (1979) reporting on the lack of classroom time devoted by teachers to actually teaching reading comprehension to students, numerous investigators have concentrated their efforts on developing instructional strategies to increase students' reading comprehension abilities. Skilled readers have been identified as those who integrate information from their own background and experiences, and information from the text to build or construct meanings. Yet, in spite of this much-needed recent emphasis on explicitly teaching reading comprehension strategies to help students construct meanings while interacting with text, many students continue to experience difficulties in the comprehension area and as a result do not reap the enormous benefits of literacy. The purpose of this paper is to present a possible explanation for poor comprehension in students and to propose a possible solution.

Time Allocated to Direct Teaching and Practice

This paper proposes that lack of direct teaching and extensive practice and application could, in part, explain the continued difficulties that many students experience in comprehending what they read. Research on how classroom time is utilised is relevant to this issue. Studies of effective teaching and effective schools have yielded two important findings regarding classroom time usage: first, the amount of time that is allocated to instruction in a particular curricular area affects how much students learn; and second, the way that this allocated time is used by teachers directly relates to student achievement. Allocated time refers to the time given to a particular curricular area. Coverage entails scheduling sufficient time for both teacher and students to cover targeted instructional goals. This aspect of time refers to quantity, that is the amount of time designated to cover instructional material.

Durkin's study provided specific data about the use of allocated classroom time by elementary (primary) school teachers.

She reported that teachers spent less than three percent of the time on comprehension instruction. Teachers in her study were found to spend most of the time testing students' comprehension, and relatively little time teaching comprehension strategies. This finding reinforces the belief that students will not learn to comprehend if they are not given the opportunity to learn through an abundance of teacher instruction and teacher-supervised practice.

The other side of time refers to how the allocated time is used by teachers in the classroom. This aspect of time is often referred to as quality time, the time when students are actually attending to the work on hand. Research on teaching clearly shows that the more time students spend engaged in learning, the higher their achievement. Again, Durkin found teachers providing some type of comprehension instruction for only a small percentage of classroom time. As one would expect, allocated time and quality time for comprehension instruction are inter-related and interdependent. The more classroom time spent on quality comprehension instruction, the more likely that learning will occur.

Difficulties in Reading Comprehension

It is proposed that many elementary students continue to have difficulties in the comprehension area because of inadequate instructional time allocation and usage in the classroom with respect to comprehension instruction and application. The argument proposed is that significant comprehension improvement will occur if classroom teachers have a multiple curricular approach to comprehension instruction, and extensive practice throughout the school day, not just during the literacy/reading period. In other words, if teachers systematically plan and implement effective comprehension instruction, and teacher-supervised practice during all periods of the day, on targetted skills and strategies, students' comprehension abilities will improve significantly. Since there is a relationship between the amount of time spent by students in actively engaging in learning to comprehend, and their comprehension abilities, it is proposed that elementary school teachers teach important comprehension goals from different vantage points throughout the day in order for pupils to use new strategies flexibly and independently. Raths (1969) discusses this very point when explaining the importance of the teacher 'showing how', one of the components of teaching. Stressing the importance of providing ample time to practice a new ability which has been demonstrated, he said:

> Without always being aware of what they are doing, many teachers tend to shorten the time for practice, the time for learning *how*. To learn a skill, to acquire some mastery of it, children must do the required actions. How much practice is enough? This can only be answered by the teacher in charge of the group. One very poor answer to the question characterised the work of some teachers; they seem quite satisfied when about half the class has learned *how*. If the genuine aim is to show the class, then just about everyone in the class should learn *how*, and the teacher should stay with the project until this goal is reached. (p. 36)

It is proposed that a curricular emphasis throughout the day on comprehension abilities (both teacher-led instruction and teacher-supervised practice) will not only address this concern for time allocation for mastery, but also will result in transfer of reading comprehension abilities to new situations. A list of major objectives of reading comprehension instruction is given in Figure 1.

FIGURE 1

MAJOR OBJECTIVES OF READING COMPREHENSION INSTRUCTION

Vocabulary Development
- Basic sight vocabulary
- Meaning vocabulary

Literal Comprehension
- Being able to understand facts (who, what, when, where), sequential development (plot structure), story theme, cause and effect relationships, fact and opinion

Interpretative or Inferential Comprehension	• Being able to arrive at the main ideas and significant details, make inferences, summarise ideas, perceive relationships and motives for characters' actions, draw conclusions, identify author's purpose and mood
Critical Comprehension	• Being able to critically analyse a story, including hypothesising, identifying assumptions, imaging, problem-solving, comparing and contrasting, applying principles to new situations • Being able to personally react to a story
Strategic Comprehension	• Being able to apply metacognitive skills to reading including pre-reading strategies (asking questions, setting purposes, making hypotheses), during-reading strategies (knowing when to shift gears – that is to slow down, speed up, skip material, answer purpose-setting questions or hypotheses and set new ones, deciding if one is understanding ideas presented or not), and post-reading strategies (summarising ideas, answering purpose-setting questions and verifying hypotheses, reviewing new vocabulary)
Content Subject Comprehension	• Knowing how to read a chapter in a content book • Knowing specific study skills such as map, table, graph, and chart reading, outlining use of various reference materials • Development of technical vocabulary • Learning how to apply specific comprehension skills and cognitive strategies to each content area (e.g., geography, science)

Whether an objective is a specific skill or strategy, literal, inferential, or critical thinking in nature, the objective can be taught and practised by the reader simultaneously in various subjects and groupings throughout the day. Even if instruction is given in the reading/literacy period, the reading strategy may best be practised in the subject matter with which it must be used. Also, relating to Rath's concern, if reading comprehension abilities are to become functional, there must be extensive opportunity to make use of them in real situations. The various subject areas provide natural situations for their application.

Teaching Students to Summarise

One primary goal in comprehension instruction is to enable students to summarise what has been presented in a chapter or story. However, this all-important ability is frequently not mastered by students. Baumann (1984) and Taylor (1985) recommended that the strategy be formally taught using an instructional sequence such as the following:

1. Identify the topic
2. Write two or three words that reflect the topic
3. Use these words as a prompt to help figure out the main idea of the paragraph or longer text
4. Select two details that elaborate on the main idea and are important to remember
5. Write two or three sentences that best incorporate these important ideas

Even if the strategy of summarising is taught in the recommended sequence, students will not master it without extensive practice and application in a variety of contexts. This can be accomplished through classroom discussions, project assignments, development of multi-media products, games, computer software, and a host of supplementary materials. The following schedule is presented as a practical example of how to provide instruction and practice in summarising throughout the school day:

Beginning of the school day. Students can be asked to review current events or to report on (summarise) a television programme.

During reading class. Students can be provided with direct instruction on how to summarise as outlined above. Then, after reading a story, they can be asked to summarise the part they like best, important events in the story, or the funniest or saddest part of the story.

During science class. Students can be asked to summarise a science demonstration performed by the teacher or other students. Alternatively, they might summarise a chapter in a science text.

During social studies class. Students might be asked to summarise a social studies experience, assign a title to a picture or photograph in the text, or summarise articles in classroom magazines that deal with current events.

During mathematics class. Students might be asked to summarise a maths lesson or the steps in a mathematical process.

Dialogue between Teacher and Students

Central to the extensive practice and application is dialogue between the teacher and students. In the early stages of learning, the teacher should take the lead in providing guided or supervised practice. Rosenshine and Meister (1995) report that in teaching cognitive strategies, 'teachers guide students by providing hints, reminders of concrete prompts, reminders of what was overlooked, and suggestions on how something could be improved'. As students become more adept at applying a comprehension strategy, they assume more responsibility for internalising the strategy. It is commonsensical; initially the teacher explains or models the new strategy to students, and after much discussion and guided practice, they gradually learn to apply the strategy independently. During this process, students need to discuss their thinking with both the teacher and other students to receive feedback on their progress.

Brown and Campione (1986) address this very point by stating, 'Understanding is more likely to occur when a student is required to explain, elaborate, or defend his/her position to others; the burden of the explanation is often the push needed to make him or her evaluate, integrate, and elaborate knowledge in new ways.'

Conclusion

Teaching students to actually master reading comprehension strategies is a difficult but critical objective in the learning process. Reading teachers recognise the importance of developing readers who can both understand printed language and strategically monitor their own comprehension. It has been proposed that students who are experiencing difficulties in comprehending or have accumulated 'half learnings' in the comprehension area need a multiple curricular focus on targetted objectives involving both instruction and practice. Effective teachers should consider designing their instruction to ensure that activities relating to a particular comprehension strategy are sustained, and extensive practice and application are provided from different vantage points throughout the school day.

REFERENCES

Baumann, J.F. (1984). The effectiveness of a direct instruction paradigm for teaching main idea comprehension. *Reading Research Quarterly*, *20*, 93-115.

Brown, A.L., & Campione, J.C. (1986). Psychological theory and the study of learning disabilities. *American Psychologist*, *41*, 1059-1068.

Durkin, D. (1979). What classroom observations reveal about reading comprehension. *Reading Research Quarterly*, *14*, 518-544.

Heilman, A.W., Blair, T.R., & Rupley, W.H. (1998). *Principles and practices of teaching reading (9th ed.)*. Columbus, OH: Prentice Hall-Merrill.

Raths, L.E. (1969). Teaching for learning. Columbus, OH: Merrill.

Rosenshine, B.V., & Meister, C. (1995). Scaffolds for teaching higher-order cognitive strategies. In A.C. Ornstein (Ed.), *Teaching: Theory into practice*. Boston: Ally and Bacon.

Taylor, B.M. (1985). Improving middle-grade students' reading and writing of expository text. *Journal of Educational Research*, *79*, 119-125.

Folk and Fairy Tales in Sanctioned Reading Schemes in Primary Schools: A Review*

. . . .

Mary Shine Thompson
English Department
St. Patrick's College, Dublin

This paper begins by exploring the values of narrative in education and then traces aspects of the evolution of folk and fairy narratives within the educational context, both here and elsewhere in Europe. The genres of folk and fairy tale are widely represented at all levels of primary reading schemes in Ireland and have occupied the privileged role of transmitter of cherished values. It might be expected that the values that underpin these stories broadly reflect those about which there is some consensus in Irish society. These might include the triumph of good over evil, the value of communitarian effort, the dangers of pursuing wealth to the exclusion of all else, and currently accepted attitudes towards gender and power.

I will suggest, through a series of readings of folk tales from sanctioned reading schemes for primary schools, that these stories do not always convey the values implicitly and explicitly articulated

*Paper presented at the 22nd Annual Conference of the Reading Association of Ireland, Limerick, September 17-19, 1998.

by society and by the Department of Education and Science. The interpretations of the tales reveal concealed ideologies, among them bourgeois individualism, the value of success over honesty, and gender imbalance. The paper draws on theory and critique of folk and fairy tale, including the works of Propp and Zipes. It suggests that the concealed ideology poses certain dilemmas for reflective teachers, and its implications are teased out in some detail.

Contrary to expectation in our economically sophisticated society, the genres of folk and fairy tale are alive and prospering. We may have dispensed with the traditional rheumy *seanchaí* by the fireside, but we enjoy media interpretations of our favourite folk, fantasy and fairy tales: throngs have flocked to the cinema to watch *Pocahontas*; *Snow White* still enjoys healthy sales after more than six decades. Neil Jordan's *The Company of Wolves*, a contemporary reinterpretation of the Red Riding Hood story scripted by the feminist writer Angela Carter, has enjoyed critical acclaim. The folk or fairy tale is now a valuable commodity in the hands of transnational corporates, as well as a means of passing an evening: witness the success of the Disney corporation. This being the case, it behoves us to review the role of folk and fairy tales in sanctioned reading schemes, and the context which gives rise to their inclusion. What importance is this genre accorded, and, why? Does the content of the sanctioned tales reflect, conceal, and/or reveal the dominant ideologies of our society? What values actually underpin the tales? What lessons can be learned from an analysis of them?

In Defence of Story

The form of story has traditionally been central to education, and with good reason. The 1971 Primary School Curriculum document's apologia for the narrative form claims that story

> consolidates and extends the child's personal experience, and often affords him compensation for the things he lacks; it fires

the imagination and broadens his language; it can provide relief from the harsher realities of life and at the same time help in coming to grips with them. Stories can attractively portray great virtue; they can stimulate interest in books and reading. They can also contribute to the establishing and strengthening of a bond between pupil and teacher (Vol. 1, p. 86).

One might go farther in defence of narrative. Because it is an intensely pleasurable activity for listeners, storytellers and readers alike, it is a sound method of transmitting values and information. Furthermore, stories, because they consist of a beginning, middle and end – even the shortest, most elemental of them – communicate the shape of the world and help to make sense of it. They represent the way events unfold in time. They form the most basic introduction to aesthetic principles by shaping events into a pleasing form. A story is a way of doing things with words, of making something happen in the real world. The word 'fiction' comes from the Latin *fingere*, 'to make' or 'to make up'. It therefore carries parallel connotations: fictional stories exist in and make an impact on the real world, but are not limited to it because they are generated by the imagination. In story, children experience conflict and the resolution of conflict, since conflict is an indispensable element of plot. Within story's relatively safe parameters and through their exploration of conflict, they are empowered to question the assumptions of their culture, and enabled to build a significant and orderly world around themselves (Hillis Miller, 1990).[1]

There is a growing awareness that storying also occupies a crucial role in the formation of personal identity, that selfhood evolves through the narrativising process. It might be said that the lives we live are enacted narratives. They too have a beginning, middle and end. We look back on events of our lives and respectively apply causation (or emplotment, to use a descriptive term of story) to the tale of self (either by ourselves or by another), thus enabling us, the authors of the lives, to imagine an ending, a future. This logical impulse co-exists with a recognition of the contingencies which are also implicated in shaping the life. Being author of one's life means selecting from the accidents and unintended consequences of previous actions in order to make sense of things. 'Life calls out for narrative recounting'; it calls out to be made and remade in that way (Dunne, 1995, p. 149).[2] The storied self is a unified, coherent being in the sense that a story is coherent; the individual is author or co-author with others in his/her own story. The stories of each individual life are embedded in the stories of communities of which the author is part – communities that are local, national or communities of enquiry. The faith which both the 1971 primary school curriculum document and its successor place in story, and in particular in folk and fairy story, is therefore not misplaced.

Definitions of Folk and Fairy Tale

What exactly are folk and fairy tales and how might they be distinguished from other narrative forms such as myths, legends, wonder tales and sagas? While it is useful to define these categories, it must be said that the boundaries between them are constantly blurring, and it is not possible to offer hard or fast definitions. The 1971 curriculum does not differentiate significantly between myth, legend, saga or folktale: for example it states that '[f]airy-tale, folktale, legend, myth and saga should all be presented [to children in standards III and IV].[3] The Department of Education's (1984) *Guidelines for Publishers of School Textbooks* specifies that '[t]he programme should include legend and mythology', again failing to draw any distinction. Even experts and analysts of folktale offer contradictory definitions. One renowned psychoanalytic critic of folk and fairy tale, Bruno Bettelheim, makes no hard and fast distinction. The theoretician Vladimir Propp uses the term 'wonder tale' in his marxist/structuralist critique of folk tales, describing it as follows: 'a [wonder] tale may be termed a development proceeding from

villainy . . . or a lack . . . through intermediary functions to marriage
. . . to other functions employed as a denouement' (Propp, 1975, p.
xxxiii). Basically, his definition involves an unhappy situation,
followed by a reversal or a transformation that leads to a happy
ending (marriage). Often this transformation is brought about by
magic or by some extra-logical means. The Brothers Grimm use
the term *hausmarchen*, which translates literally as a household
tale, but which came to be translated as fairy tale, to include
anecdote, animal tales, burlesques, folk, local, literary and religious
legends. Levi Strauss sees myth as concerned with some basic
contradiction and the way this contradiction is overcome
(Liberman, in Propp, 1975, p. xxxvi).

Fairy tales may be identified as stories that have a relaxed
attitude to the reality principle. Iona and Peter Opie (1974) have
remarked that a characteristic is that they are unbelievable, and that
they are seldom about fairies. The term originally entered the
English language at the end of the eighteenth century from the
French *conte des fées*. There the form had evolved as a literary
genre in the aristocratic salons. Women – it often was intelligent,
aristocratic women with time on their hands who adopted the form
– improvised upon and embellished a literary motif in their stories.
From this milieu came familiar stories such as Red Riding Hood
and Tom Thumb. As time went on, these stories became
increasingly the pretext for moral or cautionary tales. Many of the
originals were overtly violent and sexual, and therefore had to be
sanitised before they would be considered suitable for children. In
spite of this, and although the genre of children's literature as we
know it did not exist, they found their way into the nursery, in part
because of the morals that collectors such as Perrault insisted in
finding in them. They were a useful adjunct in the business of
grooming the young for their place in society.

Folktales are most commonly defined as an oral narrative
form cultivated by the common people to express the manner in
which they perceived nature and their social order and their wish to
satisfy their needs and wants. Therefore, they are an expression of

communal rather than individualised culture. They may reflect reality as the 'common' people perceive it, and/or they may symbolise their aspirations, dreams and wishes. They can both affirm the dominant social order *and* reveal how it needs to be changed. Because they derive from an oral culture, the impact of folktales is immediate. They appear timeless, and seem to offer universal folk wisdom uncontaminated by intellectualism, yet each historical epoch and each community leaves its stamp on them. They represent reality as it was experienced by a certain group of people at a certain time. Indeed, many folktales as we have come to know them were written down during a specific period, namely, the end of the eighteenth century, or early in the nineteenth, and rather than representing timeless truth, they reflect conditions of this transitional period in Europe – a period that is at once late feudal and early modern in many rural areas. Moreover, well-educated, middle-class intellectuals, imbued inescapably with their particular class prejudices, mainly carried out the work of collecting and cataloguing. Nowhere is this more evident than in the editing process applied to Grimm's fairy tales, which sanitised references to sexuality, but failed to exclude gruesome, violent scenes.[4] Furthermore, folktales were never exclusive to the peasantry. They provided priests with valuable, familiar, illustrative narratives for their sermons; they found their way into aristocratic nurseries and hence into shaping the experiences of young privileged people; well-to-do and well-educated travellers shared them. Folktales are, therefore, context- and time-specific, but not as class-specific (in the sense that they are not unmediated medieval peasant narratives) as might have been thought.[5]

Many of the folktales we know are related to cultural and political agendas, especially to nineteenth century nationalism. It is in the context of nurturing pride in a distinctively Irish heritage that many stories were collected by Hyde, Yeats, Gregory, Standish O'Grady, and earlier revivalists such as Crofton Croker, Kennedy, Larminie and so on. This desire to nurture national pride significantly influenced educational practice and curriculum until recent decades, and the folktales became a popular pedagogical tool.

Folktale and Primary Education in Ireland

The interest in folktale as a manifestation of emergent nationalism was manifested throughout Europe. The nineteenth century saw an immense increase in the collection, transcription and publication of folklore. Notwithstanding their temporal specificity, folktales were considered the repository of universal, time-honoured wisdom which contrasted deeply with and challenged the rapid and disconcerting changes brought about by urbanisation and the ideals of progressivism. The Grimm brothers, who were serious scholars – philologists, antiquarians and medievalists – originally saw their *hausmarchen* as scholarly work, not tales for children. For those people aspiring to independent nationhood, folklore was seen to embody the traditional, communitarian ideals upon which a nation might be founded. Irish folklore was the central impulse behind one of the most distinctive literary movements of the century, the Irish literary renaissance (Thuente, 1980, p. 1), a key factor in the cultural nationalism that was to contribute to the insurrection of 1916 and ultimately to Irish independence. This nationalist appropriation of the *volk* may have found its most sinister expression in Hitler's Third Reich.

It's hardly surprising that folktale should play an important part in education, since it plays such a crucial role in the socialisation of the young and the transmission of culture (Drudy & Lynch, 1993), p. 26). This was recognised in Germany as early as 1850 when curricula included Grimms' tales that discussed family life as well as relationships between master and servant, host and guest and between comrades. By 1938, an informing principle of German education was 'No German childhood without fairy tales; no folk specific and racial education without them'. In Ireland too in this century, the classroom has been an arena in which cultural and nationalist battles have been fought – for religious homogeneity and for the revival of the Irish language, to name but two. It was also the locus of attempts to preserve the idealised Irish identity of post-treaty Ireland – strongly agrarian, Gaelic, rural and frugal – which finds its best known expression in De Valera's famous radio broadcast. The folktale, in terms of its form and content, is a natural vehicle for these sentiments. It has particular resonance in the Irish context because much of the Gaelic culture idealised by the founders of the Irish state was part of an oral, folk culture.

Folklore played a particularly significant role in Irish education, in that there were close links between the body that collected, categorised and collated folklore, the Folklore Commission, and the primary school system. When it was founded in 1935, the Commission's staff were members of the Department of Education, and remained so until 1971 when the work was transferred to the Department of Irish Folklore at University College Dublin. One of the Commission's largest projects was undertaken in 1937-38 when senior children in primary schools in the twenty-six counties helped, as part of their school work, to collect local folklore, and it acquired about a half a million pages through that scheme.[6] Many contributors to *Béaloideas*, the journal of the Irish Folklore Commission, were national teachers, and many teachers assisted in the field work of the Commission. There was therefore a high value placed on folktale in the Irish primary education system in the formative years of the state, especially in the lean years of mid-century, when the frugality and hardship so evident in the tales was an inescapable reality. Furthermore, there is an assumption that folktales are the narrative expression of the idealised *volk*, whose ageless truth and virtue they embody. The 1971 *Primary School Curriculum* expresses this position unequivocally:

> Fairy-tales, which very often have children or animals in central roles, present kindness, truth and loyalty in a manner appealing to young children. Together with the simpler fables and folk-tales [here the handbook does not appear to

differentiate between folk and fairy tale, legend and fable], and the beginnings of legend, they provide a wide range of material from which to choose for the Junior classes. (Dept. of Education, Vol. I, p. 87).

Another attraction of the form from an educational standpoint is that folktales pay little attention to authorship and as such appear to favour more fundamental values than the bourgeois emphasis on poverty and ownership. This of course can be contested: as I will show later in this article, it is not unusual for folktale to underwrite the value of property and acquisition. A cynic might suggest that the sub-genre finds favour with educational publishers rather because it does not command a copyright fee.

The form of folktale is an attractive mode of conveying communitarian values, because, as Jakobson (1972) has remarked, the socialised sections of mental culture, as for instance, language or folktale, are subject to much stricter and more uniform laws than fields in which individualised creation prevails. The folkteller's audience operated stricter censorship over his or her inventiveness. A story had to win the approval of the collective body before it became part of the standard repertory of tales and therefore act as a cohesive influence on a society, emphasising tradition. On the other hand, a literary individual has more scope for and autonomy for flouting convention in a literary text. The written work can run counter to readers' expectations and still survive disapproval. So the folk stories concern themselves with the lives of mostly illiterate persons confronting poverty, hunger, exploitation, and injustice.

In most cases, the audience sympathises with the main protagonist in the story. Folk tales, then, can be a powerful cohering agent, binding individuals together and maintaining the sense of community. As such, they also prove invaluable in transmitting a community's values to the young. Before we explore the values that actually find their way into the tales approved for children in Ireland, let us first establish what are the values that society believes should be inculcated in the young. One way of determining this is to look to official documents produced by the Department of Education.

Value Content of Story and the Primary School Curriculum

Has the Department of Education expressed an opinion on what constitutes acceptable or suitable content of the stories taught in primary schools? The 1971 *Primary School Curriculum* makes no specific recommendation. The teacher's handbook includes a section that addresses the techniques of reading[7] but does not comment upon the value content of the sanctioned reading schemes. This is not a matter that preoccupied the Review Body on Primary Education, which published its report in 1990, or educational historians like Séamus Ó Buachalla, or more general historians like Joseph Lee. There are two assumptions implied here: the first is that there exists consensus regarding what constitutes appropriate content of reading programmes (and indeed, other aspects of the curriculum) in primary schools, and secondly, that the actual content equates with the desired content.

It is possible to identify what that desired content might be. The 1971 *Primary School Curriculum* which informed the sanctioned reading schemes that are still in use in primary schools offers some general direction as to the values that should permeate the 'whole work' of the school. It states that:

> a religions spirit should inform and vivify the whole work of the school. The teacher should constantly *inculcate the practice of charity, justice, truth, purity, patience, temperance, obedience to lawful authority, and all the other moral virtues* [my italics]. In this way he [sic] will fulfil the primary duty of an educator, the moulding to perfect form of his pupils' character, habituating them to observe, in their relations with God and with their neighbour, the laws which God, both directly through the dictates of natural reason, and through Revelation, and indirectly through the ordinance of lawful authority, imposes on mankind'. (Vol. I, p. 23)

The desire to shape the young mind in accordance with certain moral and ethical principles is further underlined when the 1971

Primary School Curriculum adverts to the need to avoid nurturing prejudice during history classes:

> The sympathy of the generous young mind will naturally lie with the oppressed and all the more so when, in the main, its own people were the sufferers. The special problem which thus arises is how to present past ill-doing without so arousing the child's emotion as to prejudice his mind in relation to existing conditions. (Vol. II, p. 88)

This prescriptive document implies a concensualist ideology. It presupposes that there is universal agreement about the scale of values that should direct our educational processes (Drudy & Lynch, 1993, p. 51).[8] One might look to the *Report of the Review Body on the Primary Curriculum* published in 1990 for modifications to the philosophy underlying the 1971 curriculum, which might also influence or reflect the subject matter of sanctioned stories. Inter alia, this report identifies the cultural and historical environment of the pupil as a valuable resource and its use as a valuable pedagogical principle (p. 21), and the importance of oral language (p. 26), the context within which the tradition of folk and fairy tale has thrived. It reiterates, albeit in less sectarian terms, certain aims: that a spirit of co-operation and a capacity to contribute to the development of society might be fostered, that children might respect their own and other cultural identifies, acquire moral and religious identifies, and respect the beliefs of others.

The philosophy that officially informs reading material may be found in a third source, the Department of Education's (1984) *Guidelines for Publishers of School Texts*. Although they do not prescribe content, the Guidelines concede that '[a]n ideal reading scheme will have to come to terms with national, cultural, environmental, social and sexual factors.' Whereas the Guidelines are generally vague about what constitutes acceptable moral or ethical material, in one area, namely that of sex stereotyping in school texts, the Department issued a specific set of guidelines.[9]

Given this relatively ample, if uneven, articulation of a moral and social framework, it is reasonable therefore to expect that the content of all aspects of the curriculum, including the English reading schemes during the last 30 years, should actively advocate a moral framework imbued with the Christian spirit and the virtues and attitudes listed (since the term 'religious' in the 1971 *Primary School Curriculum* is synonymous with 'Christian'[10]) including an awareness of gender equity. The corollary of this expectation is that the (English) curriculum should avoid presenting impressionable minds with models of unChristian, irreligious or sexist behaviour. It might be predicted that the curriculum overseers would ensure that, for example, positive character traits should predominate in the story characters with whom pupils identify, or that good should triumph over evil. It is reasonable to expect also that the stories contained in the sanctioned readers would scrupulously ensure gender equity.

Do the stories measure up to the Christian standards established in the curriculum statement? Do they reflect the dominant ideology of Irish society as outlined in the 1971 Curriculum and/or modified in the 1990 *Report of the Review Body on the Primary Curriculum*? In a tale which bears all the hallmarks of folklore, 'Sol Magee and the rich man' from the third class reader entitled *The Sea Keepers* (Educational Company, 1991),[11] the indignant Sol outwits his powerful and heartless social superiors. The starving Sol tells a rich man's butler that he wants to enquire of his master what he should do if he had a great deal of money. He is invited to join the rich man for a lunch, which he enjoys more than his host because he is hungrier. When lunch is over, he informs the rich man that the question was merely hypothetical. The moral content of this story may be deemed questionable – the underlying message seems to be that it is acceptable to be economical with the truth, for the poor to masquerade as wealthy and to rob the rich. If, as is suggested, the child sympathises with the oppressed, she or he will identify with Sol. Such an identification will hardly inculcate the practice of charity, justice and truth as the Department of Education earnestly desires. Rather, it favours dishonesty. Yet Sol Magee is portrayed as a self-styled Solomon and purveyor of folk wisdom and homely values, who, the children are told, 'became famous for doing good' (p. 17). However, he is remarkable rather for his dishonesty and pragmatism. He is guilty of impersonation, lying, of apparently putting a price on Christ's life.

One characteristic of many heroes of folk-type tales in sanctioned reading schemes is their linguistic playfulness. This is a distinctive feature of much Irish literature which has helped place Irish writers such as James Joyce and Flann O'Brien in the forefront of experimental modernism. The aforementioned Sol wants to identify a thief and does this by misleading his suspects into believing that he has hidden a cock in a freshly-painted bucket. The cock will crow, he says, when the thief touches it. In fact it is the absence of a paint mark on his hand, which identified the thief. A poor young man, Klaus, applies for a position as cook to the king whom he impresses with recipes for his unusual dragon stew. When finally the king catches a dragon with which to make the celebrated stew, it transpires that Klaus 'made up that silly recipe', he 'never made stew in his life'. After some quick thinking, he serves the king stew made by, not with, the dragon. A poor shoemaker agrees to pay over to the palace guardsmen who bully him whatever reward the king gives him for presenting him with a fine pair of shoes. The reward he chooses is ice-cold water which he orders to be poured over them. A barber, sworn to secrecy about the big ears of the rajah whose hair he has cut but literally dying to share the story, avoids the threat of jail by confiding in a tree and not a human. The citizens of a town under siege negotiate the release of their women and whatever belongings they can carry as they leave on foot. Little do the attackers know that the women plan to carry their menfolk to freedom. Protagonists-sophists such as these characters have a veritable treasure trove of half-truths, conceits and outright untruths at their disposal. In their defence, it might be said that their linguistic dexterity is evidence of flexible minds and the kind of lateral thinking that enables people to survive in the teeth of oppression. As such, the stories contain models of the critical thinking extolled in the Irish Government's (1993) *Green Paper on Education*. However, the summaries of tales cited above might lead one to conclude that the sublimated messages we give children as young as eight or nine years of age are more complex and morally confusing than a first reading suggests.

An ambivalent attitude to wealth and poverty is a theme of many stories. Some expose the misery of wealth and extol the virtues of frugal living and hard work. Misers are the object of much odium. However, close investigation suggests that the accumulation of wealth and power can also be a worthy and approved pursuit, and that humiliating the powerful, exposing their foolishness, and relieving them of their wealth, Robin-Hood style, is a laudable end in itself. This is what happens in 'The cat and the green egg', for example. Here children are initiated into the doubtful pleasures of schadenfreude as they are encouraged to watch the mean shopkeeper publicly humiliated as he clucks like a hen while the stock in his shop is distributed free to his customers. On the other hand, we are encouraged to approve of the prosperity enjoyed in 'The golden ring' by the farmer and his wife. 'The bank on the shelf jingled with silver coins' (p. 34), we are told. Ambivalence about wealth is most neatly encapsulated in 'The shepherd's treasure' (*A Postcard from the Stars*, pp. 95-101). Here, a humble but wise shepherd is made governor by the king. Everywhere he goes, he ostentatiously parades a chest whose contents are secret.

> Behind him was a camel carrying a wooden chest. The chest had a double lock and bands of iron. It was guarded by armed men, and even the camel driver carried a spear. (p. 100)

It transpires that the chest contains his old sheepskin, intended constantly to remind him of his humble origins. However, the fact that the sheepskin is thoroughly concealed behind the trappings of wealth and power – behind guards, bands of iron, the lock, the camel – conspires to deconstruct the apparent moral of the tale. The lasting impression is not of the governor's humility but of his status.

With some notable exceptions – such as 'A clever woman' (*A Postcard*, pp. 140-145) and 'My mother sends her wisdom' (*The Sea Keepers*, pp. 31-36) – the majority of stories affirm patriarchal values and revolve around men. While numerical advantage is not per se a guarantee of gender imbalance, the high proportion of stories about males nonetheless contributes to and reflects male domination and patriarchal relationships that are a feature of many folktales. Tyrants may be challenged but the underlying master/slave relationship more often is not. Sol Magee may challenge Jack Murphy's boss (the man is known only by his function, not his name) but only so that his friend may retain his job. The patriarchy is not transformed. He advises the baker's seven sons not to test their autonomy, personal or economic, but to remain subservient to their father's authority (*The Sea Keepers*, pp. 42-43). The message is that children must be socialised to please their fathers, preferably by assisting them in accumulating wealth, thus adding to patriarchal power. This top-heavy distribution of power is at odds with the belief in personal autonomy upon which contemporary education places a high value.

In many folktales in sanctioned reading schemes, the bourgeois values of thrift, diligence, and honesty are underwritten, but this is not always so. Stories such as 'The golden ring', and 'My mother sends her wisdom' actively extol industry and thrift, but what are we to make of the model of Sol Magee, a penniless, often hungry wanderer? In other stories the accumulation of wealth or position can take precedence over honesty, as in 'Dragon stew' (*The Sea Keepers,* pp. 44-45).

Many of the protagonists exact cruel vengeance for perceived transgressions, at once enforcing the attitude that both vengeance and cruelty are acceptable. The bible exhorts its readers to see the former as the province of the Lord, but the main protagonists often demand punishment that mirrors the crime (and is therefore as morally reprehensible as the original transgression), or which appears excessive or inappropriate. The dishonest guardsmen in 'The shoemaker's present' are punished twice: they serve jail sentences for their crimes, but are also made to suffer public physical indignity – ice-cold water is poured over them. The punishment meted out to the cruel Baron in 'The fiddler and his dancing bear' is that he be lured into a bear pit, intimidated by a pack of angry boars, and then be left 'cold and hungry, dirty and tired' to spend the night outside his city walls. Cruelty is revisited upon the cruel.

Conclusion

It may be asserted that folk stories should not be read as rational tracts. But the well-documented history of folktale as an instrument of socialisation implies that their messages, moral and otherwise, must be taken seriously. We may conclude that the tales discussed here are in the main morally ambivalent; often – but not always – they subliminally affirm traits and values diametrically opposed to the values which the Department of Education (and, by implication, society at large) supports. If teachers see reading-class as an opportunity for exploring values then the ambivalence may be turned to advantage. It is neither possible nor desirable, nor even Christian in spirit, to protect children from a knowledge of evil in the world. Furthermore, our national experience of nearly half a century of literary censorship highlighted the cultural debilitation that ensues from authoritarian dicta. Children are capable of confronting the serious issues and conflicts implied in the stories cited.[12] However, it behoves teachers to be vigilant to these subtexts and to facilitate dialogue on them. This in turn will demand that they explore their own stance on the problems raised. It may demand specific pedagogical approaches, of which three examples will suffice to show what is possible. Gianni Rodari has created a series of games in which the players' expectations of well-known folk and fairy tales are shattered. If, for example, Snow White were to meet a band of giants, and to organise robberies instead of keeping house, then the reader-players would be forced to re-examine their responses to the original story and to reconsider the function and meaning of certain elements of the tale. Georges Jean has experimented with card games that require children to change certain features of traditional stories in order that they relate more directly to their own lives (Quoted in Zipes, 1991, pp. 191-192). Members of the Association of Teachers for Philosophy with Children in Ireland have conducted sessions based on a method developed by Joseph Dunne and Philomena Donnelly. Children form a circle and engage or play with a story with minimal or even no direction from the teacher. Once the children have learnt the protocol of these thinking sessions, the process can be richly rewarding. Although outcomes cannot be prescribed in advance, children set seriously about reflecting and making meaning.[13] The final word on the topic of making meaning from folk and fairy tale may go to Walter Benjamin, who distinguishes between story and information. Information is verifiable, understandable in itself. Story, he says, is open to multiple interpretations because it withholds certain essential details. He contends that half the art of storytelling is to exclude explanation and concludes that this is why it cannot grow old. It is the absence of closure – of moral and social closure in this case – that exerts eternal fascination.

REFERENCES

Benjamin, W. (1983). The storyteller. In H. Arendt (Ed.). *Illuminations* (pp. 83-109). London: Fontana.

Department of Education. (1971). *Primary school curriculum: Teacher's handbook I. [Curaclam na Bunscoile, Lámhleabhar and Oide I].* Dublin: Government Publications.

Department of Education. (1984). *Guidelines for publishers of school texts.* Dublin: Government Publications. (INTO Bk 2471#3).

Department of Education. (1984). *Guidelines for publishers on sexism and sex-stereo-typing in primary school textbooks.* Dublin: Government Publications.

Dunne, J. (1995). Beyond sovereignty and deconstruction: The storied self. *Philosophical and Social Criticism, 25*(6), 149.

Drudy, S., & Lynch, K. (1993). *Schools and society in Ireland.* Dublin: Gill and Macmillan.

Hillis Miller, J. (1990). Narrative. In F. Lentriccia & T. McLoughlin (Eds.), *Critical terms for literary study* (pp. 66-79). Chicago: University of Chicago Press.

Ireland. (1992). Education for a changing world. Green Paper on education. Dublin: Stationery Office.

Jakobson, R. (1972). *Selected writings* (Vol. 4, 1-15). The Hague: Mouton.

Jean, G. (1981). *Le pouvour des contes.* Paris: Casterman.

Opie, I. & Opie, P. (1974). *The classic fairy tales.* Oxford: Oxford University Press.

Propp. V. (1975). *Theory and history of folklore.* In A.Y. Martin and R.P. Martin (Trss.) and A. Liberman (Intro). Manchester: Manchester University Press.

Review Body on the Primary Curriculum. (1990). *Report.* Dublin: Stationery Office.

Rodari, G. (1978). *Grammarie de l'imagination.* Paris: Francais Réunis.

Shine Thompson, M. (Ed.). (1998). *Arista, 1*(1). Dublin: Association of Teachers for Philosophy with Children.

Tatar, M. (1987). *The hard facts of Grimms' fairy tales.* Princeton, NJ: Princeton University Press.

Thuente, M.H. (1980). *W.B. Yeats and Irish folklore.* Dublin: Gill and Macmillan.

Zipes, J. (1979). *Breaking the magic spell: radical theories of folk and fairy tales.* New York: Routledge.

Zipes, J. (1990). *Fairy tales and the art of subversion.* New York: Routledge.

Textbooks:

_____. *The Sea Keepers.* Dublin: The Educational Company.

_____. *A Postcard from the Stars.* Dublin: The Educational Company.

ENDNOTES

1. In my understanding of narrative, as outlined here, I am significantly indebted to Hillis Miller's 'Narrative'.

2. Seamus Deane's recent novel, *Reading in the Dark*, is a testament to the model of selfhood described here, and it draws on the genre of folktale to make sense of the recent past.

3. Neither is there a distinction made when the document discusses the junior classes: 'Fairy-tales, which very often have children or animals in central roles, present kindness, truth and loyalty in a manner appealing to young children. Together with the simpler fables and folk-tales and the beginnings of legend, they provide a wide range of material from which to choose for the Junior classes' (p. 87).

4. This topic is addressed in Tatar (1987).

5. This matter is explored in Zipes (1979).

6. Microfiche copies of local collections are held in libraries throughout the country.

7. It refers to such technical concerns as sight vocabulary, word recognition skills, methods of developing mechanical reading skills, and parallel and supplementary readers.

8. My purpose here is to establish only that such assumptions are made. The work of Drudy and Lunch goes on to expose some of the weaknesses of these assumptions.

9. *Guidelines for Publishers on Sexism and Sex-Stereo-typing in Primary School Textbooks* (Department of Education, 1984). It is interesting to note that, while the general guidelines to publishers on Geography texts cautions that 'considerable care' should be exercised 'in matters touching, even obliquely on sexism and racism', the guidelines for English make no reference to these concerns. This may suggest that gender equity was not a high priority for the officials who drew up the English guidelines, or, alternatively, that it was assumed that there was consensus on the topic and that it was unnecessary for them to elaborate upon it.

10. The language of the *Primary School Curriculum: Teacher's Handbooks I and II* is distinctively Christian, if not Catholic. 'Each human being is created in God's image. He has a life to lead and a soul to be saved. Education is concerned, not only with life but with the purpose of life' (Vol. 1, p. 12).

11. For example, the stories 'Sol Magee and the Rich Man' (pp. 29-30) and 'Sol Magee and the Bakers' (pp. 42-43) in *The Sea Keepers*.

12. The work done by the Association of Teachers for Philosophy with Children under the direction of Joseph Dunne of St. Patrick's College, Drumcondra is evidence of this.

13. This method is described in several articles in M. Shine Thompson (Ed.). *Arista*.

Language Play and Vocabulary Development in the Primary School*

. . . .

George Hunt
University of Reading, England

This paper addresses some issues involved in the learning of vocabulary, and relates these issues to the more general phenomenon of language play. The paper has arisen from concerns about the way in which vocabulary learning has been represented in the current National Literacy Strategy in England, and the ways in which the vocabulary strand of this strategy is being implemented in some classrooms.

What Does It Mean to Know a Word?

Perhaps the minimum conditions for knowing a word are that the learner should be able to use the word in the same range of contexts that other members of the speech community would use it, and recognise its meaning, or a part of its meaning spectrum, when it is used by another person (Wittgenstein 1953). Word learning, at least with younger children, begins with speaking and listening; they need to have the word in their oral language (even if they can't pronounce it 'properly') before they can usefully recognise it in reading or use it in writing. This implies that new words need

*Paper presented at the 23rd Annual Conference of the Reading Association of Ireland, Limerick, September 17-19, 1998

to be 'demonstrated' in conversation or in other oral events such as story-reading or recital, and their meanings discussed. This should be obvious, but there is a danger that this essentially oral, meaning-oriented stage in word learning might be neglected in practices which prioritise immediate recognition of words in reading and the ability to spell them. Neither of these practices necessarily imply understanding of the word. However, once a child has learned to read independently, he or she will begin to encounter many words which are not in oral vocabulary. The acquisition of vocabulary by learning words from context in the process of reading is discussed below.

Another aspect of word knowledge is awareness of the web of relationships that binds the word to other words. It seems clear that words are not arranged as individual items in the word-hoard, but as clusters of terms linked by principles such as inclusion, entailment, synonymy and antonymy (Miller, in Anglin, 1993). Word learning can therefore be seen as a gradual process of integrating a new item into a semantic field of related terms, a process which involves a restructuring of this field. For example, a child beginning to learn a word like *grotesque* might start off by assimilating it to known words like *ugly* or *hideous*. The lexicon is expanded, but because no two words are ever completely synonymous, shades of difference between the new term and the old are gradually acquired – the fact that *grotesque* may have suggestions of the bizarre and ridiculous for instance, and that its metaphorical use has different connotations to the metaphorical use of related words. This restructuring of the semantic field depends of course on the learner having opportunities to use the word and to see it used in a range of contexts.

If new words are assimilated to clusters of known words according to the semantic relationships mentioned above, it seems likely that they are also related by sound to known words. Children's fascination from an early age with rhyme and alliteration has been well documented, as has their ability to make sound spelling analogies between known and unknown words encountered in reading (Goswami and Bryant, 1990).

To summarise, knowing a word means being able to use it in a variety of contexts or 'language games'. Learning a word is not just a matter of adding a new lexeme to the word-hoard; it involves knowing how the new word's range of meanings interconnect with those of the words that we already know, and being able to orchestrate these relationships in order to communicate.

How Do Children Learn New Words?

The child's first recognisable word is uttered at about twelve months, and after this, words are acquired with remarkable rapidity and apparent ease. At eighteen months the 'average' child can produce about fifty words, and understand five times as many (Crystal 1986). After the child passes the 200 word mark (typically at around two years old) estimates of vocabulary size are extremely variable, but some studies have put the recognition vocabulary of children starting school at roughly 10,000 words (Anglin, 1993). Vocabulary development is a lifelong process. The recognition vocabulary of an educated adult probably exceeds 50,000 words (Aicheson, 1987), and it is a common phenomenon for adults to acquire new items through reading and social interaction.

Unlike phonological and grammatical development, in which most progress is made in the pre-school years, vocabulary development is at its most dramatic during the early and middle years of schooling. Anglin's study of vocabulary growth in American school children (1993) indicated that between grades one and five the 10,000 items known when the child enters school quadruples to 40,000 words, a phenomenon which implies an average rate of growth of some twenty words per day during these years. Clearly, this represents more words than can possibly be taught through direct instruction, so what *are* the processes by which children achieve this growth?

There is evidence that in the pre-school years, vocabulary acquisition, along with other aspects of language, is facilitated by interactive routines with a more mature speaker in which learner and interlocutor share a joint focus of attention. Circumstances which have been researched include picture-book reading (Snow & Goldfield, 1983) and mealtimes (Beals, 1997). In these situations, the impact of the traditional 'naming game' appears to be augmented by physical and imaginative involvement in social exchanges and rich sensory experience.

In the classroom, claims have been made for direct instruction (Beck, Perfetti & Omanson, 1987), learning from context during reading activities (Nagy & Anderson, 1984; Shu, Anderson & Zhang, 1995) and morphological problem-solving (Anglin, 1993). There is strong evidence that traditional dictionary exercises, in which children look up definitions of items from prescribed word lists and then attempt to use the words in sentences, are ineffective (Miller & Gildea, 1987).

The study by Beck, Perfetti and Omanson (1987) suggested that effective programmes of direct instruction in vocabulary feature the following characteristics:

- words are grouped according to meaning;
- learners receive multiple exposures to words in a variety of illustrative contexts;
- they receive rich and varied information about each word, including how it relates to words already known, and to other aspects of current knowledge and experience;
- the learner should have an active role in integrating this information. For example, in Beck et al's study, tasks included discussing what a *hermit* might have a *nightmare* about, describing an occasion on which learners had *consoled* somebody, and deciding whether or not a *miser* could be a *tyrant;*
- a strong word play element is advisable. For example, in Beck et al.'s study, a 'Word Wizard' game motivated children to explore the use of words outside the school context.

The latter two aspects suggest that the instructional programme should focus as much on attitudes towards vocabulary as on target words, fostering a curiosity about and appreciation of words. The benefits of well planned direct instruction are not so much in the efficacy with which a particular set of target words are learned, as in the development of a long term predisposition to be interested in words in general.

Studies of vocabulary acquisition through reading have indicated that with appropriate support reading can be an effective route for word learning, but only when fluent reading has been achieved. Before this, the learner's energies are largely expended on the decoding of print. Chall (1987) makes the point that in the early stages of reading, a child can understand and use in speech many more words than she can recognise in print. As the child's reading becomes fluent, recognition vocabulary 'catches up' with oral vocabulary. Thereafter, wider reading and progress through the curriculum is likely to bring the child into contact with words that can be read from the page but not necessarily understood. It is at this point that the child is confronted by the challenge and the opportunity for expanding vocabulary through reading. In order to benefit from this, the child needs to learn strategies for working out the meanings of unfamiliar words. These strategies will include applying prior knowledge to the context in which the new word occurs, but this is a high risk strategy unless it is augmented with feedback and discussion of inferences (Miller and Gildea, 1987).

Another set of strategies involves analysis of the word itself. Morphological problem solving is the process used by learners to derive word meanings from their knowledge of root words and inflections. Anglin (1993) coined this phrase to describe how children figure out words which are 'potentially knowable' by relating them to the 'psychologically basic' words and word parts that they have already learned and arranged in their mental lexicons. His study was based on a categorisation of English words into five different types:

1.   Root words consisting of single morphemes (meaning units). Examples from Anglin's study are *closet, flop, hermit* and *pep.*

2. Inflected words consisting of a root word plus one of the eight types of inflectional suffixes that occur in English: the plural *-s*, the possessive *-'s*, the third person singular *-s*, the progressive *-ing*, the past tense *-ed*, the past participle *-en*, the comparative *-er*, and the superlative *-est*. The addition of these suffixes produces grammatical variants of the root word, rather than a change in meaning or part of speech. Examples are *boy-boys, cat-cat's, jump-jumps, jump-jumping, jump-jumped, fall-fallen, poor-poorer, poor-poorest.*

3. Derived words consisting of a root plus one or more derivational prefixes or suffixes, creating a related but distinct word and often a change in the part of speech. Examples are *muck-mucky, talk-talkativeness, compare-incomparable.*

4. Literal or transparent compounds – words made up of two or more smaller words. The meaning of a literal compound is determinable from the meanings of its component words. Examples are *payday, seabound*, and *live-born.*

5. Idioms or opaque compounds – consist of two or more component words, but their meanings are not determinable from the meanings of their parts. For example, one cannot deduce from simple word analysis that a *redhead* is a person with red hair rather than a head which is red.

Anglin found that much of the vocabulary growth that occurs in the school years can be explained by children's growing awareness of the morphological structure of words, and in particular of derivational morphology. He found that with both transparent and opaque compounds, children actively construct meanings by identifying whole word components and blending the meanings together. In the case of idioms, the most difficult of the five categories to learn, this process is, of course, likely to be misleading. Anglin argues, however, that 'in the case of some relatively transparent idioms, it may be that such an approach might provide a base from which the child could guess their non-literal meanings, possibly through metaphorical reasoning' (p.147). It is easy to see how this could work in the example of *redhead* given above.

Anglin's findings are important for teachers in that morphological problem-solving indicates an active and creative role for the learner in the construction of meaning (in this sense, there is a similarity with Beck et al.'s direct instruction model). This study also emphasises that the learner's lexicon or personal word-hoard is highly structured. As Miller, (in Anglin, 1993) says:

> the mental dictionary is not a homogenous list of concept utterance pairs that have been memorised by rote. Words are related to one another in many ways, and it is by taking advantage of those relations that children are able to develop their vocabularies so rapidly (p.173)

An emphasis on the learner actively discovering and creatively developing relationships between words and meanings underlies the classroom activities outlined in the latter part of this paper. They are aimed at stimulating curiosity about words, willingness to play with them, and aesthetic response to their sounds and connotations. If, as Meara (1996) argues, we should as teachers be paying less attention to isolated words and more attention to the personal lexicons that learners construct with them, then this entails a concern for how the learner engages affectively as well as cognitively in the structuring and restructuring of his/her word-hoard. For the child, play is central to these processes.

The Role of Language Play

No sooner do young children acquire the rudiments of language than they begin to play with them. This is hardly surprising, given that speech is so often acquired within a playful context. Studies of the earliest interactions between parents and children show that at the heart of the register variously known as baby-talk, motherese or child-directed speech is a set of features that emphasise its playfulness. These include exaggerated pitch range, the use of 'nonsensical' and reduplicative vocabulary (*dumdum; weewee; bow-wow*), and semi-linguistic vocalisations like clicks and coos (Crystal, 1998).

Children begin to engage in phonetic play from around the age of one, often in spontaneous soliloquies which include onomatopoeic lexicalisations of environmental sound (*brumbrum, neenaw, wuff*). An awareness of rhyme and a readiness to experiment with it characterises the speech of children in their third and fourth years (Bradley & Bryant, 1985). From this age, children will often home in on an 'accidental' rhyme in conversation, then attempt to outdo each other in brainstorming variants of the rhyme, often producing strings of nonsense words in the process. Play with morphological features of words has been identified in the conversations of five year olds, as in the example below where the adjectival function of the -*y* suffix is playfully extended (Garvey, 1977):

> A: Cause it's fishy too. Cause it has fishes.
> B: And it's snaky too cause it has snakes and it's beary too because it has bears.
> C: And it's . . . its hatty too cause it has hats.

During the school years, language play continues to develop and diversify. Children collect and invent taboo and exotic words; they deliberately misname everyday items and make up silly names for people and things; they experiment with phonology through the use of play voices; they engage in riddles and puns and knock knock type jokes that juggle with the syntax and semantics of everyday speech; they memorise rhymes and other verbal formulae to ritualise a range of social events from farting to courting; they inherit play languages such as pig Latin and spoonerism-talk which are based on sophisticated rearrangements of onsets and rimes; some children even teach themselves to talk backwards.

All of this suggests that children exhibit what appears to be a natural tendency to play with language at all levels, from the phonological to the pragmatic. Many of the games mentioned above require quite highly developed metalinguistic awareness, relying as they do on facility in manipulating semantics, syntax and sublexical aspects of spoken and written language (for a fascinating cross-cultural survey of a selection of such games, see Schwartz 1982). As Crystal (1998) has pointed out, this tendency and the underlying skills involved would seem to have significant educational potential. High levels of oracy and literacy require dexterity with language, and dexterity with language is exactly what children exhibit in their linguistic play. Yet linguistic play has traditionally been seen as something that children should do in the playground rather than the classroom, and in the prescriptive, target-oriented atmosphere that surrounds current innovations in the Literacy curriculum in England, it is likely to remain marginalised.

Implications for Instruction

To summarise the arguments of the preceding section:

- Knowing a word implies being able to use and understand it in a variety of contexts.
- Early vocabulary is acquired through social interactions which afford access to the meaning and pronunciation of words; such contexts frequently involve conversational routines around a joint focus of attention, and rich sensory experience.
- Words are assimilated to meaning- and sound-based networks rather than learned as discrete items.
- An active, problem-solving approach to learning, which encourages investigation of both the contexts in which new words occur and the internal structure of words, appears to be more effective than rote learning and traditional dictionary work.
- An attitude of curiosity towards words appears to facilitate word learning.

- Children's spontaneous play with language incorporates activities and levels of awareness which have the potential for facilitating vocabulary acquisition.

An ideal programme of vocabulary instruction would therefore be as socially interactive and as experiential as possible. The traditional nursery school approach, in which children encounter words and their designata in the course of active, talkative, multi-sensory *play* is perhaps as near to this ideal as we can get. But it is difficult to extend this type of practice into the later years, and no amount of direct experience in itself will necessarily afford access to the comprehension of the abstract vocabulary which characterises the academic reading and writing tasks which older pupils are required to master.

A sound programme for primary-age children would focus on semantic and phonological word families rather than arbitrary or frequency-based word lists; it would teach children about the history and anatomy of words and the relationships between them; it would foster curiosity about words as objects of interest in their own right. Most importantly, it would encourage children to play with and savour words, enjoying their sounds and speculating about their possible meanings; it would emulate the procedures children use in their games by helping them to investigate the effects of splitting words into phonological and morphological elements and recombining them in new patterns, generating nonsense, then creatively infusing this nonsense with meaning.

Although the English National Literacy Strategy supports such strategies in its small print, the word-level strand of its programme of objectives is dominated by a heavily prescriptive sequence of sub-lexical spelling and phonic elements, with no reference to meaning. This is supplemented by year-on-year frequency-based word lists to be taught as sight vocabulary. The semantic and phonaesthetic elements of vocabulary learning are neglected, and the heavy emphasis on graphic and phonic elements of printed words risks reducing the field of vocabulary instruction to procedures for the teaching of spelling and decoding skills.

In the rest of this paper I would like to offer some suggestions for classroom investigations which incorporate the programme features suggested above, while at the same time offering ways of fulfilling objectives in spelling and decoding.

These investigations are based on three interconnected aspects of language which feature frequently in children's language play: sound symbolism; onomastics; and the exploration of sense and nonsense through the segmentation and reordering of word parts into new words.

FIGURE 1

EXAMPLES OF SOUND SYMBOLISM

sl-: sleazy, slippery, slime, slop, slum, slug, sly
DO ALL SL- WORDS HAVE SLEAZY CONNOTATIONS?

-ng: bang, clang, bong, ding, dong, gong, ping, ring
DO ALL -NG WORDS RESONATE METALICALLY?

-ash: bash, clash, gash, gnash, lash, mash, slash, smash, thrash
DO ALL -ASH WORDS DENOTE VIOLENT ACTIONS?

-sh: gush, slosh, flush, splash, mush, slush, wash
HOW DO THESE WORDS DIFFER FROM THE PREVIOUS SET?

-ump: bump, clump, dump, hump, lump, mumps, plump, stump
DO ALL -UMP WORDS HAVE LUMPY CONNOTATIONS?

st-: stable, stagnant, stand, stay, steadfast, still, stop, stun
WHAT MEANING DO THESE ST- WORDS SUGGEST?

Sound symbolism refers to the way in which the sound of some words appears to suggest their meanings. Onomatopoeic words which 'echo' natural or artificial sound are straightforward examples. More nebulous examples are families of words where particular sounds seem to correspond with meanings in a not quite echoic manner (see Figure 1). As mentioned above, onomatopoeia is one of the sources of children's early language play, and onomatopoeic words are common in popular children's reading material, particularly comics. (For an interesting discussion of this phenomenon, see Brown, 1958, chapter 4.)

Onomastics is the study of names of people and places, and of 'personal' names given to animals, ideas, products and other objects. Names loom large in the consciousness of children, and are amongst the first words that they learn. A child's own name is often the first string of letters that they learn to read and write. Making up comic names for people and things is a common childhood practice, and the appeal of this is echoed in popular fiction where character and place names often incorporate the alliterative, reduplicative and sound symbolic aspects of language play (see Figure 2).

FIGURE 2

**NAMES THAT COULD BE USED TO ILLUSTRATE
SOUND SYMBOLIC ASPECTS OF LANGUAGE**

Wee Willie Winkie, Desperate Dan, Teletubbies, Micky Mouse, Willie Wonka, Bilbo Baggins, Mrs Wishy Washy, Hagar the Horrible, Mr. Creep the Crook

Luke Skywalker, Mrs Trunchbull, Scrooge, Krindlekrax, Mort, Puddleglum, Silverfax, Gollum

Grimpen Mire, Lothlorien, Gormenghast, Toytown, Narnia, Hogwarts

Nonsense words are common in children's playground chants and invented languages, prefiguring their ubiquitous role in the titles and refrains of popular songs (see Figure 3). Many children appear to be adept in splicing and shuffling sublexical elements in spoken words in order to make up neologisms, a skill which might be applied to written words to raise awareness of both graphophonics and morphological structure.

There is a sense in which the principles of sound symbolism, onomastics and sublexical shuffling go against the tide of language development. Children have to learn that links between most words and their referents are arbitrary rather than imitative; that most words are not names for individual things; that spelling systems rely on stable sequences for letter strings and morphemes. However, by enabling children to work outside these constraints, we provide them with a metalinguistic perspective from which to view language at one remove from practical usage.

FIGURE 3

EXAMPLES OF CHANTS THAT USE NONSENSE WORD

Eeny meeny macka racka rara raya dominacka chicka pocka lollipopa im pom push aye!

Michelle fifichelle chickelichelle bombichelle bombichelle fifichelle-
That's how you spell Michelle!

My mavourite feal is pashed motatoes with bausages and saked seans in somato tause.

Jack-sack-lack and-sand-land Jill-sill-lill went-sent-lent up-sup-lup the-se-le hill-sill-lill.

ethay atcay atsay onway ethy atmay.

Ten Classroom Strategies

1. Identify or invent characters whose names suggests sound symbolism (Mrs Wishy Washy would be a good example). Discuss the origins of the name with the children and help them to collect words with similar associations (for example *slosh, gush, splash; trickle, drip, drench* and so on). Emphasise similarities in spelling patterns and sound associations, and use the word groups collected to compose short stories or poems.

2. Conduct further investigations into other sound symbol families, such as those set out in Figure 1. Draw children's attention to both the similarities in association and the exceptions. Encourage the children to invent new words sharing the selected spelling pattern, and compare the subjective associations generated by these new words: do they conform to the specified trend or are they 'exceptions'? Again, these words and neologisms can be used to make character names and can inspire other types of creative writing.

3. Invent neologisms, including onomatopoeic words, by permuting onsets and rimes, using a combination matrix like that shown in Figure 4.

FIGURE 4

MATRIX INDICATING VALID COMBINATIONS OF ONSET AND RIME

	-ash	-ump	-ong	-oof	-ush
sl-	x	x			x
st-	x	x			
scr-		x			
squ-	x				
str-			x		

These words can be used for the same purposes outlined above. After the children have considered possible meanings for new words, you might also encourage them to write dictionary definitions and illustration sentences, based on a critical reading of their school dictionaries.

4. Invent new onomatopoeic words for 'lexical gaps' in the vocabulary of sound: for example, a word is required that expresses the sound of a computer saving data. How should such a word be spelled?

    With older children, you could prompt neologising to fill other lexical gaps: in recent years, humorous pseudo-glossaries have been published, presenting neologisms for hitherto nameless phenomena such as the puddle of beer on the counter that the barman always manages to put your change into, the quivering sensation that precedes a sneeze, and the propensity of traffic lights to change to red as the motorist approaches them (Crystal 1998). Showing children appropriate examples might motivate them to seek out and fill their own lexical gaps.

5. Provide frequent opportunities for children to play with phonological similarities and contrasts between words, and to integrate this kind of attention to word-level knowledge with a readiness to use the highlighted patterns for creative purposes. For example, the simple word webbing activity shown in Figure 5 can be used as a resource for writing alliterative and rhyming ABCs, nicknames, tongue twisters and variants on nursery and playground rhymes. The nonsense words created by such activities can be given definitions, or used as ingredients in song choruses, spells and concrete poetry.

FIGURE 5

WEB ILLUSTRATING PHONOLOGICAL CONTRASTS BETWEEN WORDS

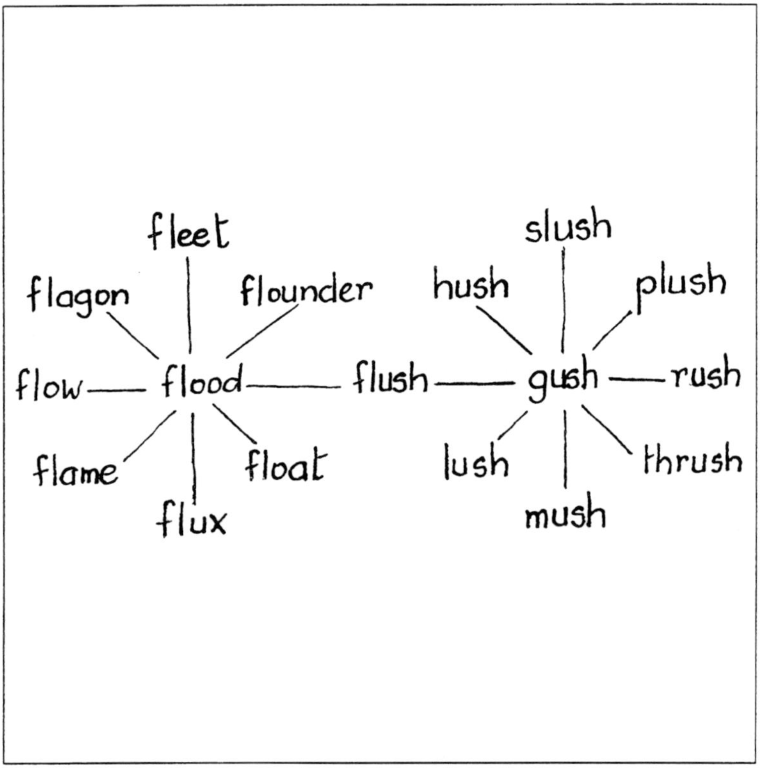

fleet
flagon   flounder   hush   slush   plush
flow — flood — flush — gush — rush
flame   float   lush   thrush
flux   mush

6. Compound words are a fertile source of analysis and synthesis. The structure of many of the compounds that children are most familiar with (*teapot, wristwatch, lighthouse, football*) are transparent, and thus their analysis provides an accessible way of introducing the children to the idea of morphology. Children can generate new compounds by analogy or by splitting and shuffling (*football - fingerball - toeball; football, eggcup - eggball, footcup*) and integrate the outcomes into creative writing and dictionary work.

   By encouraging learners to speculate about and then research the origins of more opaque compounds (*cupboard, wardrobe, butterfly*), we can provide insights into the evolution of words over time. Children can also try to coin poetic compounds after the model of kennings, the metaphorical terms used in Anglo Saxon poetry. A sword, for example, might be referred to as a *battle-torch*, the sea as the *whale-road*, the body as the *bone-house*. Nineteenth century traditionalist attempts to rid English of classical influence fell back on this approach, renaming caution as *forewit*, musicians as *tonewrights*, grammar as *speechlore*. (My own use of the term *word-hoard* for personal lexicon in this paper is another example.) Older children might be interested in playing with similar picturesque translations.

Looking at modern usage, children can research the hyphenated compounds that are often used as alluring adjectives in the language of advertising (*custom-made, state-of-the-art, long-lasting*). They can also look at the prolific neologising made possible by hyphenated elements like *-friendly* and *-rage* (*user-friendly, child-friendly, novice-friendly; road-rage, parking-rage, restaurant-rage*).

7. Similar investigations can be conducted with idioms as the raw material. These expressions can be problematical for learners because their meanings cannot be derived by analysing the meanings of their component words. When *you make up your mind*, for example, you neither use make up, nor make anything. Idioms can be collected and their origins guessed at and researched. Children can then have a go at making up their own, perhaps starting with analogies to known idioms. For example, given the meaning of *feeling under a cloud*, what might *feeling over the rainbow* mean?

8. Teaching children some basic derivational morphology can be an effective way of helping them to embark on the problem-solving procedures researched by Anglin. It has been estimated that understanding of 30 high frequency roots and affixes can 'unlock' the meanings of some 10,000 English words (Shaughnessy, 1977).

Morphology can be made vivid by engaging with children in the kind of semantic and morphological word webs illustrated in Figure 6. These can start off with very simple word families and be extended into interconnecting webs of great complexity (see McNamara et al., 1998 for lively classroom examples of this procedure). A playful approach can be encouraged by asking children to generate new words by combining a selection of morphemes (see Figure 6). The meanings of the new words must be derivable from an analysis of their roots and affixes (see Figure 7).

FIGURE 6

EXAMPLES OF SEMANTIC MAP AND MORPHOLOGICAL WEB

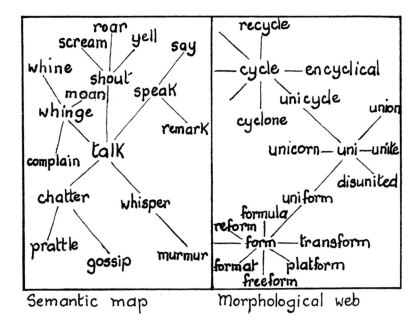

Semantic map   Morphological web

9. Children can be helped to research the origins of the names of people, places and things around them. Browsing through a map of the local area will provide a wealth of examples of how history and folklore are represented in place-names. The very concrete manner in which meanings are structured into the spellings of place-names provides opportunities for reflecting on the etymology of words in general. Dictionaries of forenames, surnames and eponyms (from *atlas* to *zeppelin*)

will provide similar insights. As in previous examples, analysis can be followed up by synthesis: children can be encouraged to rename local streets and institutions with more appropriate titles, or to offer new eponyms to the language, based on contemporary characters.

FIGURE 7

MEANINGS OF COMMON PREFIXES, ROOTS AND SUFFIXES

Prefix	Meaning	Root	Meaning	Suffix	Meaning
pre-	before	form	shape	-able	adj
inter-	between	port	carry	-er,-or,	agent
in-	not	tract	stretch	-less	without
ad- *	towards	graph	write	-ful	adj
un-	not	bio	life	-ology	study of
com-*	with	cycl	circle	-ion	noun
pro-	in favour of	phon	sound	-ise	verb
sub-	under	psych	mind	-ist	agent
ex-	out of / formerly	therm	heat	-ness	noun

* spelling frequently changes to match first letter of root (as in *approve, account, appoint, collect, connect*)

10. Finally, there is a consensus in many studies of vocabulary acquisition that the teacher's own love of words is a crucial factor. Enthusiasm for words needs to be manifested in as many educational contexts as possible, formal and informal. An inquisitive approach to the terminology of different subject areas may help to motivate pupils whose first love is not English. Collecting 'fad words' as they go in and out of fashion

is an enjoyable way of demonstrating the fluxionary nature of language, as is tracing the birth-stories of relative newcomers to the dictionary (*kodak, googol, hobbit, quark*). As Beck et al. (1987) suggest, a regular time and place for children and teachers to report lexical discoveries to each other is essential, but so is a permanent readiness to pause in the process of teaching, just to talk about words.

REFERENCES

Aicheson, J. (1987). *Words in the mind.* Oxford: Basil Blackwell.

Anglin, J. (1993). *Vocabulary development: A morphological analysis.* Chicago: University of Chicago Press.

Beals, D.E. (1997). Sources of support for learning words in conversation: Evidence from mealtimes. *Journal of Child Language, 4,* 673-94.

Beck, I., Perfetti, A., & Omanson, R. (1987). The effects and uses of diverse vocabulary instructional techniques. In McKeown, M. & Curtis, M. (Eds.) *The nature of vocabulary instruction.* Hillsdale, NJ: Erlbaum.

Bradley, L., & Bryant, P. (1985). *Children's reading problems.* Oxford: Basil Blackwell.

Brown, R. (1958). *Words and things.* London: Macmillan.

Chall, J. (1987). Two vocabularies. In M. McKeown & M. Curtis (Eds.). *The nature of vocabulary instruction.* Hillsdale, NJ: Earlbaum.

Crystal, D. (1986). *Listen to your child.* London: Penguin.

Crystal, D. (1998). *Language play.* London: Penguin.

Garvey, C. (1977). Play with language and speech. In S. Ervin-Tripp and C. Mitchell-Kernan (Eds.). *Child discourse.* New York: Academic Press.

Goswami, U., & Bryant, P. (1990). *Phonological skills and learning to read.* Hove: Erlbaum.

McNamara, M., Colgan, D.M., Johnson, B., & Nanni, L. (1998). *In a word.* Barrington, IL: Excel.

Meara, P. (1996). *The vocabulary knowledge framework.* University of Wales, Swansea: Virtual Library.

Miller, G., & Gildea, P. (1987). How children learn words. *Scientific American, 257,* 94-99.

Nagy,W.E., & Anderson, R.C. (1984). How many words are there in printed school English? *Reading Research Quarterly, 19,* 304-330.

Schwartz, A. (1982). *The cat's elbow and other secret languages.* Toronto: Farrar, Straus and Giroux.

Shaughnessy, M. (1977). *Errors and expectations.* New York: Oxford University Press.

Shu, H., Anderson, R., & Zhang, H. (1995). Incidental learning of word meanings while reading: A Chinese and American cross-cultural study. *Reading Research Quarterly, 30,* 76-95.

Snow, C.E., & Goldfield, B.A. (1983). Turn the page please: Situation specific language acquisition. *Journal of Child Language, 10,* 551-569.

Wittgenstein, L. (1953). *Philosophical investigations.* Oxford: Blackwell.

Perspectives on Learning Support Policy and Practice in Irish Schools: The Urgency of a Whole-School Initiative*

. . . .

Antóin Ó Dubhghaill
Mary Immaculate College/University of Limerick
Limerick

Policy and practice in learning support provision have undergone considerable change in Irish schools since remedial teachers were first appointed over three decades ago. While there have been significant improvements since that time, it is important at this stage to consider how effectively the system is responding to pupils with learning difficulties, with a view to improving the learning support provision where necessary. In this context it is also necessary to address the urgency of planning and implementing a whole-school approach without which learning support initiatives are unlikely to meet with a great deal of success.

According to the *Report of the Special Education Review Committee* (the SERC Report), 'Pupils in need of remedial teaching are those pupils in ordinary first-level and second-level schools who

*Paper presented at the 23rd Annual Conference of the Reading Association of Ireland, Limerick, September 17-19, 1998

have clearly observable difficulties in acquiring basic skills in literacy and numeracy, or who have some difficulties in learning of a more general nature' (Department of Education, 1993, p.76). For the purpose of this paper 'pupils with learning difficulties' will be the generic term used to describe the above category as well as other general broad categories such as disadvantaged pupils, emotionally or behaviourally disturbed pupils and children of the travelling community.

How Effective is the Provision of Learning Support in Irish Schools?

Learning support provision has evolved from the initial appointments of learning support teachers (or 'remedial teachers' as they were then called) in large primary schools in the 1960's to a situation where there are now 1242 learning support teachers (plus 76 resource teachers) serving 3227 schools, large and small. Further learning support posts (60) and resource posts (26) are being allocated for the 1998/'99 school year. At present there are 350 *ex-quota* learning support teachers in service in post-primary schools, though it is very difficult to ascertain the numbers of those teachers who actually provide a learning support service. It is a fact that in many post-primary schools, trained learning support teachers are almost entirely engaged in subject teaching – a situation which represents a grave misuse of this resource (ARTI, 1995a). According to the *Warnock Report* (Great Britain, 1978), one pupil in six is likely to need learning support provision at any one time. The SERC Report estimated that the broad categories of pupils with special needs who do not necessarily have a disability represent approximately 15-18% of the pupil population. The Report also estimated that 11-12% of pupils were receiving learning support where it was available. Nationally, 8.35% of the pupils were availing of learning support provision (Department of Education, 1993, p. 51).

There are many pupils in the system at present who do not have access to learning support teachers (Shiel, Hartnett &

Morgan, 1996). Furthermore, access to learning support does not guarantee adequate provision based on need (INTO, 1994). While all pupils with learning difficulties should have access to learning support, there is little value in this support if it is not very effective. It is a matter of concern that despite the increasing provision of learning support for many years, a recent report, *Literacy Skills for the Knowledge Society* (Organisation for Economic Co-operation and Development, 1997) estimated that 25% of the adult population of this country were functionally illiterate. Of further significance was the finding that 17% of the 16-25 age cohort were functionally illiterate, as this cohort of young adults had only recently passed through the education system. While one may not entirely agree with the literacy criteria used in this report, one must accept that a significant proportion of young adults have literacy problems.

Another possible measure of the effectiveness of learning support provision would be the numbers of pupils with learning difficulties who no longer require learning support after periods of specialist intervention in a withdrawal setting. While the *Guidelines on Remedial Education* (Department of Education, 1988) suggest that two or three years of withdrawal support should suffice, it is clear that several pupils attend learning support teachers throughout their primary schooling (INTO, 1994; Shiel et al., 1996). Ideally pupils should complete withdrawal programmes by the end of fourth class but this does not appear to be the case. Far from being a temporary measure therefore, this practice in a sense constitutes a form of streaming where some pupils with learning difficulties are never fully re-integrated into mainstream classes. Lack of resources and large numbers of pupils have been cited as possible contributing factors to this practice, while interpretation and implementation of Department of Education policy and the formulation of that policy in individual schools have also been cited (Shiel et al, 1996). In this context, the extent and quality of learning support provided in mainstream and in learning support rooms must be seriously examined.

Addressing inadequacy of provision at post-primary level, the *SERC Report* refers to the numbers of pupils who do not make the transition from primary to post-primary and acknowledges the significant numbers who do not even complete their years of compulsory schooling. The Minister for Education and Science recently stated that as many as 1000 children did not transfer from primary to post-primary schooling, and that between 3000 and 4000 pupils did not complete the Junior Cycle Course (Minister for Education and Science, 1998). Many of the pupils who drop out come from socially and economically disadvantaged backgrounds and from the traveller community.

The *SERC Report* highlights the exam-oriented second-level system of education in this country. 'The post-primary system of education, being mainly geared towards success in examinations leading to entry into third-level education and training, presents a climate which may inculcate a sense of failure and inadequacy in students of low academic attainment' (Department of Education 1993, p. 67).

The SERC Report acknowledges that despite efforts by the NCCA and other agencies to devise alternative courses, the curricula are still too academically biased and unsuited to the abilities and interests of these lower-achieving students. The problem is a persistent one. Murtagh (1988) cited the huge numbers of pupils leaving the system ten years ago, estimating that between 4000 and 5000 pupils would drop out from an age cohort of 67,000 students. Pupils who needed learning support (approx 18-20 %) mostly came from disadvantaged families and tended to be concentrated disproportionately in vocational schools. While some schools were providing a degree of learning support, Murtagh felt that the whole thrust of the educational system at second level was to cater for the needs of the 'top fliers' who were given the best teachers as well as the best facilities. In spite of the awareness of the problem 10 years ago, it would appear that there has been little progress in the area to date.

Perspectives on Present Policy and Practice in Schools

As a consequence of professional experience in working with cohorts of primary and post-primary learning support teachers on a college campus and in their respective schools for the past five years, during their participation in a Graduate Diploma in Remedial Education, some perspectives on present school policy and practice are offered which point to the urgency of developing a whole school initiative for learning support for pupils with learning difficulties.

Responding to pupils with learning difficulties. At times, too many pupils are referred for learning support, thus presenting learning support teachers with huge unmanageable case loads. In certain cases the contact time with the learning support teacher for individual pupils is as little as 30 minutes per week. Learning support teachers feel that very little can be achieved during such infrequent short 'booster lessons'.

Some pupils with learning difficulties are not identified or referred for learning support until third or fourth class. In a number of schools there are pupils in need of learning support who do not receive it.

Because of time constraints, the majority of pupils with learning difficulties in the area of literacy receive some learning support, while those who have problems with numeracy are largely uncatered for by learning support teachers.

Despite obvious reading deficits, pupils are often compelled by mainstream teachers to undertake reading tasks which they are unable to cope with. As a result, they may experience continuing failure and frustration in these situations.

Because curricula are not modified to meet the needs of certain pupils, they are uninvolved in the work of the classroom and may eventually opt out of many curricular areas. Mainstream classes are of little benefit to a significant percentage of pupils with learning difficulties.

Pupils' self-esteem may be damaged when their attendance at withdrawal sessions is insensitively dealt with by mainstream teachers. Negative and contradictory comments from mainstream teachers in reporting on pupils with learning difficulties compound their poor self-esteem and sense of failure. Sometimes, these pupils are labelled as lazy, inattentive and uncooperative by their teachers.

It is unfortunate that many pupils with learning difficulties have potential and talents that are never recognised in school. Teachers focus too much on pupils' weaknesses, while ignoring their strengths and positive attributes. As a consequence, many pupils with learning difficulties are not fully included in mainstream activities.

There is a lack of co-operation and continuity between some primary and post-primary schools with the result that the earlier work and expertise of the learning support teacher at primary level may be overlooked when pupils with learning difficulties arrive at post-primary schools. In certain post-primary schools some pupils are not selected for learning support in first year in the belief that all pupils should be exposed to the full range of second-level subjects for one year without any intervention.

A number of post-primary schools have a disproportionate share of pupils with learning difficulties and do not have adequate resources to cater for those pupils.

Models of learning support. A number of schools do not have learning support provision at all, while others offer very limited provision in terms of restricted contact with learning support teachers. The model of learning support most commonly used is based on withdrawing small groups from mainstream classes for 20-45 minute sessions, ranging from one session per pupil to six or seven in the course of a week. Where learning support is confined to very limited contact periods, it is questionable if any real progress is made without the co-operation of mainstream teachers. Some pupils seem to be condemned to withdrawal classes for the duration of their schooling.

There appears to be very little team-teaching and some learning support teachers feel they do not have the confidence to initiate this practice with their colleagues in the absence of a whole-school strategy in this regard.

In some post-primary schools there is streaming where the lowest stream comprise the learning support group. There is also withdrawal from streamed classes and from mixed ability classes, but there isn't always a recognition of the disparity of this group.

Learning support teachers and colleagues in mainstream. Traditionally seen as an appendage to the school staff, some learning support teachers in primary school still feel isolated from mainstream colleagues (INTO, 1994). Shared learning-support teachers complain of not being invited to staff meetings in the schools they visit.

For some post-primary teachers who enter the learning support system, there is an initial culture shock, many being unaware of the extent and range of literacy and numeracy problems. Toolan noted that the philosophy, methodology and terminology of learning support was largely alien to post -primary teachers and that a huge paradigm shift was required by them (Toolan, 1997).

Learning support teachers at all levels often feel that there is a lack of awareness on the part of their colleagues as to the actual levels of development of pupils with learning difficulties. At post-primary level, learning support teachers feel that their colleagues do not realise that some of the pupils have reading ages as low as 8 or 9 years, so that they are unable to cope with textbooks in most curricular areas.

Very often learning support teachers believe they do not have the same status as their colleagues in the schools. Learning support teachers believe that, for the success of learning support policy they must have credibility as good practitioners among their colleagues. There is an assumption in certain schools that the needs of pupils with learning difficulties are catered for when the learning support teacher is appointed. It is the view of learning support teachers that they are left by their colleagues with total responsibility for the needs of pupils with learning difficulties in the school.

There appears to be a lack of cohesion regarding the strategies and programmes employed by learning support teachers and the role of mainstream teachers regarding same. Some learning support teachers have specific programmes in such areas as phonics, comprehension, spelling, oral language and writing, but feel their efforts are often ignored by colleagues who expect a topping up of certain curricular areas in the withdrawal sessions. There is generally an absence of a collaborative approach by school staffs in catering for pupils with learning difficulties. Many learning support teachers and mainstream teachers know very little about each other's work.

Some primary schools oblige learning support teachers to administer screening tests to several classes with the result that they are pre-occupied with this function for weeks on end. At post-primary level, where teachers commencing learning support work often have difficulties with screening and diagnostic testing, there are problems occasionally in gaining access to assessments conducted by career guidance teachers which would be helpful in compiling profiles of many of the pupils in need of help.

There is a huge variation in the systems of record-keeping, progress reports and profiles devised by learning support teachers, while most appear to be left to their own devices to establish recording strategies if they wish to do so. Where records are kept, they may be inaccessible to a significant number of mainstream colleagues.

Learning support teachers often have difficulty in getting colleagues to release pupils in time for withdrawal sessions and complain of continuing problems with timetabling arrangements where mainstream colleagues are dissatisfied with ongoing disruption and the fact that pupils miss certain classes repeatedly. At post-primary level some subject teachers refuse to permit pupils to leave their classes to go to learning support sessions.

Where there is consultation and communication, it is done informally for the most part during coffee or lunch breaks. Despite the best efforts of teachers participating in the Graduate Diploma Courses, only half of them were able to engage in a consultative role with colleagues due to time constraints and lack of support and organisation within the schools (Toolan, 1997). Very few formal staff meetings are held where learning support issues are raised, and most of the learning support teachers do not get an opportunity to share their expertise with colleagues.

Up to now very little has been done regarding the use of IT to support pupils with learning difficulties – due in part to lack of training, resources and support, though there is much evidence to show that IT has a major role to play in supporting pupils in improving literacy and numeracy skills (Holland, 1997).

While some learning support teachers endeavour to involve and work with parents, others find it extremely difficult especially where parents are used to attending only the formal parent-teacher meetings that take place annually.

It is a matter of concern that, in a significant percentage of schools, teachers assigned to learning support are untrained for this task. A further problem arises when learning support teachers have to absent themselves from school for certain periods and are replaced by untrained substitutes.

Accommodation, resourcing, and funding. Problems relating to inadequate accommodation, resourcing and funding have been comprehensively highlighted (Lynch & O'Sullivan, 1986; INTO, 1994; ARTI, 1995a, 1995b). Learning support teachers have been observed working with pupils in corridors, general-purpose rooms, staffrooms, small portacabins and in dilapidated rooms not conducive to good working-conditions for teacher or pupil.

Many post-primary learning support teachers have no base room from which to operate, where materials (if they have same) can be stored, with the result that these materials have to be transported continuously from one classroom to another. In many schools teachers do not have adequate supplies of readers, workbooks, language kits or even test material because of lack of funding.

Recent positive developments and initiatives. Not withstanding the apparent lack of cohesion, organisation and planning and the misuse of expertise in the learning support situation, there have been recent welcome developments and initiatives by the Department of Education and Science:

- An increase in the numbers of learning support teachers and educational psychologists for primary schools
- Intervention strategies such as the Breaking-the-Cycle initiative, the Home-School-Community Liaison scheme, and initiatives on 8-15 year old early school leavers
- New revised curricula from the NCCA, intended to ensure that all pupils will have access to and benefit from the experience of schooling. Regarding those pupils who hitherto had difficulties with literacy and numeracy at primary school, the White Paper, *Charting Our Education Future*, guarantees that 'the objective will be to ensure that, having regard to the assessment of their intrinsic abilities, there are no students with serious literacy and numeracy problems in early primary education within the next five years' (Ireland, 1995, p.20)
- New national programmes of training in remedial education for primary and post-primary teachers. Between 1995 and 1998 the numbers of learning support teachers who participated in these programmes were 288 (primary) and 202 (post primary)[1]
- A significant increase in the provision of in-career development courses for teachers in coping with learning difficulties in mainstream classes.
- Improved library services to many schools
- The schools IT 2000 Initiative and a range of Incareer Development courses on the use of IT in supporting pupils with learning difficulties.

A Whole-School Approach

There is increasing research overseas on school effectiveness achieved through whole-school planning, to the extent that the focus has shifted somewhat from learning difficulties and under-achievement of pupils to effective teaching and learning (Harris, 1996). Where it was previously assumed that due to certain socio-economic disadvantaged backgrounds, a school could not significantly improve pupil performance, research findings in the UK show that school effectiveness does make a positive difference regarding pupil attainment (Harris, 1996; Dyson, 1994; Ainscow 1988).

The practice of looking on pupils with learning difficulties as pupils unwilling or unable to avail of the opportunities offered by schools is now being questioned. In this regard Ainscow argues that we should begin by asking what is wrong with the school rather than what is wrong with the child. Slavin (1996) cites evidence from research to show that with certain programmes it is possible to ensure success in the area of reading for practically all pupils in the elementary grades.

In view of the perceived difficulties highlighted earlier, the recent developments and initiatives at system level by the Department of Education and Science, and in the light of current research, it is imperative that all schools develop and implement a whole-school strategy for learning support to ensure school effectiveness in responding to the needs of pupils with learning difficulties. Most of the difficulties highlighted would be ameliorated if the entire staff of schools werè adequately involved. According to the *Guidelines on Remedial Education* 'the involvement and co-operation of the whole staff are essential for the success of the school's remedial programme' (Department of Education, 1988, p.29). It is further pointed out in that publication that the class teacher has the first line of responsibility for all pupils with learning difficulties in his/her class (p.13). The White Paper, *Charting Our Education Future*, recommends that all schools be required to include in their school plan a strategy with defined objectives and associated performance measures for achieving basic literacy and numeracy targets (Ireland, 1995).

At post-primary level the White Paper recommends 'that the identification of special needs should be a collective responsibility of all the relevant subject teachers having collaboratively considered the students' needs' (Ireland, 1995, p. 53). Ten years ago Murtagh advised principals and staffs of all post-primary schools to sit down as a team to develop and implement appropriate educational programmes for pupils with learning difficulties. This was to have involved every teacher with whom such pupils had contact and was intended to cover every subject in the curriculum (Murtagh, 1988).

If a whole school approach is to succeed, then all of the teachers must be effective in teaching all of the pupils in their classrooms. Schools must therefore focus immediately on the whole-school issues which relate to school effectiveness and in this respect detailed updated guidelines on learning support should be issued to primary and post-primary teachers. School-based in-career development courses should be provided to assist schools in preparing whole-school policies, and all teachers should be encouraged to participate in In-career Development Courses on coping with pupils who have learning difficulties in mainstream education.

Teacher Guidelines and In-career Development programmes are crucial to ensure that all schools are empowered to undertake the following:

- to conduct a proper analysis of learning support needs
- to implement realistic prevention strategies
- to identify all pupils with learning difficulties as quickly as possible
- to utilise suitable screening and diagnostic procedures
- to define clearly the roles and responsibilities of learning support and mainstream teachers
- to introduce models of learning support appropriate to the needs of the pupils

- to consider and address in detail the timetabling complexities associated with learning support
- to ensure proper learning support in mainstream, through modification of curricula and through specific programmes reflecting the diversity of pupils' needs
- to evaluate programmes and whole-school policies on a continuing basis to secure maximum parental involvement
- to address the issue of transition from primary to post-primary schools and from post-primary schools to college and work
- to utilise IT as a priority in learning support situations
- to acquire essential pedagogical resources for learning support programmes
- to undertake profiling and record-keeping in an adequate professional manner.

The rights of all pupils will undoubtedly be enshrined in the forthcoming Education Act as a result of which school policy and practice in all areas will be scrutinised as never before. In not preparing adequately to cater for pupils in an equitable way so that all have access to meaningful curricula, schools will be challenged for contributing to and perhaps even exacerbating problems for pupils with learning difficulties. Notwithstanding the shortcomings in the system, schools and teachers can and do make a huge difference where they *include all* pupils in meaningful and fruitful learning experiences.

In an era of increasing accountability, the expectation is that schools will have realistic policies so that their implementation will ensure effective practices, which will prevent many pupils from having learning difficulties in the first place, while providing adequate learning support for those pupils who may still need it.

REFERENCES

Ainscow, M. (1988). Exploring links between special needs and school improvement. *Support for Learning*, 13(2), 70-75.

Association of Remedial Teachers of Ireland. [ARTI]. (1995a). Survey of current remedial teaching practices. *Learn, 17,* 70-85.

Association of Remedial Teachers of Ireland. [ARTI]. (1995b). *Submission on the development of Remedial Education to the Minister for Education.* Dublin: Author.

Department of Education. (1988). *Guidelines on remedial education.* Dublin: Stationery Office.

Department of Education. (1993). *Report of the Special Education Review Committee.* Dublin: Stationery Office.

Dyson, A. (1994). Towards a collaborative learning model for responding to student diversity. In C. Gains (Ed.), Collaborating to meet special educational needs. *Support for Learning, 9(2),* 7-14.

Great Britain. Department of Education and Science (1978). *Special education needs (Warnock Report).* London: HMSO.

Harris, A. (1996). Raising levels of pupil achievement through school improvement. *Support for Learning,* 11(2), 62-87.

Holland, M. (1997). Extending learning opportunities: An analysis of the contribution of information and communications technology for pupils with learning difficulties. Unpublished M. Ed. Thesis, University of Limerick.

Ireland. (1995). *White Paper on Education: Changing our educational future.* Dublin: Stationery Office.

Irish National Teachers' Organisation. [INTO]. (1994). *Remedial education.* Dublin: Author.

Lynch, P. & O'Sullivan, A. (1986). Remedial teaching in Irish primary schools. In V. Greaney and B. Molloy (Eds.), *Dimensions of reading.* Dublin: Educational Company.

Minister for Education and Science. Interview on 'Morning Ireland', RTE Radio One, July 16th, 1998.

Murtagh, L. (1988). Remedial education at the crossroads: Meeting special needs. *Learn, 10,* 8-19.

Organisation for Economic Co-operation and Development. [OECD]. (1997). *Literacy skills for the knowledge society.* Canada: Author.

Shiel, G., Hartnett, M., & Morgan, M. (1996). Access to and participation in remedial education. *Learn, 18,* 93-101.

Slavin, R. (1996). Neverstreaming: Ending learning disabilities before they start. *Support for Learning, 11(2),* 74-76.

Toolan, E. (1997). Evaluation of the graduate diploma course in remedial education, 1996-1997. Unpublished M. Ed. Thesis, University of Wales.

Adler, Froebel, and Reading Pedagogy: A Spirituality of Children's Literacy*

. . . .

David J. Carey, Froebel College, Sion Hill, Co. Dublin
Séan Griffin, St Nicholas Montessori College, Dún Laoghaire, Co. Dublin

Our meddling intellect
Misshapes the beauteous forms of things:-
We murder to dissect.
(Wordsworth)

Recent research (Hay & Nye, 1999) has outlined the natural language of children's spirituality. Coles (1989, 1990) has written about the spiritual life of children and the importance of story in the development of the moral imagination. Here, it is argued that the teaching of reading and literature is of the utmost importance to children in communicating a way of being human. Contemporary education appears to largely ignore the higher calling of literature and reading and reduce both to a level which focuses on fluency, comprehension, and technical proficiency in teaching. Teacher training programmes conspire in this process as they merge reading and literature into methodology. This paper calls for a wider view of reading and literacy and relates both to the spiritual lives of children.

*Paper presented at the 24th Annual Conference of the Reading Association of Ireland, Dublin, September 29-Oct. 1st, 1999.

A definition of spirituality which removes it from religious dogma and creed is presented and related to the everyday lives of children. The importance of story to young children is outlined and instances of children's story as both autobiography and personal theology are presented. The use of story to develop a vocabulary of spirituality is discussed with specific examples from senior primary school classes. Reference is made to the educational spirituality of Froebel and Adler.

Why do we teach children to read? Why do we choose the stories we read to them or encourage them to read themselves? What purpose does reading serve in the child's life? Why is it, that after so many decades of research into the teaching of reading, so many adults lack basic literacy skills?

While the answers to these questions are not the most profound we may seek at the end of the millennium, they are critically important none the less. On reading the works of the historical founders of what has come to be called 'child-centred education', we find precious little written about the methodology of reading. Pestalozzi, Froebel, Montessori, and others had what they perceived as a 'higher calling'. Indigenous populations continue to this day to pass stories from one generation to the next, trusting that the words speak to the heart of the child and communicate something essential about what it means to be a human being. Yet teachers in training are presented with the methodology of reading, the technology of literature, and the curriculum of objectives as though the child were a computer waiting for a programme.

This paper is concerned with the spiritual dimension of the child's life. It is based on a psychological theory that is essentially spiritual, the individual psychology of Alfred Adler, and an educational theory which is equally spiritual, that of Friedrich Froebel. Embedded in the underlying philosophy of this paper is the idea that children are whole beings, a unity of diverse parts. Children are not a totality, they are a unity. Although the foundation upon which this paper is written rests on a view of the child as a unity of body, mind, and spirit, the paper itself focuses more on the spiritual dimension as opposed to the other two. As such it does not offer technical solutions and methodological innovation. The authors rely on others to do that work. Instead it attempts to provoke and instigate educators towards a broader view of their calling, one which recognises that when it comes to the spiritual dimension of human life, as Chopra (1993), has stated, 'We are, after all, human beings not human thinkings [sic]' (p. 25). He concludes we are more spiritual beings having occasional episodes of thought, than thinking beings having occasional episodes of spirituality. It is on this foundation that all that follows is laid.

What is Spirituality and Why Is It Important?

Attempts to define spirituality date back over a lengthy period. During that time considerable debate has ensued attempting to secure an adequate definition. The debate has centred on a continuum of issues such as secular vs. religious values, political interests in multicultural societies, and dogmatic, theological matters. In attempting to end this debate, Carey (1997) has taken as a starting point a definition of spirituality provided by Savary (1988) who writes that it is '. . . one's way of being and acting in light of ultimate values, of which we may be consciously unaware, as opposed to everyday values' (p. 5). By rooting his definition in the realm of both human action and being, Savary has avoided the difficulties inherent in the sectarianism that had characterised the debate up to that time. Savary speaks to an innate ability of Homo sapiens to be and act in conformity to ultimate values and adds that for the most part, we are consciously unaware of these values. Savary's definition bears striking similarity to the psychology of Adler and philosophy of Froebel, as we will see later.

Others have addressed the issues of spirituality's essence far more elegantly. One of the most intriguing solutions to the conundrum of defining spirituality was offered by Alister Hardy (Hay & Nye, 1999). In 1965 Hardy delivered the Gifford Lectures at the University of Aberdeen. He spoke about the relationship between biology and religion. Taking the position that what he called 'religious experience' was an evolutionary process, he postulated that it must have survival value for the individual. Hay (1999), discussing his interpretation of Hardy's lectures, concludes that Hardy is speaking about spiritual awareness when using the term 'religious experience'. Hay explains that Hardy's hypothesis is that religious experience is biologically based and that individual variations in this experience all arise out of cultural responses to the humans' natural spiritual awareness (p. 10). It will be noted later that there is more than a little similarity between Hardy's supposition and the theories of Adler and Froebel.

In Hay's investigation of the language of children's and adults' spirituality, he discovered that awareness of a spiritual experience is almost universally accompanied by a heightened awareness of the inter-connectedness of all things and the desire to put this awareness into some form of action. He cites many examples of people relating their interest in social and community affairs to the onset of a spiritual experience. Hay has labelled this phenomenon 'relational consciousness' (p. 113). We will see later than Adler had a term to describe the same concept and that Froebel, in his educational philosophy, addressed this issue as well. For now we can conclude that spirituality just is; it is an innate potentiality in all human beings. It is not uncommon for it to become hidden from the view of others, like a wound, because of society's bias against such experience. I will argue that it is education that creates this wound and it is the responsibility of education to heal it.

By defining spirituality in a broader sense it is hoped that we can end the debate and move on instead to what is the essence of spirituality, that is, what form it takes. We view all children, indeed all people, as spiritual beings whose daily experiences in the spiritual realm transcend religious orientation, secular community, and the intellectual life so rife with doctrinaire differences. Spirituality, in this definition, is a felt sense involving our highest values, values which often lie outside our everyday awareness.

Spirituality is driven by the human need to feel at home in the world, to feel as though we are part of something larger than ourselves, to believe that life has purpose and we are part of this purpose, and to feel the ever-present need to move towards fulfilment, unity, and wholeness. Our spirituality is a call to our destiny and the destiny of the world. It is vivified through both happiness and pain and is a call which we feel, cannot explain, but which transcends all we do, think, and feel.

The Spiritual Psychology of Alfred Adler

Alfred Adler, contemporary of Freud, creator of the phrase 'inferiority complex', and social psychologist, is one of the most influential of the founding fathers of the psychodynamic approach to human behaviour. According to Adler, psychology has '. . . for its proper goal the understanding of human nature by every human being' (Bottome, 1957). Most of contemporary cognitive psychotherapy owes considerable debt to Adler (Ellis, 1962). Ellenberger (1970) has stated 'it would not be easy to find another author from which so much has been borrowed from all sides without acknowledgement than Adler' (p. 645). His approach is essentially one which emphasises human connectedness and purpose. Personality theorists such as Maslow (1954), Jourard (1963), and Hall and Lindzey (1957) all recognised Adler's importance as a social theorist. The last two stated, 'By endowing man with altruism, humanitarianism, co-operation, creativity, uniqueness, and awareness, he restored to man a sense of dignity and worth that psychoanalysis had pretty largely destroyed' (p. 125). The cultural anthropologist Ernest Becker (1962) has written, 'It is incredible that human behaviour can be discussed from a psychoanalytic point of view without mentioning Adler's name or that some so-called 'neo-Freudians' can deliver ostensibly 'fresh' ideas with an air of discovery, when many of these ideas were adumbrated by Adler over a half-century ago' (p. 200). A recent publication elucidates the importance of Adler and is entitled *The Forgotten Prophet* (Gray, 1998).

In addition to his influence as a social psychologist and humanitarian, Adler was the first of the great psychologists to take an active interest in education. He recognised that it was through education that children could be taught to co-operate and become 'fellow men' (Adler, 1930). He valued education as a means towards creating people who can change the world even while they must, at times, co-operate with it. He stated that love was not enough and added, 'The healing process must begin with winning the erring human child for co-operation' (Ansbacher and Ansbacher, 1956, p. 306). So important did Adler view the educational process that he centred much of his work in Vienna in the schools and focused on teachers. He established child guidance clinics throughout the city and before World War II there were at least thirty in operation. Adler valued teachers and said their role was to replace the mother '. . . and make corrections where she has made a mistake' (Ansbacher and Ansbacher, 1958, p. 399).

'Everybody can accomplish everything' (Ansbacher and Ansbacher, 1956, p. 400) was Adler's way of emphasising the corrective influence of education. His focus was on the power of encouragement in the learning process and its healing potential to resolve feelings of inferiority and discouragement. He believed that an emphasis on heredity and genetics was an obstacle to proper education. While he did not deny the relevance of inherited potential he emphasised the use to which it was put. His psychology was a psychology of choice and use, founded in optimism and hope. For Adler, correct education was a method of developing the whole individual and, if done properly, Adler believed '. . . disabilities may be so compensated that they even become great abilities' (Ansbacher and Ansbacher, 1956, p. 400). Adler brought his community focus into the classroom and believed that the success of one member of the class was an advantage to the entire class. Throughout the teachings of Adler, one sees the healing power of hope and the vital force of community at work.

Adler's insights into human psychology articulate a process of holism, inter-dependence, co-operation, encouragement, and hope. They speak to the creative power of individuals to alter their personality and move from the useless to the useful side of life. The main tenet of Adlerian thinking is that human beings are self-creating, goal-striving individuals whose behaviour is purposeful. For Adler, the sine-qua-non of mental health is one's capacity to manifest what he called Gemeinschaftsgefühl, commonly translated as 'social interest' but translated here as 'community feeling'. He believed that human beings were born with a certain predisposition towards community feeling but that it must be developed and trained. Adler saw the schoolhouse as the second training ground, after the family, the place where this most vital element would be developed and guided towards perfection. For Adler the perfection of the individual's community feeling intersected in the future with the perfection of the cosmos (Ansbacher and Ansbacher, 1956).

Components of Adlerian psychology include the following: all behaviour has social meaning, all behaviour has purpose, holism is the interconnectedness of everything, creativity is the power to make choices and change, all humans have a need to belong, life is lived potentiality, and life is unity. Among the themes that are prominent in Adler's work are: strving for significance, the need to overcome, the psychology of use and teleology, community feeling, and subjectivity.

Froebel Education: Inter-connectedness and Unity

Friedrich Froebel, forester, mineralogist, and spiritual seeker, came across his vocation for education by a happy accident. As a student of architecture in Frankfurt in 1805, he was invited by a friend to try his hand in a classroom of 40 boys. He wrote (Liebschner, 1992, p.4):

I have to tell you how much I enjoy my new occupation. From the very first hour, the children were not strangers to me. It

> seemed as if I had been a teacher for a long time and been born to the job. . . . You should see me in my work, how happy I am. . . . This happiness is derived from the knowledge of the high purpose of my activity: the education of men – but also because of the children's love and affection towards me

In teacher education, our quest must be to discover the doorways and pathways which lead to this experience of the joy of teaching and learning. Perhaps a vital element is the reciprocal element in the teaching-learning relationship hinted at by Froebel in his reflection on his first encounter with a class: the adult must be prepared also to learn from the child.

Froebel's insights into education articulate a process of give and take, activity and passivity, a recognition of duality which yields to a confluence of opposites helping us to pursue purpose and resolution in apparently irresolvable situations (Herford, 1900). The challenge for teacher education in circumstances of political encroachment, financial stringency, and the demands of a utilitarian or technological society are some of the tensions which may require a spiritual alignment which is robust, accessible, and practical. Reviewing Friedrich Froebel and English Education, Dent (1947) remarked that all teaching was inherently a spiritual activity and that school should provide a living proof '. . . . of the laws of love which are the nature of God' (p. 17).

Problems in Teacher Education

Carey and Griffin, (1998) have outlined a brief history of Froebel education in Ireland and the difficulties ensuing from its introduction. They cite Dean (1952) addressing the National Froebel Foundation at its convocation on New Year's Day, the centenary celebration of Friedrich Froebel's death:

> A good [Teacher] Training College is now a democratic community . . . where everyone counts and everyone contributes. It is in such an atmosphere that we try to train

> our students for personal responsibility not as artisans but (some of them at least) as artists, not merely as teachers but as educators. . . as guardians of our best traditions and never as mere agents of some external authority.

Dean outlines laudable aspirations and we have no doubt that in some situations it must have had an expression in reality. Shortly after the time of Mr. Dean's address, the Council of Education, an advisory body reporting to the Minister for Education in Ireland, complained that schools were largely places of narrow curricular exposition, unchanged in didactic practice for over a hundred years. Training Colleges also tended to operate under a traditional technical/rationalist model.   Since 1943, however, a small Dublin college under the stewardship of the Dominican Congregation of Sisters had affiliated itself with the National Froebel Foundation in London. They had a mission to provide for intending teachers a community of co-operative learning which would incorporate the educational principles of Friedrich Froebel.

During the 1970s, Ireland adopted explicitly a child-centred, integrated activity-based national curriculum for primary schools strongly influenced and upheld by the progressive experience of the Froebel College. Ironically, however, the associated reform of teacher education at that time which saw the introduction of the B.Ed degree and an affiliation with the universities, led to an inevitable diminution of the flexible, humanistic, collaborative practices between staff and students which had served to nourish and sustain a vision of qualitative classroom communities.

What do we mean by education? Rather than embark on waters that would take us into involved philosophical discourse, let it be sufficient to state simply that 'At the heart of the educational process lies the child' (Plowden, 1967). In the context of our specific focus on spirituality let us see the special significance of the word 'heart'. Hogan (1995) has proposed an analysis of education which recognises the custodial conceptions of learning enforced by the temporal and spiritual authorities of Western Christendom. He invites us to reclaim insights from the unavoidable play of influences and motives in the process of teaching and learning which are expressed as a dance of courtship between teacher and learner. Education is a drawing, a teasing out in 'e(x)-ducare' into movement which is at once liberating, sustaining, invigorating and challenging. Education should be the music which resonates with the heartbeat of the child, helping each to keep in step with an inner dance and leading outwards to a recognition of individual action in a greater belonging.

Research over the last quarter decade has indicated a high level of dissatisfaction regarding the whole area of teacher training. Criticisms have pointed to the too theoretical and academic weighting of courses. There has been a sacrifice to practicalities and the psychological needs of the teacher in the face of the impact of social change on school communities (INTO, 1994). Serious concerns have been expressed about the relevance and overload of the present teacher education curriculum with its lack of meaningful opportunity to engage in reflection on experience (INTO, 1995). More worryingly, it would seem that the pace at which children are being driven through the curriculum in primary schools in recent times bears a close resemblance to what has been demanded of students in teacher education. How is it possible in this treadmill climate to give emphasis, resources or enthusiasm to the development of the inner life, insight and vision? As Brennan (1997) states in an article entitled *The Contribution of School Management to Spirituality*: 'No school can function educationally with only vertical values; we need horizontal values to create a balanced and creative school' (p. 54-55). It echoes what Dent said fifty years earlier in his hard-hitting book *To Be A Teacher*:

> A teacher's business is, in the last analysis, to guide his pupils towards spiritual values; to teach them how to recognise such values, how to assess them, to respect them, if need be to change them, but above all to be committed to those in which they can believe (1947, p.40).

Back to Basics: A New Look at the 'Three R's'

In 1998 Carey and Griffin called for a new look at traditional primary education. The basic skills of the 'three Rs' (reading, writing, 'rithmetic) may have been given grander appellations but they are still the recognised 'stuff' of schools. Where competition, individualism, passivity and predictability reign supreme, creativity, questioning, choice and accountability may have been seen as unprized qualities. In such a culture the tendency would also be to gravitate towards the rigidity of rules and regulations. Alternatively, there may be a retreat into a rut and perhaps regrets and even recriminations. What is proposed is a distillation of concepts based on Froebelian-Adlerian principles in education which offers instead an approach to the teaching-learning process based on a new 'three R's': relationships, respect and response. These are wedded to a spirituality of teacher training.

1. Relationships – Roles, Reconstruction and Reaching Out

Froebel's insight into what he described as the spherical view of all aspects of nature and human life represented for him a law which recognised that however much one action is differentiated from another, they will all lead to an 'allsided [sic] harmony and unity of life of the self' (Liebschner, p.9). For Adler, the recognition of the unity of the personality required seeing the child and his/her relationship with the world 'as a continuous thread interpenetrating all the incidents of his existence'(Adler, 1930, p. 64). In a world where fragmentation and individualism appear to be everyday realities, how can aspiring teachers be led to appreciate the spiritual inter-connectedness of things: the relationships between persons, objects and ideas?

Roles. Student teachers need to re-examine the teaching role. They need to retrieve through autobiographical writing images of the teacher from their own experience and to reconstruct attitudes and approaches consistent with their emerging consciousness of connectedness. Pupils love to play teacher. It provides for them a powerful possibility to enact what Adler calls the 'striving for superiority'. Children in classrooms can be taught to take on teaching roles, whether in whole-class or in group situations, imitating the sensitivities and skills deliberately modelled by the teacher. For this to occur, students in teacher education need the experience of co-operative seminar style presentations in which they exercise collaboration, creativity and confirmation of communication skills.

Reconstruction. School and classroom settings may tend to reflect traditional and functional arrangements; classroom routines and conventions may remain constant for generations. Adaptability and change, if fostered even in small ways in the classroom, tend to open children's perceptions to larger possibilities. Froebel's introduction of the school garden with its individual and communal plots was intended to illustrate how the results of self-activity mediate in and modify the larger laws of nature.   Classroom seating, display areas and use of space may – along with teaching styles and techniques –   offer opportunities for creative reconstruction, not only in the physical sense but intimating also the possibilities of psychological and spiritual renewal.

Reaching Out. Froebel always insisted that life itself was the most important school for man and that unless a school was related to life it had no claim to its name. The centrality of the local and immediate environment to the teaching-learning process was paramount in this approach. Many children see their book-learning as unrelated to their immediate world. Yet, the classroom, playground, and surrounding streets offer all the ingredients to illustrate and concretise the entire curriculum.

2. Respect – Receptivity, Resilience and Resolve

Receptivity. Teachers in their position of power are perceived as givers of knowledge, skills and ideas. Children are considered to be the recipients of learning. Froebel, however, reminds us that 'every genuine educator and teacher has to be always in every detail, two-sided; to give and to take . . . The child or pupil is to be likewise' (Herford, p.9). Teachers must learn to receive as much as to give. A climate must be established where objects, feelings and ideas are received and welcomed – and that includes parents. True respect comes from a sense of being valued.

Resilience. How can flexibility and irrepressibility be encouraged in schools? How can teachers learn to teach encouragement and in turn receive encouragement themselves? Adler (1930, p.173) speaks of the dangers of competition and rivalry in the classroom if overlooked or tacitly encouraged by the teacher. A perception that striving will not succeed may cause children to suffer a retreat into disappointment, despondency and a rigid subjective view of things. Froebel taught that good education was not a matter of establishing laws and pressures from without but love and self-determination from within (Liebschner, p.69). Student co-operation rather than competition in teacher education must pave the way for classroom progress.

Resolve. Respect, with its hope-enhancing window on the world, will not happen in the educational process if it remains at the level of aspiration. It must translate into concrete promises, preparedness and practices. Children must invited to make surmises and intuitions, take decisions and to make friends with mistakes. The teacher too must recognise that he or she will make errors – more often in the affective domain – and that the admission of mistakes with a simple request for forgiveness will be noted and internalised in a way that no other lesson will. Froebel wrote specifically: 'Let us learn from our children, let us give heed to the gentle admonitions of their life, to the silent demands of their minds. Let us live with our children; then will the life of our children bring us peace and joy, then shall we begin to grow wise, to be wise' (Froebel, 1899, p.42).

3. Response – Recognition, Responsibility and Reinterpretation

Recognition. Response, in this sense, requires a willingness to receive, respect and relate to the pupil's place in the world, whatever or wherever it might be. It incorporates a belief that the child's environment and experiences can be mediated for the purposes of learning and drawn outwards in further discovery. Froebel's dictum was: 'I always start with the child'.   Careful observation of children help teachers to recognise that assumptions about children's attitudes cannot always be accurately drawn from their behaviour. Froebel (1826) noted 'The child who appears rude and self-willed is often involved in an intense struggle to realise the good by his own efforts'. Adler (1930, p.61) argued that 'the basis of differentiating between useful and useless manifestations of the striving for superiority (in children) . . . is interest in the community'. The child must be recognised in the context of his/her world as an essential member of the community.

Responsibility. Helping children to take responsibility means assisting them to make choices and to reflect on the outcome of their choices and actions. Can the curriculum be mediated to the child in such a way that alternatives are on offer? Is there only one way of presenting a solution to a problem? What would the implications be of doing something differently? Froebel's concept of freedom in education is based not on license but on the idea that children must be given the right kind of environment which allows them to see relationships, to draw inferences and to make decisions. A truly free person is one who ultimately lives in harmony with him(her)self and his surroundings and perceives the 'unity of all things' (Liebschner, p.69).

Reinterpretation. The principle of reinterpretation recognises that there is no established 'method' that will bring about the education of children in spiritual harmony. Guidelines must warn against too rigid or prescriptive an approach which might end in frustration and disillusionment. Student teachers must also be led to see that the guiding principles of Froebel and Adler may not be dismissed as the sentimental aspirations of a less complex world. Just as the curriculum must be interpreted for each age and community, so must the teacher's response be a reinterpretation for our own time.

A Spiritual Orientation to Teacher Education

A spiritual approach to education is essentially an optimistic one. It recognises that as human beings – teachers and pupils – we are drawn out of ourselves towards goodness, wholeness and fulfillment; it recognises also that we are regularly confronted with our shadow sides – our weaknesses, oversights, failures and wrongdoings. A spiritual orientation to education must be a hopeful one. Adler (1930) emphasised that 'an educator's most important task – one might almost say his holy duty - is to see that no child is discouraged at school' (p.83). For Froebel, creative activity was the key to discovering this way towards hope-giving wholeness. Each child, each person, has a particular gift which will become visible if brought to the light by a perceptive teacher. The expression of the 'gift' in creative activity appropriate to the abilities and inclinations of the child becomes in turn a spiritual response to the prompting of the Creator (Liebschner, p. 36).

Student teachers are just as vulnerable to discouragement as their pupils are – perhaps more so. If dynamism, idealism and a genuine affection for children inspired the student in the first instance, there is a real danger that the crushing weight of the curriculum, the narrow but necessary focus on examinations, and the unreality of teaching practice might serve only to sour and unsettle a healthy spirit. Initial employment may bear further burdens of textbook-driven teaching, perceived parental pressures to meet standards in basic competencies, competition and cynicism from colleagues, and pressure from inspections. A biographical case study of a practicing teacher noted: 'The curriculum is overloaded – parents seem to think they are qualified teachers, inspectors have their own pet little plans, and the clergy also demand their pound of flesh. I find I am a 'jack of all trades' and master of few, and am drawn in many directions simultaneously. Probably the most helpful strategy I've found to help me cope with teaching is the ability to switch off at 3.00pm and find a quiet hour by myself to unwind' (INTO, 1994). How can teacher education, drawing from the spiritualities of Froebel and Adler, help focus the student on 'ultimate values' in their work while grappling with the day-to-day difficulties in the contemporary reality of school and classroom experience?

At the outset it must be stated that a spirituality of teacher training is not based on technique alone. Of course all lecturers must rely on pedagogy to an extent and pedagogy can ultimately be translated into technique. However, in approaching teacher education from the perspective of spirituality it needs to be recognised that the whole is greater than the sum of the parts. Bennet wrote about the spiritual education of children: 'Never attempt to teach children directly about high and deep spiritual questions, including questions of religion. If we did so, they. . . would not penetrate into the deeper understanding of the child' (1984, p. 71). The authors believe that we will benefit from a renewed look at some of the basics, some of the tenets upon which Froebel education is founded, and some of the psychological suppositions which underlie it. These principles include:

- The concept of inner connectedness out of which derives the principle of integrated learning and the relevance of thematic and project-based curricular opportunities
- The spiritual basis of education, in that the drawing outwards of the pupil in 'e(x)-ducare' by the enlightened teacher mirrors the unobtrusive, life-enhancing work of the Creator in all of nature
- Reverence and respect for the child by which the teacher learns to recognise and cherish his or her own inner childishness and love of the playful
- The understanding of the importance of the early years and of self-activity and the purpose of play during these years – promoting a move from the traditional didactic teaching to more life-enhancing forms of learning
- The use of concrete materials and activity-based methods of inquiry which embrace the need for children to externalise

before they can internalise many basic concepts, particularly in mathematics

- The emphasis on the deliberate construction of a happy and harmonious environment both in the physical arrangements of the school and classroom and in sustaining a climate that incorporates a welcoming space for pupils, parents and colleagues.

Was Adler Influenced by Froebel?

Norman Brosterman's book, *Inventing Kindergarten* (1997), makes invigorating reading for anyone schooled in the Individual Psychology of Adler. Brosterman's thesis is that the Froebel method of education had a significant influence in the development of modern art and architecture. In his book, Brosterman enumerates the guiding principles of Froebel's educational theory:

- Froebel believed that learning. . . would provide a common ground for all people. . . and advance. . . into a realm of fundamental unity' (p.96).
- One universal law upon which Froebel based all of his principles was unity or inner connection. The inter-connectedness of all things was the governing force in Froebel's philosophy and pedagogy. . . (p. 13)
- More than any teacher before him, [Froebel] recognised the unity of an individual's physical, intellectual, and spiritual powers. . . (p. 32)
- The study of nature sensitised children to. . . the interdependence of all things (p. 34)
- The habit of pointing out the moral of the story, which was traditional in education, and in particular religious education, was anathema to Froebel, as he thought it robbed the child of the opportunity of drawing his or her own conclusions. . . (p. 35)

Since Adler was born in Vienna in 1870, it is possible, even probable, that he attended a Froebel Kindergarten. No reference to Froebel has been discovered in Adler's writings, but he offers an intriguing hint in an article written in 1937, the year of his death, where he quotes Pestalozzi, 'The environment moulds man, but man moulds the environment' (Ansbacher & Ansbacher, 1979, p. 28). It appears, therefore, that Adler was at least influenced by one of the major influences on Froebel. So much of Adler is reminiscent of Froebel, such as his use of the Socratic method in his therapy, and the principles of unity, perfection, interconnectedness, and interdependence, that it is not far-fetched to see a relationship between the two. Indeed, it is my contention that Adler provides the necessary psychological underpinning to the Froebel method of education.

It is unfortunate that Froebel's method of education and Adler's view of human nature have such limited influence today. Adler is now either a footnote or a brief section in psychology texts and a minor historical figure in the development of psychotherapy. His significance and influence are rarely cited. Additionally, in certain quarters and among certain individuals, Froebel education has mutated into 'Froebelianism', and espousing his methods makes one a 'Froebelian'. Both are cultist terms suggesting restricted entry and elevated superiority among a chosen few. This view is, quite simply, contrary to everything Froebel, and Adler, believed. Both spoke of the necessity of sharing knowledge, not restricting it for private use or claiming ownership over it. According to Ansbacher and Ansbacher (1956), Adler viewed his psychology as primarily a liaison activity and would have taken these developments as symptoms of neurotic safeguarding activity at the institutional level. Froebel would have viewed them as yet another form of restrictive education which artificially segments knowledge into parts.

The core components of Froebel's educational philosophy include: centring the curriculum in the classroom, schoolhouse, and local environment; creativity – utilising materials and ideas in new and varied forms; connectedness – seeing unity in everything, activating integration; co-operation and collaboration by meaningful groupwork; concrete materials and clear practical activities over abstract didactics; celebration and communion through play; calling forth respect by displaying respect for child, family, and community; and concern for the inner life of the spirit and its outward drives

Children, Spirituality, and Literature

Among the most valuable contributions of Hay and Nye (1999) is that their research actually uncovered the language children use to describe spiritual experiences. It has been mentioned previously that they have dubbed the spiritual experience of children 'relational consciousness' which they take pains to note is not a narrow concept but rather pertains to 'I-Self', 'I-World', 'I-Others', and 'I-God' (p. 114). Adler went further than they, and was more specific, when he wrote, 'Community feeling remains throughout life. It becomes differentiated, limited, or expanded and, in favourable cases, extends not only to family members but to the larger group, to the nation, to all of mankind. It can even go further, extending itself to animals, plants, and inanimate objects and finally even to the cosmos' (Ansbacher & Ansbacher, 1956, p.138).

Additionally, and perhaps most importantly they have noted that children's spirituality is most definitely not confined to a religious word-view. Hay and Nye stand as heirs to Adler who stated, 'The goal should be that no child could leave school without the assurance of being a real fellow man [sic]', and added, 'Self-boundedness is an artefact thrust upon the child during his education and by the present state of our social structure. . . . Teachers. . . . must be freed from their own self-boundedness and, together with all those who want to work honestly for the common welfare, must prevent these seductions of the child' (Ansbacher & Ansbacher, 1956, p. 138). The authors' research has been focused on the expression of spirituality in children. Standing on the shoulders' of Savary and Hardy, we are interested in what it is that children do which demonstrates the spiritual nature they possess as a biological endowment and living potentiality. We have been guided in this work by the words of Adler who wrote, 'Community feeling is not inborn as a full-fledged entity, but it is an innate potentiality which is to be consciously developed. . . . and the dominant purpose of education is to evoke it.' (Ansbacher & Ansbacher, 1956, p. 134). Our view of the core components of this applied spirituality as follows (Carey, 1997):

- Compassion – the call to action aimed at healing a broken world
- Creativity – the call to wholeness and integrity
- Communication – the process of constructing self and world
- Co-operation – the call to collective action through community building
- Contribution – the call to collective concerns as opposed to private agendas
- Commitment – the call to participate in the fulfilment of the world's destiny
- Courage – the call to non-conformism and the need to overcome

It is our contention that through skilful observation of children at play, and at times in the classroom, one can see these seven attributes of the child's spiritual life in action.

Coles (1989) has written about the importance of story and literature and tells us,

'Novels and stories are renderings of life; they can not only keep us company, but admonish us, point us in new directions, or give us the courage to stay a given course. They can offer us kinsmen, kinswomen, comrades, advisers – offer us other eyes through which we might see, other ears with which we might make soundings' (p. 160).

Coles, eminent child psychiatrist and perhaps the world's most skilful listener to the stories children tell about themselves is pointing us toward the powerful gravity field of the spiritual meaning of story and literature (Coles, 1990). He recounts being told by his psychiatric supervisor while in training, 'Remember, what you are hearing is to some considerable extent a function of you, hearing' (p. 15).

Coles reminds us that no story, no book, in fact no learning, takes place in the absence of relationship. This is a point that Palmer (1983) has made effectively. He points out that, 'Ultimately, an ethical education is one that creates a capacity for connectedness in the lives of students' (p. xviii). When we tell or read stories to children we are wise to realise that the story belongs equally to the teller as to the listener.

So what use are stories and reading to the child's spirit? It is our belief that the highest purpose of story and literature for children is their ability to point towards a solution to the existential problem of what it means to be human. We take strong exception to those who use the language of helping children become 'more fully human' or who introduce any sort of hierarchy into the spiritual development of children. Children are fully human from the moment of conception. But it is through story and literature that we learn to discern the various manifestations of living the human life. Stories fill our earliest days. We hear them from parents and relations, thereby learning about our personal and family history and the direction towards which it is heading. We learn to read and discover the lives of other people in other places, and internalise those lives into an ever-changing view of self. All of life is story and the quest for the discovery of the meaning and purpose of the life force itself. It could be argued, indeed has been argued, that autobiography is a form of theology. Keen (1970) quotes Elie Wiesel, 'God made man because he loves stories' (p. 83)

If God made man because he loves stories then there must be more to story-telling and reading than literacy, phonics skills, and comprehension. But what is it exactly? Bettelheim (1982), writing from a doctrinaire psychoanalytic perspective, has provided the seminal framework from which any discussion of children and story must proceed. This is not the place to dissect his work or to introduce his philosophical heirs. Rather it is sufficient to note his own words of warning, 'The acquisition of skills, including the ability to read, becomes devalued when what one has learned to read adds nothing of importance to one's life' (p. 4). He cautions us about the importance of moral education '. . . which *subtly*, and by *implication* only [emphasis added] conveys. . . the advantages of moral behaviour. . .' (p. 5). He speaks of 'safe stories' and cautions against their simplistic view of the world, a world without struggle, sorrow, pain, and forgiveness. While writing about fairytales, Bettelheim is teaching us something important about all forms of story; he is emphasising that they speak to the human soul with all its fantastic intricacy.

Reading and Story in School

Teacher training, as has been pointed out, is currently in the throes of tensions between political, social, cultural, and ethical forces. As a result, it tends to focus on the more practical, skill-oriented aspects of the art of teaching. In the area of literacy, student teachers are taught about phonetic or whole-word approaches as they relate to children's reading. The writing of lesson plans helps maintain the illusion of objectivity and creates distance between teacher and learner. Quantum physics long ago did away with the notion of objectivity which Hay and Nye refer to as '. . . the myth of objectivity' (p. 79).

Last year a sixth-class group of boys, thirty-two in number, engaged in a discussion about prayer with one of the authors. It was nearing confirmation time and the boys had been presented with endless lessons about the importance of this sacrament and had been urged to create all sorts of posters and activities related to it. For no particular reason whatever, the boys were asked if those who prayed would be willing to raise their hands. Of course, every hand went up immediately. We began to discuss the nature of prayer and what is it we do when we pray. The general consensus seemed to be that prayer is a form of talking to God. At this point, it occurred to us that it might be interesting to ask a question about this business of talking to God. We inquired if there was any boy who had ever had the experience of God talking to them. One boy in the front of the class immediately raised his hand. He told the class that he had heard God speak to him. He was then asked what God's voice sounded like. He responded, 'God has the voice of my dead brother in heaven'. When asked how old his dead brother in heaven was he replied, 'Let's see, he was 14 when he was killed by the car, I guess he would be 18 now'. He was then asked just what God's voice had said to him and he told us, 'God just said it's all right, I'm happy here and you don't have to worry about me'. A lively classroom discussion followed.

One can see, of course, the cultural and religious background of this boy's story and also the effectiveness of religious upbringing. However, what is noteworthy is the telling of the story. In a classroom of doubting peers, he had the courage to recount a spiritual experience of a highly personal nature. We wondered just how often we had not bothered to ask children to tell their stories and how seldom we make ourselves available to listen to them. Personal narrative is the entryway to the spiritual life of the child. Hay and Nye have quantified this in their research. By asking the proper questions we can gain powerful insight into the child's inner world, the world of the spirit.

Literature in the classroom can serve the purpose of opening the child's mind and allowing children to internalise a spiritual world view while at the same time giving life to it by talking about it. The children's classic, *The Wizard of Oz,* can lead to this process. Unfortunately most children and adults are far more familiar with the film version than the book itself. In the film, the Tin Woodsman's story is never properly explained. In the book, the Woodsman is given time to tell his story, which revolves around jealousy, possessiveness, separation, lost love, and culminates in the recovery of the ability to love. The journey to Oz is, like all great spiritual journeys, a healing journey which requires the ability to endure hardship, loss, grief, and strife before reaching wholeness. In the Froebel classroom, the moral of the story is never told. Children are trusted to internalise the essence of the tale in a way that has meaning and purpose for them. Adler reminds us that when one child learns, the entire class benefits. So from the perspective of Froebel and Adler, spiritual wisdom is reached in community through the process of one individual's struggle to open up to life's meaning. In other words, when the teller tells the story, listener, teller, and observers engage in a dialectic of spiritual discovery.

If we are to take the teachings of Froebel and Adler seriously, we recognise that children's literature must not be dissected or analysed for doing so is like cutting the nightingale's throat to see what makes it sing. Literature is its own song and needs no additional music to make its meaning clearer. If we are to begin to use literature to provide the child with a clearer view of what it means to be human, we could benefit from taking a look at what research has shown us about the spirituality of children. Hay and Nye articulate a four-step process in nurturing the child's spirit. The four steps are:

1) Helping children to keep an open mind
2) Exploring ways of seeing
3) Encouraging personal awareness
4) Becoming personally aware of the social and political dimensions of spirituality.

They caution us, that '. . . matters can be closed off in the classroom. . . including discovering a purpose in life, understanding their dependency on the community in which they find themselves, what it means to be just, facing the reality of their own death, the need for meaning, what it is to be a free human being and how to stand alone' (p. 163).

By choosing literature that embodies some of these themes we increase the likelihood of opening the inner eyes of the child to the spiritual dimension of life. Likewise, when we ask children to tell their story, or their family's story, we focus their eyes inward towards the still-point in the human heart wherein lies the spirit. Children are constantly re-creating themselves; adults do the same. All life is, according to Froebel and Adler, constant creation replicating itself towards ultimate perfection. Literature and story in the classroom must be recognised as an essential component of the process of helping children recognise this essential fact of life.

We spend too much time teaching about religion and not enough about the life of the spirit. In Bennet's compilation about children's spirituality, he quotes one author who believes that the teaching of religion to children is almost always damaging to their souls.

What about Instructional Objectives?

The process of training future teachers is a minefield of difficulty. Perhaps one of the most obvious is the area of instructional objectives in the writing of lesson plans. If one is to attempt to help teachers understand their responsibility to the spiritual development of the child, how are we to incorporate proper training into this imperative? Can we write instructional objectives that address the spiritual life? Although the authors are not certain that such an undertaking is necessary or appropriate, we offer some suggestions to those who might wish to do so.

Let us suppose we have read or told one of Wilde's fairytales to children, for example, *The Nightingale and the Rose* (1994). This is a story about love, self-sacrifice, the shallowness of human beings, and the giving which goes unseen. If we read this story to children, how are we to know if it has touched their spirit? We might formulate an instructional objective which reads, 'The children will be asked to discuss their understanding of the word 'sacrifice'. The children will then be asked to write or tell a story, using their own personal experience, about sacrifice.' There are multiple paths to the child's spirit but the first step begins with asking the correct question. One could make an entire week's lessons out of this story by asking children to focus on how they might make some small sacrifice for the class and if they wish to have it be known publicly. Drawing up action plans about sacrifice and making written commitments to follow through can be part of the overall aim. To demonstrate the unity of all knowledge, the lesson can be brought into the world of nature study. All of this is difficult and tricky. No less so because much of what we often call cross-curricular integration is forced and shallow, speaking more to inter-connectedness than to unity. We must also not forget the caution of Froebel about never telling the moral of the story to children.

Conclusion

We have spent considerable time setting the spirituality of children into a theoretical context, using the educational philosophy of Froebel and the psychological theory of Adler. It is our hope that the integration of these two schools of thought is not forced or shallow, but a true unity, each demanding the other in the search for higher meaning. We believe that the integration of these two disciplines reveals a unity of knowledge about children and helps us look at education in the classroom in a different context. We have touched upon reading, story-telling, and literacy only to a small degree. We do not wish to create yet another technology and apply it to the spiritual life of the child. We do not wish to create another curriculum to be 'delivered' to children. We are calling for a re-visioning of the importance of story and literature to children, a re-visioning which recognises that these aspects of children's education go right to the core of the child's being.

It is important for us to recognise that not all stories must be told. There are many untold stories, and other stories which have been told long after their heroes have left this mortal life. Bettelheim wrote about the untold story of Freud's interest in the soul (1982). Matthew Fox (1986) wrote a book about a stream of Christian spirituality overshadowed by mainstream orthodoxy. The children in our classroom have stories to tell, stories about life, love, family, home, joy and sorrow. Perhaps children resist reading at times because we have not created space for them to tell the greatest story of all, the story of their unfolding life.

Coles (1990) reminds us that the story belongs as much to the listener as to the teller and has written about the spiritual life of children. Stories unfold on a daily basis in our classrooms. The more we focus on the technology of reading the less space we create for stories to unfold. Palmer (1983) tells us to make a space where learning can begin, a space for the unfolding of the human spirit in the educational process. Froebel and Adler gave primacy to the spirit of the child, its ever-creative unfolding and development, and its importance to the re-creation of the world which is headed towards ultimate perfection. As teachers, and as teacher-trainers, we need to re-vision our view of what literature is about and recognise that the stakes are high. When children grow up in a world which does not provide for them an innate sense of purpose and belonging, it is no wonder some of them turn to chemicals in their search for oneness.

Bettelheim wrote about the use of the formulaic 'Once upon a time. . .' in fairytales and tells us that it serves to distance the reader from the tale in a sort of defensive manoeuvre for the service of ego protection. But there is another, more radical conclusion one can draw for this formula, and all forms of forced distance. Watts (1972) speaks of the need to believe we are separate from the other. He writes, 'The fact is that because no one thing or feature of this universe is separable from the whole, the only real You, or Self, is the whole' (p. 48). He comments on children's books, 'Children's books are written by serious ladies with three names and no imagination. . .' (p. 105). Perhaps he is being too harsh. But it is not unlikely that his prime thesis, the conspiracy to convince people that each and every one is separate from all others, begins in primary school and is introduced through literature that stifles the spirit's silent movement.

Chopra, in a book concerned with the spirituality of parenting (1997), has written of the importance of teaching children that success in life depends more on who you are and less on what you do. He speaks of human being and states, 'But being can be over-looked, since it is completely silent, like a master choreographer that never joins the dance' (p. 15). Powerful implications leap from this premise and connections can be made with Savary's definition of spirituality with its focus on being and action, and Hogan's notion of the dance of courtship between teacher and learner. 'We are, after all, human beings, not human thinkings', Chopra reminds us. Yes, we are human being, once children, born fully human, born with a biological drive towards the spiritual which cannot be stifled but can be twisted and distorted towards useless ends. We need to be, to dance in celebration of joy in the act of learning. Re-visioning the role of story and literature in the child's life is one path towards helping the spirit grow straight and strong.

The authors sound one cautionary note: if the spiritual life of the child is seen as part of the remit of public schooling, it must not be reduced to a curriculum. Spirituality is a lived essence, not a taught subject. If we reduce spirituality to the level of a subject, if it will be goverened by inspection and supervision, if it begets the development of workbooks, videos, and computer software, then we have taken the highest potentiality of humankind and rendered it impotent. We are not calling for the addition of anything new in an already over-crowded national curriculum. We are suggesting that educators rethink their remit, recall that they are responsible for the education of the whole child, and become mindful of the ever-present spirit of education in the classroom community.

REFERENCES

Adler, A. (1930). *The education of children.* South Bend, Indiana: Gateway Editions.

Ansbacher, H.L., & Ansbacher, R. (Eds.). (1956). *The individual psychology of Alfred Adler.* New York: Basic Books.

Ansbacher, H.L., & Ansbacher, R. (Eds.). (1979). *Superiority and social interest.* New York: W.W. Norton.

Baum, L.F. (1997). *The Wonderful Wizard of Oz.* Oxford: Oxford University Press.

Becker, E. (1962). *The birth and death of meaning: Perspectives in psychiatry and anthropology.* New York: Free Press of Glencoe.

Bennett, J.G., et al. (1984). *The spiritual hunger of the modern child.* Charlestown, West Virginia: Claymont Communications.

Bettelheim, B. (1982). *Freud and man's soul.* New York: A.A. Knoph.

Betteliem, B. (1991). *The uses of enhancement.* London: Penguin.

Bottome, P. (1957). *Alfred Adler: A portrait from life* (3rd ed.). New York: Vanguard Press.

Brennan, J. (1997). The contribution of school management to spirituality. *FORUM for Promoting 3-19 Comprehensive Education, 39 (2).* London.

Brosterman, N. (1997). *Inventing kindergarten*. New York: Abrams.

Carey, D.J. (1997). Squaring the sonnet: A spirituality of special education. *SPES, 7,* 18-23.

Carey, D.J., & Griffin, S. (1998). *Adler and Froebel: Towards a spirituality of teacher education.* Paper presented at the Third Conference on Education, Spirituality, and the Whole Child, Roehampton, England.

Chopra, D. (1993). *Ageless body, timeless mind*. London: Rider.

Chopra, D. (1997). *The seven spiritual laws of success for parents*. London: Rider.

Coles, R. (1989). *The call of stories*. Boston: Houghton Mifflin.

Coles, R. (1990). *The spiritual life of children*. Boston: Houghton-Mifflin.

Dean, A. (1952). *Reflections on the training of teachers*. London: National Froebel Foundation Bulletin.

Dent, H. (1947). *To be a teacher*. London: University of London Press.

Ellis, A. (1962). *Reason and emotion in psychotherapy*. New York: Lyle Stuart.

Ellenberger, H. (1970). *The discovery of the unconscious*. New York: Basic Books.

Fox, M. (1986). Original blessing. Santa Fe, New Mexico: Bear & Co.

Froebel College of Education, Sion Hill. (1982). *Friedrich Froebel, 1782-1982*. Dublin: Author.

Froebal, F. (1899). *The education of man* (translated by W.N. Halliman). New York: D Appleton.

Gray, L. (1998). *Alfred Adler, the forgotten prophet*. Westport, CT: Praeger.

Hay, D., & Nye, R. (1999). *The spirit of the child*. London: Fount.

Hogan, P. (1995). *The custody and courtship of experience*. Maynooth: Columba Press.

Hall, C.S., & Lindzey, G. (1957). *Theories of personality*. New York: Wiley.

Herford, W. (1990). *The student's Froebel*. London: Isbister.

Irish National Teachers Organisation. (1994). A career in teaching. Dublin: Author.

Irish National Teachers' Organisation. (1995). *Education of teachers, reform and renewal*. Dublin: Author.

Jourard, S. (1963). *Personal adjustment: An approach through the study of healthy personality* (2nd ed.). New York: Macmillan.

Keen, S. (1970). *To a dancing God*. New York: Harper and Row.

eibschner, J. (1992). *A child's work*. Cambridge, England.

Maslow, A. (1954). *Motivation and personality*. New York: Harper.

Palmer, P. (1983). *To know as we are known*. San Francisco: Harper and Row.

Plowden, B. (1967). *Children and their primary schools* (Vol. 1). London: HMSO.

Savary, L. (1988). Dreams and spirituality. *Common Boundary, 6*(2), 5-7, 26.

Wilde, O. (1994). *The complete short stories*. London: Penguin.

Reading in Romanian Schools: New Directions*

. . . .

Adela-Luminita Rogojinaru
Institute for Educational Sciences
Bucharest, Romania

During the 30 years of Ceausescu's regime, reading never was a controversial issue in the Romanian education system. As part of the mother tongue acquisition, and supported by the 10 years compulsory education, it seemed that, at a minimum, all students finished school with an acceptable level of literacy. We, the teachers, lived within the culture of the 'passing mark': all students had to achieve the minimum literacy level of '5' (the minimum school performance). The reading method of the primary school (7-10 years of age), an analytical-synthetic one, focused on phonics and on literal understanding of a text's meaning. The strengths and weaknesses of this method had never been debated at any length. In both the reading curriculum and textbooks of the gymnasium (middle school) and of the high school, the specialists interpreted the process of literacy development as simplified literary criticism, and acquisition of the rules of grammar. Moreover, between 1977 and 1990 research activities in specialised academic fields were stopped for ideological reasons. Similarly, no pedagogical research was undertaken between 1982 and 1990.

After 1990, educational research pointed to the low literacy levels in Romania, and attention was directed to reading methodology.

*Paper presented at the 23rd Annual Conference of the Reading Association of Ireland, Mary Immaculate College, Limerick, September 17-19, 1998.

The low literacy levels and high dropout rates were alarming and still are. The concerned educators raised two main issues: a political one (policy of education) and a technical one (curriculum development and reading methods). Political activity focused on three broad areas – *textbook diversification, curriculum restructuring*, and new *school policy*. Unfortunately, the pedagogical changes (in particular, the methods for teaching reading) have not changed during the post-revolutionary years. This might be one reason for the teachers' current resistance to non-traditional textbooks or to instructional approaches other than the ex-cathedra one.

The first formal interventions in language acquisition occurred in foreign language didactics. Foreign language teaching benefited from international exchanges and the introduction of the first communicative-based methods. Following them, the Romanian language curriculum prescribed four aspects of language competency: *reading, writing, listening,* and *speaking.* At the primary level, the subject 'communication' replaced 'speech development'. And yet the Romanian language didactics, subverted by the continuous debates on mother tongue versus national (official) language, ignored innovation. Public opinion considers that the Romanian language – as the official language of the country – should keep the tradition in both values and methods of instruction. Besides, what we call 'reading' implies exclusively the linguistic side – the language skills – and does not take into account the social aspects of learning to read.

The publication of the text, *Introduction to the Theory of Reading* (Cornea, first edition, 1988, second edition, 1998) marked in a positive sense the emergence of the literary reading, but it had very little impact on reading pedagogy. It is fair to say that the author's intention was truly aimed at developing pedagogical insights. But if we looked into the methodological details, we could see that, for instance, in the chapter dedicated to the reader's functions, the least consideration is given to the 'real' reader. Also, if we examine the reading strategies and models reviewed in the book, we would see that it would be difficult for a primary or even a secondary teacher to apply the principles of literary criticism in the daily classroom activities. Again, the reading theory is refined, while reading practices continue as before.

Initial Attempts at Reform: 1994-1998

Starting in 1994, educational reform has been implemented in the school system at large, with the assistance of a loan from the World Bank. This reform covers all the strategic components of educational change: curriculum, teacher training, textbooks, evaluation and assessment, management and finance. However, while textbooks were intended to be 'alternative', in fact, a lot of them are only 'repetitive'. At the primary level, the ABCs and the reading textbooks, including those approved by the National Commission of Textbook Evaluation, do not differ either in concept or in method. They make use of similar textual conventions, in spite of the fact that curriculum is now less prescriptive. Moreover, they preserve the same idiosyncratic difference between 'citire' and 'lectura', both words meaning reading in different etymology (Slavic, in the first case; Latin, in the second one). The two meanings tend to divide the fields of reading into 'didactic' and 'specialised', or 'literal' and 'literary', or 'basic' and 'complementary', or 'classroom reading' and 'leisure reading'.

As for the gymnasium textbooks, some differences do show up, many because the authors are specialists in educational research, as well as having a sound practical knowledge. Yet, even these do not include an emphasis on teaching reading strategies, even though they incorporate the new communicative approach recommended by the curriculum. However, two of the latest textbooks issued – a textbook for fifth-grade published by Humanitas Publishing House, and one for 6th grade one, published by the ALL Publishing House – have included some reader response strategies. With no provision of appropriate in-service training during the last school year, the teachers of the 5th grade have tried the reader response methodology with very little success. Not surprisingly, in a recent survey, 80% of the teachers expressed a preference for more conventional textbooks, leaving out what they called the 'innovative' issues. Instead of feeling empowered by the reader-based methods, teachers became intimidated by the complexity of the learning tasks, and by the new teaching roles which they were supposed to take on. They could not appreciate the benefits of the new methods which seemed to be appropriate for the highest achieving (and most competitive) students. According to teachers, student-centred learning works only for the best students or for the ones living in cities, who have access to additional reading materials. The other students are perceived to need direct instruction from their teachers and less complex reading tasks. So called 'self-steering' tasks were found by teachers to be difficult to implement and manage.

We must then conclude that strategies for teaching reading have not really changed in day-to-day classroom practice. We can also notice that reading didactics is considered a personal concern rather than a scientific one. Much discussion centres around the question 'What should students read?' instead of focusing on 'How do students learn to read?'. Metacognitive approaches, although recommended by research, are far from being part of the formal teaching of reading. However, the new curriculum that the Ministry of Education launched at the beginning of this (1998) school year makes the change irreversible. New procedures have been introduced to ensure that the teaching of reading will change and that the system will absorb its own idiosyncrasies.

The 1998 Curriculum Change

The curriculum changes introduced in 1998 have been coming on stream for some time. Real intervention at the level of structure and content is part of the broader movement towards authentic reform that the new Minister of Education initiated at the beginning of 1998. The new curriculum framework includes the following innovations:

1. The school year is divided into two semesters (terms);

2. Curricular areas have been introduced instead of individual subjects;

3. There is a core curriculum with some cross-curricular options;

4. A specific amount of time has been allocated to each curricular area, with some optional time available also;

5. There is room for selection of curricular areas at the school level;

6. A new assessment system, aligned to the semester structure, and focusing on flexible, student-based learning, is to be introduced;

7. Changes are being implemented in the design of teacher training;

8. There are proposals to implement new system-level evaluation.

There are seven curricular areas:

- Language and communication;
- Mathematics and sciences;
- The human being and society;
- Technologies;
- Arts;
- Physical education and sports;
- Vocational guidance and counselling.

Related to each curricular area is a set of options, including those of a cross-curricular nature, from which individual schools may select, following consultation with parents. The option recommended under the 'language and communication' area for grades 1 to 5 is concerned with the following (suggested) topics:

- Children's literature;
- Foreign languages;
- Minority mother tongues;

- Concrete situation communication;
- Child philosophy;
- Folklore and oral history.

How do these curricular changes affect the status of reading in schools and classroom? The following positive aspects are evident:

- reading is essential to the whole curricular area 'language and communication';
- reading can be integrated into a range of curricular areas and hence is a suitable candidate for cross-curricular integration of subjects;
- reading can be integrated into all school activities.

Apart from these broad assumptions, reading instruction is still controversial:

- there is no evidence whatsoever that teachers will reconsider the teaching of reading and writing under the new curriculum;
- there is no explicit statement that methodology is crucial to the implementation of the reading curriculum;
- there is no explicit statement on how children's engagement in communicative approaches would help to improve their reading and writing processes;
- the inclusion of children's literature as an optional component for primary school children suggests that traditional divides between classroom reading and leisure reading will persist.

Moreover, at least for the first year of implementation, the language curriculum and syllabi will not be correlated to the existing reading/writing textbooks. It appears that specific approaches to implementation are dependant on the new teacher-training system. The following issues are likely to affect implementation:

- the quality of teaching is viewed as depending on how much the teacher is in control of the classroom; consequently, the teaching of reading depends more on the particular texts that are selected and on strict guided instruction, rather than on students' motivation to read;
- acquisition of language (namely, the Romanian language) is the result of classroom reading and writing instruction; there is little action yet in the reading classes towards considering the reading habits of young people outside of school, and even less towards family literacy;
- adults, parents and teachers decide upon the content of the reading, and continue to focus on reciting and reproducing sections of texts by heart as techniques for understanding.

Development of Alternative Reading Programmess (1991-1998)

Due to the fact that the official curriculum offers a good framework for the development of all types of methodology, non-governmental bodies initiated alternative reading and writing programmess. The oldest initiative (called 'Expanded Reading') belongs to the Romanian Reading Association (RoRA), which launched the programme of teacher-training for applying reading as a cross-curricular tool in 1992. Unfortunately, at the time the project was launched, the formal curriculum was less responsive to such an approach. Ideas from the project can now be offered for integration of the subjects across any of the curricular areas.

RoRA's project proposed a twofold action research approach – one side concerned with developing proficiency in reading, the other with the methods of teaching reading. The programme was initiated because of concerns with literacy standards. A research study conducted by the Institute of Educational Sciences in Romania, as reported on in UNESCO's (1995) *Education for All,* found that 10.3% of graduates of the basic compulsory education systems are functional illiterates. These young people, aged between 14 and 16, cannot perform the regular social tasks that require reading, writing and calculation skills. Among the 10.3%, four groups in particular were over-represented: girls, young people from rural areas, young people from families with literacy problems, and young people from families engaged in agriculture.

A defective mode of classroom reading instruction can contribute to functional illiteracy. Young people cannot transfer skills acquired in formal reading classes to the social literacy tasks that are necessary for basic functioning. Lacking this social response leads to political illiteracy and to civic misconduct. A lot of TV satirical shows disclose the incapacity of the people to discriminate between nuances of public discourse. RoRA's programme, 'Expanded reading', therefore reflects the principle of using authentic symbols of the social milieu, and helps individuals to develop life-long learning skills. Indeed, labour market studies show that unemployment is highest among those aged between 15 and 24 – a group that needs to value reading, especially the use of non-fictional texts, for their personal and work-related development.

Other programmes have been initiated by the Foundation for an Open Society: 'Step by Step' and the 'Reading and Writing for Critical Thinking' (RWCT). Although involved in the preliminary stage of the RWCT – at that time called 'Reading for Understanding' – neither RoRA nor other Romanian specialists gave advice on the reading methodology underlying these programmes. The programmes are effectively packages of strategies and reading techniques developed in North America, which, it is assumed, can eventually be applied in any context, with appropriate assistance and teacher training. The same goes for the 'First Steps in Reading and Writing' whose goal is to produce and publish children's books to suit each reading level. The difficulty in implementing this programme is that Romania does not have a standardised description of reading levels, which makes it potentially difficult to match the reader with books for the appropriate level of reading skills.

More practical outcomes have resulted from the implementation of a programme called 'Equal Chances for Roma Children through Education', also sponsored by the Foundation for an Open Society. The principles of this programme draw on the results of previous studies and research reports, such as the Institute for Educational Sciences' *Education in Disadvantaged Areas*, and the Romanian Reading Association's *ECOLECT: A Methodology of Reading for Mutual Understanding*. The programme addresses Roma and at-risk children in small rural communities and urban districts. The programme aims at developing intercultural attitudes and community-based strategies to assure school enrolment andattendance as well as the minimum school performance for the target groups. The programme components assure that attention is given to the following:

- School development and institutional partnership;
- Classroom management (learning by co-operation);
- Parents' involvement in school activities;
- Folklore and oral history oriented curriculum;
- Roma history and culture;
- Intercultural education.

These reading programmes provide opportunities for peer work and group activities in which children themselves create an environment for mutual understanding. Children discuss, for instance, the values that literary characters carry symbolically through the text and their relevance to the readers' own personalities. They also learn the ethical attitudes of the characters by considering the moral of a story's events, and try to relate it to their family and community experience. The children are invited to either retell the stories or to make short compositions with argumentation of their views. They are also invited to create stories based on authentic experiences and share their compositions in small groups or in front of the whole class. Besides reading classes, the children are invited to write compositions and short essays on non-fictional texts, related to the Sciences or Civics topics.

Closely linked to the 'Roma Equal Opportunities Programme,' the Foundation invited me to run a Reading Club for children in one of the two pilot schools in Bucharest. The project lasted for one school year (1996/1997) and was aimed at enabling and empowering children to reflect symbolically upon their own values and experiences. The Club mentors – two persons, primary teachers, one of them Roma by ethnic origin – conducted reading sessions, in which children of 6, 7 and 8 years of age listened to, read, retold and illustrated stories. Though delayed, the intention is to publish these children's stories and to use them as authentic reading material in the classroom. The Reading Club addressed two groups of about 10-12 children each, Roma and Romanian together. These were extra-curricular activities that will eventually be part of the optional subject areas in the 1998 curriculum.

The Vocational Educational and Training (VET) Curriculum under the EU Phare VET Program has contributed also to the expansion of alternatives to the formal reading programmes. Since 1994, at the same time that the World Bank assisted Reform Project was initiated, the EU Phare donation of 25M ECU has come on stream, to assist the vocational educational system in 75 pilot schools all over the country. VET structure (upper secondary level) covers three years of study, which gradually grows from 'basic training' (first year) to 'general training' (second year) up to 'specialised training' (third and, in some cases, fourth year). The individuality of the VET curriculum is reflected in its modular format. The basic, core curriculum consists of two parts: general education (focussed on the personal and social development of the students) and the specialised, technical education (assisting the development of vocational capacities and skills). Besides the basic curriculum, the optional areas consist, on the one hand, of modules for upgrading skills or for occupational mobility, and, on the other hand, of cross-curricular themes.

The VET curriculum does not allocate a special place to reading programmes. However, the learning methodology is very much focused on technical reading skills. Both mother tongue and foreign language education enable students to use the technical symbols, such as technical drawing, schemes, tables, figures, diagrams, etc. These skills are basic for a future qualified worker, and help such a person to perform job tasks in real settings. The learning process is entirely standardised, in terms of both occupational (working) and training (educational) standards. The evaluation of the standardised competencies is prescribed under the curriculum by means of 'performance criteria'. From this point of view, VET provides the only curriculum in which student capacities are discriminated in assessable units. Teaching and Learning Portfolios provide the teachers and students with appropriate strategies for problem solving, critical thinking, self-steering tasks, analysing logical situations, constructing similar examples and implementing solutions in practical situations.

The Routine of Reading Pedagogy

Reading is not a topic that one can easily overlook. Nevertheless, reading research and development is not a topic of research in Romania today, even though it is implicit in the general reform of the curriculum structure. Consider, for example, the difficulties I encountered as an author of a 6th grade reading textbook.

The process of textbook specification, approval, editing and publication are entirely the Ministry of Education's formal task. The Commission for Textbook Evaluation, appointed at the central level, oversees two aspects of textbook assessment: first, preliminary approval of the textbook during a bidding process; second, final approval before publication and promotion in the educational textbook market. In the first phase, three textbooks (including my own) were selected from among about twenty presented. The criteria for selection included curriculum relevance, pedagogical relevance, originality and cost. Prior to final approval, the Commission can call the authors and sharewith them any concerns they may have. In my case, their judgements at this juncture confirmed a canonical approach to the teaching of reading:

- The selection of the literary texts (classical, by curriculum) was not an over-riding concern; the intrinsic value of reading appeared to be neglected;
- The articulation of grammar exercises (also required by the curriculum) produced statements about accuracy of definitions of concepts or of the number of examples; evaluation ignored the practical articulation of the language actualisation through the literary texts that were provided;
- The conversational exercises, meant to assist the development of reading awareness and the construction of understanding were perceived as a potential content overload, a likely burden on students' individual learning, and too complicated a technique for the teacher;
- The composition exercises, meant as writing and rewriting exercises, passed unnoticed; instead, the literary commentaries were remarked on;
- The organisation of the textbook by modules, though common in the case of foreign language textbooks, was a cause for concern; the communication module in particular raised a lot of concern among the Commission's members.

The whole concept of this textbook was based on a model of 'fuzzy reading', on the premise that children today are less eager to follow linear text and instead live as bricoleurs within a cross-cultural world. Also, the new ideas about hypertext confirm the capacity of contemporary reader to process different, mixed textures, instead of decoding separately icons and alphabets. The textbook develops, from this point of view, a heavy design, challenging the reader to get a global impression of the page. It really implies a different type of reading, and encourages the application of this type – a logographic one – in classroom instruction. Apparently, 'fuzzy reading models' contradict the orthodox approach to didactics. They might not, if the right attention were paid to the learner's motivation and interests, and nowadays playing video games represent a much more familiar task than reading literature for many students. In this respect, the social codes appear to act in a more powerful way than the literary ones.

Clearly, old conceptualisations about textbooks and the teaching of reading persist in Romania and elsewhere too. Nevertheless, reading becomes the main problem of the 'learning society', and yet there are no effective solutions to low literacy levels. I have earlier spoken about the Roma child's education. Their parents use to live in a complete oral, non-literate world. Reading for them is symbolical more than practical. As for the practical side, they need reading and writing to sign the checks for the social security, or to fill in the form for the driving license. Romania used to report on a high literacy rate. Nowadays we are more doubtful.

Conclusion

To conclude, we would say that reading in Romania is still not a systematically researched topic, unless we restrict reading to language development. The specialised field of reading is still philological, not pedagogical. Poetics is much more advanced and frequent than studies on literacy. Such elitism neglects the real cultural problem: we do complain that the greater group of the reading public prefers best sellers, soap opera or telenovela. The intellectuals would like to see an interest in major classical works. Too busy to assess the quality dynamics of the book market, we tend to forget that reading practice itself becomes a marginal habit. Adult reading has decreased a lot; the Publishing Houses complain about selling fewer books than ever. The costs of purchasing books has increased in a dangerous way. All these happen in a society that requires skill in reading.

By the time my RoRA colleagues and I developed a model of extended or multiple readings, we had in mind the plurality of the signifiers in the contemporary world. We referred to literal reading, to symbolic reading, to metaphorical reading, to reading signs, to environment reading, to social and emotional reading. Other specialists in education preferred to make use of the concept of 'multiple literacies'. However, there is chasm in Romanian pedagogical development between the theoretical complexity of the models and the implementation of appropriate practices. The definition of a literate person is still minimal for the school, while society requires computer skills, strategic thinking, fast decision making, and greater adaptability.

REFERENCES

Bârzea, C. (1993, 1995). *Educational reform in Romania: Opportunities and trends.* Bucharest: Institute for Educational Sciences.

Cornea, P. (1988). *Introduction to the theory of reading* (2nd ed.) Bucharest: Iasi, Polirom.

Foundation for an Open Society. (1977). *Romathan (Roma studies) (Vol. 2).* Bucharest: Author.

Jigau, M. (1996, 1997). *Education in disadvantaged areas* (First and Second Reports). Budapest: Institute for Educational Sciences.

Vasilescu, A., Rogojinaru, A., & Vasilescu, M. (1997). *Romanian language and literature* (Textbook for the 6th grade). Bucharest: ALL.

UNESCO/Institute for Educational Sciences. (1995). *Education for all in Romania.* Bucharest: Authors.

SECTION 3

Writing

Undergraduate Academic Writing: An Analysis of Errors and Weaknesses in Syntax, Lexis, Style and Structure*

. . . .

Anne O'Keeffe,
Arts Department, Mary Immaculate College
University of Limerick

Essays are a common currency of assessment at third level. They serve to evaluate what students have learnt and, more importantly, to assess how learners can critically apply, evaluate and discuss this knowledge. Writing tasks at third level also help students to clarify and to externalise their thinking about a given topic. It has been argued that writing about a topic helps students to discover what they really believe (Moran 1997, p. 119). Within the genre of academic writing, there is a qualitative difference between what is required of a secondary school composition compared with a university essay. In order to succeed in third-level writing, students need not only to be adept in the established process of writing, they also need to become accustomed to this genre of writing. Some students intuitively sense this 'culture', picking up implicit tacit knowledge as they progress, but unfortunately, many do not. This

*Paper presented at the 23rd Annual Conference of the Reading Association of Ireland, Limerick, September 17-19, 1998.

167

paper sets out to examine a sample of first-year history essays in order to detail the types of weaknesses which frequently occur accross a sample of data. The analysis will focus mainly on problems at sentence and paragraph level in the areas of syntax, lexis and style; it will also examine how ideas within the essay are structured.

Background

There are many reasons why students underachieve at third level. Barrass (1995) states that many students perform below their ability not because of low motivation or lack of effort, but because they do not pay enough attention to improving their competence in communicating their thoughts in writing.

The genesis of this study comes from dissatisfaction on the part of lecturers with undergraduate essay-writing skills at a third-level institution in the south-west of Ireland . It was felt that students needed some academic support in their transition from second- to third-level writing. A needs analysis was carried out and a foundation course in academic writing was designed and implemented for first year Liberal Arts undergraduates.

The Data

Data for this study come from a large corpus of undergraduate essays collected for analysis since 1996. For the purposes of this paper the sample has been limited to twenty-five history essays. Only pass grade essays were examined, in which students scored less than an honours mark of 55 out of 100. All informants were in their first college year in the academic year 1996/97. The essays were typed by requirement and had a word limit of 1000 words. The essay titles were: *'Women in early Ireland were given unequal but not unfair treatment. Do you agree?'* and *'Estimate the impact of the Vikings on Ireland'*. Henceforth, *H1* will be used after examples to indicate the former essay, and *H2* will denote the latter.

Method of Analysis

Error analysis was conducted at the levels of syntax, lexis, style and essay structure. Error types were tagged in the case of syntactic, lexical and stylistic problems but structure was viewed qualitatively – for example, in terms of how an essay dealt with the central question posed in the title. It must be stressed that the results of this analysis remain tentative. In this initial analysis, the objective is to examine, in an intensive way, a small sample of empirical data in order to identify typical weaknesses. In the future, the results of this pilot investigation can be tested longitudinally against a much larger sample. It is a fair criticism that an analysis based solely on writing as a product is never complete since it takes no account of the recursive processes involved including planning, drafting, revising etc. (see Kavanagh 1995, p. 75).

Outcomes

There are four main areas under which the data are analysed: syntax, lexis, style and structure. Under each of these, there is an outline of typical errors and weaknesses with authentic examples.

Syntax

Richards et al. (1992) define syntax as 'the study of how words combine to form sentences and the rules which govern the formation of sentences' (p.370). This category is sub-divided into the constituent error types most commonly found in the data.

(1) Spelling

Spellchecker-proof errors. As stated earlier, students were required to submit their essays in typed form. Obviously, the use of word processors greatly reduces spelling errors. However, spellchecker-proof errors still exist. Here are some examples of homophone-type errors that go unnoticed:

*Of course, **there** arrival would have caused initial confusion*
[H2.2/4]

*. . . Irish women **faired** particularly well* [H1.18/1]

*The Vikings did **steel** from the monasteries but* . . . [H2.10/2]

The presence of this type of error could be symptomatic of writing which has not gone through a review and editing process. Equally, it could be indicative of poor spelling skills for which a spellchecker cannot fully compensate. In order to avoid the above errors, the writer needs to have an awareness of homophones (their/there; fared/faired; steal/steel). It could be argued that the spellchecker facility is disempowering because it lures the writer into a false sense of security about the accuracy of spelling.

Bound grammatical morphemes. There is evidence of spelling errors which result from students' lack of language awareness. In the examples below, the writers are not aware of the morphological difference between *-ice* (noun: practice) and *-ise* (verb: practise). Spellchecker software will not always 'notice' these errors.

*A woman had to be monogamous but a man could **practice** polygamy.* [H1.3/2]

*Polygamy was widely **practiced** in early Irish society. . .* [H1.19/1]

Possessives. Oversimplification may explain some of the confusion in this area – that is, where a writer over-extends a rule and is not aware of exceptions and variations. For instance, in an essay on the impact of the Vikings on Ireland, the following errors were found:

*. . . and enriched **it's** existing culture.* [H2.11/2]

*At the same time, their **idea's**. . .* [H2.11/1]

We see that *'s* is used in every context of possession. In the same text, we find *it's* used in the normal way meaning *it is* (see below).

> *I believe it's due . . . to the communal sense . . .* [H2.11/1]

Another error-type in this area comes from avoiding the issue of where to put an apostrophe (see examples below). From the writer's point of view, omitting the apostrophe will not have as negative an impact as inserting it in the wrong position. In any case, it stands a good chance of not being noticed by the corrector.

> *. . . on the **Vikings** effect on Ireland.* [H2.2/3]

> *. . . her **husbands** actions . . .* [H1.1/1]

> *. . . her **fathers** land.. . . **womens** rights* [H1.2/2]

> *. . . the **mans** honour price* [H1.19/1]

It is worth noting that spellcheckers are very inconsistent in picking up these errors.

American versus British English conventions. Mixing of American and British English spelling conventions is evident:

> *These included clothes and **jewelry** which could be given as a pledge . . .* [H1.8/1]

> *. . . it is evident that the **center** of Irish intellectual life. . .* [H2.10/2]

The earlier example of the *practice/practise* error under the heading of 'Bound Grammatical Morpheme' could also be a result of confusion between British and American conventions.

(2) Punctuation

The 'Breathing Method' of punctuation. It is a widely pronounced dictum that punctuation can be based on where you would take a breath if speaking. Some writers assume that if you can say a sentence without taking a breath, then you can write it without using any punctuation. This may sometimes be the case, but it would be far more enabling for students if they were introduced to the notion of sentence structure and how it relates to punctuation. In the corpus of essays, many instances can be found where students avoid punctuating a sentence. One can deduce that either they simply do not see the need for punctuation or that they are using the *'breathing method'*.

So if there was a break up in the marriage then the woman would be compensated and would receive compensation in accordance to the amount of work she would have done. [H1.3/3]

Also for example it was considered a much more serious crime to murder a woman rather than a man and the offenders hand or foot could be cut off as punishment. [H1.14/1]

The records of the Norse/Irish co-operation suggested that the Norse of the coastal settlements filled into the political structure of the country very much as if they had been Irish tribes. [H2.9/3]

The following examples might be plausible when spoken, but they clearly do not work when written. Elements of prosody, such as intonation and word stress, would disambiguate these sentences in spoken form. Unfortunately, these writers may not be sensitive to the nuances of writing as a distinct medium:

When the Vikings began to settle their metalwork was copied by the Irish. [H2.7/2]

In conclusion I would like to point out that much of the evidence we have of the Vikings is while contemporary severely biased. [H2.11/3]

(3) Maintaining Grammatical Parallelism

Good writing style demands that corresponding ideas within a sentence be expressed in parallel grammatical form (for a detailed treatment, see Mohr 1998, p.120). An example of a problem in this area is the lack of parallel between the nouns '*marriage*' and '*unions*' in the following:

> . . . *a detailed description of the many different types of* **marriage** *and* **unions** *that were permitted in Irish law.* [H1.20/1]

It would be better to have both nouns in plural form: '*marriages and unions*'. In the example below, we see parallel between '*. . . result of a man being*' with the adjectives '*sterile*' and '*impotent*', but this does not extend to the third item '*spoke to others about the marital bed*'.

> *A woman could divorce her husband for varied reasons for example divorce could be result* [sic] *of a man being sterile, impotent,* **spoke to others about the marital bed** *or . . .* [H1.14/3]

If it were grammatically parallel, it would be: '*speaking to others about the marital bed*'.

(4) Concord

Concord refers to a grammatical relationship in which the form of one element requires the corresponding form of another, for example, agreement between subject and verb: **she** eats, the **boy has** . . . and so on. Many instances of such agreement errors were found:

> *Was there* [sic] **attacks** *exaggerated?* [H2.9/3]

> **Women** *were not capable of sale, purchase, contract or transaction without the authority of* **her** *superior.* [H1.3/2]

> Women *also had half the honour price of* **her** *male superior . . .* [H1.4/1]

> . . . *e.g. Greece and Rome where women had not as* **much** *rights . . .* [H1.4/1]

> There **was**, *however, good* **aspects** *to their presence . . .* [H2.1/5]

(5) Tense

Writers display widespread problems with tenses. Most notable is the lack of consistency with time references.

> *If a woman **marries** a stranger her freedom **was curtailed** she **has** only a land interest while she **is** alive* (Present Simple, Past Simple, Present Simple X 2) [H1.1/2]

> *The husband **cannot buy** or **sell** without first consulting his wife, she **is** completely free to eradicate any deals her husband **has made** without her knowledge. The wife **is** constantly aware . . . They **must consult** each other at all times. On the other hand, females **were** also **allowed** to retain their common property . . . If the husband **takes** her land and **sells** it, she **can** immediately **divorce** him for compensation . . . These profits **were divided** . . . The wife always **received** some amount as she **provided** some of the labour.* (Present Simple X 2, Present Perfect, Present Simple X 2, Past Simple, Present Simple X 3, Past Simple X 3) [H1.2./1]

> *But out of the decline of metal work **appeared** . . . stone work, . . . there **is** a revival of metal work in the 11th and 12th centuries which **has** a strong Viking influence . . .* (Past Simple, Present Simple X2) [H2.9/2]

Lexis

Lexis refers to the vocabulary of a language as opposed to its grammar. In this paper, the area of lexis is dealt with as a separate item even though the errors overlap with other categories.

(1) Register

Register can be generally defined as the relationship between language features and their context (McCarthy 1998, p. 26). Aspects of register include levels of formality and differences between written and spoken language (see Halliday, 1978; Biber, 1988; Biber, 1995). Biber (1995, p. 7) defines register in the general sense of situationally defined varieties. In the current analysis, we are examining the genre of academic writing where the level of language is formal and where certain lexical items and syntactic structures are more frequently used (for further details see Carter and McCarthy 1997, p.115; Biber et al., 1998, p.135). The formality demanded in the context of academic writing limits writers in terms of the words and expressions they can use. Experienced writers have absorbed these limits. In the corpus of essays analysed in this study, there is substantial evidence that some students are not aware of the contextual parameters of register within this genre. One obvious area of weakness is lexical choice. In the examples below, we see lexis chosen from outside the formal register of academic writing:

*If a man **'blabbed'** about his marraige* [sic] *bed, he could be divorced by his wife.* [H1.21/3]

*The Vikings were **tremendous** at adapting to their environment. . .* [H2.2/3]

*. . . from the coasts and islands of the Baltic, came forth groups of honest traders and **swarms** of daring robbers . . .* [H2.2/1]

*Both partners commonly provided goods and were in the marriage **50/50*** [H1.2/1]

. . . the importance of the Vikings can be parrelled [sic] *with Ireland's joining the E.E.C. in 1973. Joining the E.E.C. in 1973 **propelled us onto the playing pitch of Europe** and instantly allowed us **'catch up' with the rest of Europe.*** [H2.9/2]

*The Vikings it seems assimilated quite easily into Irish society through intermarriage, fosterage, trade etc . . . they were at first, **difficult to digest.*** [H2.11]

(2) Contracted Forms

Contracted forms, such as *can't, won't, it's,* are commonplace in spoken language and in many written registers, but they are not the norm in academic writing. As discussed above, third level academic essay writers are often without such tacit knowledge of the register, for example:

> *I don't think their impact was as huge as . . .*[H2.5/1]

> *As the years progress it's paid to the woman . . . Women didn't separate . . .*[H1.15/1]

> *. . . if they raided and took everything, then there wouldn't be much left for the other raiders.* [H2.13/1]

(3) Idioms

Here the term *idiom* refers to what McCarthy (1998, p. 130) describes as a string of more than one word where all elements are fixed in the phrase, for example, the expression *rough and ready.* Idioms are generally associated with informal situations where they provide colloquial alternatives to their semantic equivalents (see McCarthy, 1998). Below we can find some interesting examples of idiomatic expressions not normally used in this register; again, there is evidence of undergraduates' lack of the norms of the genre:

> *The partnership was further protected by the fact that they had to make contracts or business deals together, no party was allowed to be left in the dark.* [H1.2/1]

> *. . . they would not stand for it and they would fight tooth and nail for their rights . . .* [H1.3/2]

> *. . . So basically wherever a woman turned there was a male there to crack the whip* [H1.9/1]

(4) Ellipsis

Ellipsis is a well-established feature of spoken English. Speakers choose to omit certain language. Pronoun subjects, for instance, are very often excluded where there is no danger of ambiguity. Carter and McCarthy (1997, p. 16) give the following example:

A: What's the matter?
B: Got an awful cold. (ellipsis: *I've*)
A: Just seen Paco. (ellipsis: *I've*)
B: Did he say anything?
A: Nothing.
B: Interesting isn't it? (ellipsis: *It's*)

This phenomenon occurs across many speech genres and, in almost all cases, it is indicative of informality (Carter and McCarthy 1997, p. 17). Obviously, pronoun elipsis is not a feature commonly found in the formal register of academic writing. Among the data, this example arose:

*What is unequal is that promiscuous women were offered no protection by law and if **became** pregnant, **had** to solely rear the children* . . . (two examples of subject ellipsis) [H1.2/2]

Style

A sentence may be grammatically valid, yet for reasons beyond syntax, it may not read well. Pirie (1985, p.95) asserts that inefficient writing simply fails to communicate. Unless one's style is clear, no other virtues or skills which one may possess can be recognised. Under the heading of 'style', this paper attempts to identify areas where weaknesses commonly occur.

(1) Redundancy

Redundancy may be defined as the degree to which a message contains more information than is needed for it to be understood (Richards et al., 1992, p. 310).

> *They soon found out that many of the monasteries were rich in* *works of art,* ***such as crosiers, shrines, books and bells, which were*** ***ornamented with much gold, silver and precious stones*** [H2.1/1]

Tautology, or the use of words which mean the same thing, also adds to redundancy:

> *The above statement is both* ***true and accurate.*** [H1.2/1]

> *It would be difficult to doubt the Vikings initial impact was* ***sudden,*** ***unexpected*** . . . [H2.2/1]

(2) Repetition

Repetition of words and ideas is a very common symptom of poor style. Examples are found where students use the same word without any attempt to vary their expression, even in cases such as the first example below where repetition could cause ambiguity:

> ***Evidence*** *exists which shows that females were banned from giving* ***evidence*** *and their oaths were useless.* [H1.2/3]

> *Although women could never have full ownership of* ***land*** *they* *could inherit a life interest in* ***land*** *if her father had no sons. They* *were not free to pass it on like men but they did have the control of* *the* ***land*** *during their lifetime. The only way in which she could* *pass the* ***land*** *on to her husband or sons was if she was related to* *them.* [H1.17/1]

'Nervous writers', according to Pirie (1995, p. 107) 'prefer to dress each concept in at least two words as if one on its own might fail to prevent indecent exposure.' He refers to this as 'the belt and braces strategy', that is, making the same point more than once, lest one idea should fail to function.

Within the space of twelve lines in the same essay on the Vikings, we find the following example of repetition:

> *... They soon found out that many of the monasteries were rich in works of art, such as crosiers, shrines, books and bells ...*

> *... they plundered churches, monasteries and libraries, both on the islands and on the mainland ...*

> *... The monasteries in Ireland were favourite targets for the Viking raiders, for they were rich in treasure and the monks put up little resistance [H2.1/1]*

(3) Lack of Clarity

Clarity is usually achieved by expressing a point in the most straightforward way. The process of making sentences clearer for the reader forces the writer to refine his/her ideas. The following examples clearly show that the writer in each case did not go through a process of redrafting or editing:

Referring to the Vikings:

> *Only those who were raided had to bear the brunt of the raids.* [H2.7/1]

> *Inthe* [sic] *the Irish literary movement seems to have remained aloof from the Vikings, and* [sic] *little intercourse on literary as distinct from the popular level seems to have taken place between the two peoples.* [H2.11/2]

> *Still more positive is the renaissance of Irish art in the 11th and 12th centuries. With Irish art work taking on more characteristics such as spiral lobes. The Vikings paid* [sic] *both a negative and positive effect on Irish art work.* [H2.12/2]

On women in early Irish society:

> *... Considering the time period we are discussing I feel women emerged well out of it, today in many developing and underdeveloped countries women are shackled and bound to laws*

which treat them as sub-human and we are citizens of the twentieth century. [H1.10/1]

(4) Long Sentences

In the process of writing, an experienced writer will usually refine and clarify long sentences either by breaking them up or by deleting unnecessary phrases. As we can see from the examples below, long sentences which have not been redrafted are a stylistic vice:

Referring to women in early Irish society:

> *If her husband became a vagrant or propertyless so he couldn't support her she could divorce him if he mocked her in public or told malicious rumours about her she could get a divorce if a divorcee* [sic] *was sought and the fault lay with the husband the coíbche or bride price remained with the bride but if the divorce was the brides fault* [sic] *the coíbche was returned.* [H1.16/3]

> *In Early Irish Society anybody of any importance was given an honour price, this price represented their status in society a king or Rí had the highest honour price and from the first wife had half the honour price of the husband, this was called a Díre husbands also bought their bride from her father and this bride price or coíbche was calculated to the wife's Díre.* [H1.16/2]

On the Vikings:

> *Around AD850 there are records of the arrival of the Danes, from England, and their confrontations with the Norse, many argue that these Danes were in fact hired and Norsemen also began.* [H2.2/3]

Parenthesis can be used in writing to add an explanatory or qualifying phrase within a sentence. However, many students use parenthesis as a substitute for thinking things through. What results is usually a 'premature' idea:

If rape resulted in a child, the rapist was responsible for rearing the child as children were prized in Early Ireland (the whole purpose of marriage was to produce children) this maybe explains the absence of illegitimacy. Punishment for rape was to do with payment. [H1.1/5]

(5) Spoken Voice

The use of a 'spoken voice' is connected with the area of register; it is also indicative of poor language awareness. From the examples, it is clear that some writers communicate in an informal register. They write as if they are speaking about the topic. Most obvious is the use of the first person:

*This may be viewed as degrading **but as I heard it argued** before women gained their status from this...* [H1.14/2]

*Early Irish women **I feel** were treated fairly* [H1.10/1]

I have come to the conclusion *that the Vikings did have an influence on Ireland* [H2.5/6]

Below are samples of language which are obviously written with a listener rather than a reader in mind. They contain typical spoken discourse markers, such as *well* and *of course*:

Why monasteries? Well, they were. . . [H2.13/1]

Of course, if this was a male heir there would be no suggestion of such a thing. [H1.19/1]

Exclamation marks appear frequently in the corpus. Writers use them to add a prosodic dimension to the message. Their use further suggests that the writers have not conceptualised the formality of this genre:

When a man wants to marry a woman it is necessary that he gives a 'coibche' or bride price to her kin. **Simply hand the money over and receive the goods!** [H1.6/1]

. . . Despite the certain amount of fairness that existed in early Ireland being a woman in that period certainly does not appeal to me. **Thank God for the twentieth century!!** *. . .* [H1.6/2]

. . . it is amazing how even in the sixth and seventh century they managed to figure that one out . . . **'womens lib' must have been campaigning even then . . . !** [H1.8/1]

A woman could leave a man if he was impotent; 'because an impotent man was not easy for a wife'. Other circumstances were obesity, the reasoning being that excessive obesity prevented sexual intercourse thus preventing fertilisation . . . **Wouldn't that keep the 'couch potatoes' of today fit!** [H1.8/1]

This type of marriage was more of a business arrangement than a love relationship! [H1.8/1]

Below are examples where writers respond to the title as if in a speaker-hearer relationship:

Equality? A non chauvanistic[sic] male dominated society? [H1.6/1]

I would have to agree that women . . . [H1.18/1]

Structure

Some of the essays in the corpus are more deficient in structure than in the areas of syntax, lexis and style as discussed above. Most commonly, these essays fail to address the core question posed by the task. Their authors wander through the essay without a thesis statement and lapse into description rather than discussion and analysis. These essays may have been well written and adequately researched, but the writers display little or no ability to analyse. Such essays, no matter how few syntactic or stylistic weaknesses they contain, will never rise to honours standards.

Unfortunately, this type of weakness can often come from diligent students who get little reward for their efforts. We need to question why this is the case. This is perhaps not a question of writing but more to do with thought processes – if our students are not equipped with the ability to dispute, argue and critically analyse, then it is not surprising that many of them will not rise to the challenge of a discursive essay.

At this point, it is worth returning to the study conducted by Kavanagh (1995) in a selection of Dublin primary schools; he found that children were not exposed to a wide range of writing. The results for argumentative and persuasive writing are particularly notable:

TABLE 1

PERCENTAGES OF TEACHERS PROVIDING INSTRUCTION IN VARIOUS WRITING GENRES

Genre	Percentage of Teachers
Narrative/story writing	95%
Descriptive writing	71%
Expository writing	23%
Drama	9%
Argumentative writing	7%
Persuasive writing	3%
Poetry	0%

Kavanagh (1995, p. 82)

A recurring point throughout this paper has been writers' lack of genre-based awareness; they do not know what is expected of a discursive essay, either stylistically or structurally. They not only lack the norms of the genres of argumentative and persuasive writing but also of the 'cultural' aspects of the genre, such as register.

To further substantiate this inadequacy, it may be pointed out that many essays show a pattern of 'chunking' or bulleting of ideas. Fragmented ideas are substituted for paragraphs. The lines below are presented by one student as a paragraph:

> *It was within this second settlement that the great town of trade was properly established in Dublin. The coins produced were exact copies of an English coin and were therefore primarily in use for trade.* [H2.2/4]

It could be speculated that excessive fragmentation found in essays is a by-product of an exam-driven secondary school system where, in certain subjects, memory of facts takes precedence over the ability to synthesise and critically analyse. This tendency also results from viewing writing as a product. Perhaps if students were to undertake collaborative writing projects, interaction with their peers might force them into the process of planning, drafting, revising, reflecting and editing.

Conclusion

Overall, one of the most salient reasons for poor writing appears to be writers' lack of genre awareness. Quite often, they do not know what is expected. At its most general, 'genre awareness' ranges from cognisance of appropriate essay structure to sensitivity to relevant style and register. Inadequate awareness inhibits the writer's ability to reflect, develop and ultimately learn from the process of essay-writing at third level. Some of the deficiencies such as register, subside as students progress through their college programme. Many gain tacit knowledge of the genre through reading academic texts or from their peers. Unfortunately, in every academic cohort, there are students who do not acquire the norms of academic writing and it is reasonable to presume that their motivation and quality of learning are adversely affected as a result.

Being a college graduate is equated with having a high level of literacy; however, universities do not see themselves as responsible for remediating inadequacies in undergraduate written expression. It became obvious within the Liberal Arts degree programme at Mary Immaculate College, however, that essay writing could no longer be left to chance. As well as subject-specific tutorials, a mandatory course is now in place as part of first-year Foundation Studies. This course aims to provide some support for students in their transition to the more formal genre of academic writing. The programme is supported by a learner support service which was established with the purpose of empowering students through developing awareness of their learning process through learner training. Clearly there is enormous scope for further research in this area of writing – such research could illuminate the range of difficulties encountered by undergraduates who have to grapple with a foreign 'academic culture' when they enter third-level education.

REFERENCES

Barrass, R. (1995). *Students must write: A guide to better writing in coursework and examinations (*2nd ed.). London: Routledge.

Biber, D. (1988). *Variation across speech and writing.* Cambridge: Cambridge University Press.

Biber, D. (1995). *Dimensions of register variation.* Cambridge: Cambridge University Press.

Biber, D., Conrad, S., & Rippen, R. (1998). *Corpus linguistics: Investigating language structure and use.* Cambridge: Cambridge University Press.

Carter, R. and McCarthy, M. (1997). *Exploring spoken English.* Cambridge: Cambridge University Press.

Kavanagh, J. (1995). A survey of writing instruction in Dublin primary schools. In G. Shiel, U. Ní Dhálaigh and B. O'Reilly (Eds.). *Reading development to age 15: Overcoming difficulties* (p. 73-85). Dublin: Reading Association of Ireland.

Halliday, M.A.K. (1978). *Language as social semiotic.* London: Edward Arnold.

McCarthy, M. (1998). *Spoken language and applied linguistics.* Cambridge: Cambridge University Press.

Mohr, R. (1998). *How to write: tools for the craft.* Dublin: University College Dublin Press.

Moran, A.P. (1997). *Managing your learning at university.* Dublin: University College Dublin Press.

Pirie, D.B. (1985). *How to write critical essays.* London: Methuen.

Richards, J.C., Platt, J. & Platt, H. (1992). *Dictionary of language teaching and applied linguistics* (2nd ed.). London: Longman.

Schiffrin, D. (1987). *Discourse maters.* Cambridge: Cambridge University Press.

Developing Self-Esteem through Writing Activities: A Unit of Work for Pupils with Learning Difficulties at Senior Primary Level[*]

. . . .

Finian O'Shea
Church of Ireland College of Education
Rathmines, Dublin

This paper is based on an assignment I undertook as part of an MA programme I completed some time ago. The assignment involved a critical appraisal of some aspect of *Curaclam na Bunscoile* (Department of Education, 1971). Part of the appraisal was to include recommendations on how the curriculum might be adapted to cater for the needs of pupils with learning difficulties.

Recently I chose to examine the English Curriculum (*Curaclam na Bunscoile,* Department of Education, 1971) with special reference to the teaching of writing. My analysis of the existing programme showed an approach to writing which was quite revolutionary in its day though rather heavily weighted in terms of the personal experience of the child, and of 'creative writing.' This is not a criticism of the 1971 curriculum but rather an observation of the thinking that prevailed at the time..

[*]Paper presented at the 23rd Annual Conference of the Reading Association of Ireland, Limerick, September 17-19, 1998

I set out to design a unit on the teaching of writing which could help children have a successful experience of writing and thus develop their self-esteem through successful learning. Developing each child's self-concept as a writer was at the core of this programme. I wanted to shape the unit in such a way that it could be used with any pupil in the senior classes, and with younger pupils when relevant adjustments had been made for age and writing experience.

The unit was written from the perspective of a practising classroom teacher who saw that children with literacy difficulties were reticent about engaging in any activity where these difficulties could be manifested.

Writing was accomplished using the Process Approach where children were encouraged to write for a known audience and work through several drafts of a text until they were ready to display/ show/share their writing. I acted as a model for writing and we engaged in collaborative writing on a daily basis. Children were also encouraged (and directed) towards experimenting with various forms of writing – fiction, non-fiction, poetry, letters, etc. This involved exposure to a wide variety of texts – children were encouraged to read (and listen to) various texts as part of their reading programme. It has been difficult to put this unit together as 'writing' because it is difficult to separate writing from oral language, reading and literacy in general.

I have divided the unit into seven themes (see Figure 1). Each theme is titled so as to include the kind of learning outcomes to be experienced by the children. The themes are not discrete, nor do they represent a hierarchical progression. Rather they are themes which a teacher could use to augment work in other areas of the curriculum, where the development of self-esteem is an integral part of the objectives to be reached. The work is designed so that the pupils can be involved in meaningful activities, where they stand a good chance of success and can validate their status as successful learners.

FIGURE 1

OUTLINE OF WRITING PROGRAMME

Thematic Unit

Theme 1. Writing Which Says 'I am'

Theme 2. Personal History

Theme 3. My Life Experience

Theme 4. I Can Create Fiction

Theme 5. I Can Create Non-Fiction

Theme 6. Poetry Writing

Theme 7. Interactive Writing

The Thematic Units

Writing Which Says 'I am. '

The purpose of this section is to allow the pupils to use themselves and their experiences as the stimulus to write . . . i.e., to write about themselves. Such activities include:

a) *Silhouettes* – the construction of a simple silhouette of themselves in profile mounted on coloured paper.

b) *Family photographs* – using a family photograph as the stimulus to write about the pupil's personal life. When a photograph was not available I gave pupils my camera and asked them to photograph one another. Disposable cameras are very useful here. Several drafts of the 'biography' are gone through and pupils are told that a display will be mounted using their photographs and pieces of writing.

c) *Hand/foot prints* – this idea I 'borrowed' from the RE programme where the pupil is asked to write about all the things they can do with their hands etc. I have broadened it out to include other possibilities (see Figure 2).

FIGURE 2

IDEA CHART

Things I Can Do With My Hands	Things I Can Do With My Feet
Things I Can Think About	Things I Can Say

Personal History

Two activities are described here: Writing about one's own memories and writing about the memories of other people:

a) *One's Own Memories – 'I remember when . . .'* This activity involves encouraging the pupils to use their own past experiences as the impetus to write. I used this idea with pupils to help build up a sense of who they were – they all brought in their oldest toys and used these as an impetus to write about childhood memories – who had given them the gift, etc. When the pupils read their pieces to one another, they frequently thought of things that they might want to write about.

b) *Other Peoples Memories* – This also involves the idea of memory as an impetus to write, except that the pupils are encouraged to look at the memories of older people in their lives – parents, grandparents, teachers etc. Pupils are encouraged to think about what they want to know (e.g., to compare their own memories with those of their parents) and to prepare questionnaires accordingly – survey questions etc. Tape recorders, camcorders etc. can be used to compile the information and it can be presented in a variety of media, including writing.

My Life Experiences

a) *Things which happened to me. . . diary/log* – This activity differs a little from 'personal history' in that it looks at the 'now' as well as at the past. I have used this idea to get the pupils to make up their own 'time lines' – selecting an event from their lives for each year – resulting in the development of a time line. The most useful 'event' was to focus on the teachers they had over the years, and recall an event particular to each year.

FIGURE 3

CHART FOR RECORDING PAST EVENTS

1995: My teacher was	1996: My teacher was	1997: My teacher was	1998: My teacher was
I remember ...	I remember ...	I remember ...	I remember ...

This idea can be expanded to include such activities as making a personal photograph album (using photographs or drawing pictures), making their own family tree, or a book about a local football club, Girl Guides, a Judo club etc.

b) *Things I would have liked to happen* – This is a 'what-if?' idea where the pupil is offered the chance to alter outcomes, re-arrange events and explore possibilities. The old essay ideas of 'If I Won The Lottery' or 'If I Could Change One Thing in the World' were the starting point for this and were fuelled by the notion of setting new endings for stories, or retelling stories with altered events and characters, often in the context of an oral language activity. It broadened out to looking at how we might alter the plot-lines of various TV shows and films and narrowing down the focus to how this change would have consequences for other characters/events – all within the parameters of the story-line.

I Can Create Fiction

a) *The stories I absorb, make my own and retell.* This is one of the least used methods of encouraging writing – allowing pupils to retell stories they already know. It allows them to concentrate on the form and shape of the story and to be able to spend time on the 'surface features' – spelling, punctuation etc. It also allows the pupil to tell a story without having to worry about 'having it right'. Later the pupil can be encouraged to tell the story from various characters' points-of-view, retelling folk/fairy tales in modern settings, composing modern-day fables etc.

b) *Stories I tell.* This would involve pupils giving voice, form and shape to their imagined narratives. Such stories could be presented as books, compilations, essays etc. and would be followed through several drafts before being 'published' – should that be the intent in the writing. The pupils could work collaboratively on the production of a single story to begin with, before branching out on their own, should such support be required. T.V. shows, film, etc., could be used as a stimulus as could stories that the children are exposed to in their reading.

I Can Create Non-Fiction
Many pupils experience difficulties and need additional help in making the move to non-fictional writing. The activities described here are designed to support that move:

a) *I will show you.* This can take the form of scrap-books made around hobbies and interests of the pupils. The amount of text to accompany pictures and illustrations will vary from child to child. This idea can be expanded to having the pupils compile books relating to their shared hobbies, or a book detailing their lives both in and outside school. Some discussion will have to be introduced to look at how this kind of writing (genre) differs from the narrative form they would be more familiar with.

Another possibility is to have the pupils write about what they have learnt – keeping track of what they have learnt by maintaining a learning log. A class diary or a record of the weather can be kept by each child in turn.

Individual diaries can be kept, but I would suggest that the activity be a definitely timed one – a week, fortnight, or a month. Pupils find it difficult to maintain the impetus for diary writing on an on-going basis. Fictional diaries are often interesting to explore with pupils, but this is a fairly complex and sophisticated form of writing.

'Learning-logs' or 'I-Can-Do Books' are very useful ways of getting pupils to document what they have learnt/accomplished. It allows them to display their knowledge and take a more independent role in what they are doing, Further, it allows the pupils to examine their understanding of what they are learning and clarify aspects which may be difficult.

b) *Things I need to know.* This would be very much in sympathy with the project idea which is advocated in the 1971 Curriculum. It involves the pupils selecting a topic and locating information relating to it. This material is then presented with the explicit intention of informing the reader. Projects are presented and pupils are questioned by their peers.

Writing Poetry

Pupil self-esteem can also be fostered by engaging them in writing poetry. Here I would include rhymes, jingles, rap, as well as verse. I use a lot of set pattern poetry – haiku being the most used one (see Figure 4). But I also allow the pupils to collect and illustrate compilations of their own favourite poems. They use this as a source for read-alouds from time to time. But the main emphasis in allowing the pupils to experiment with language and with poetic forms is to express their feelings as well as celebrate the use of words by others.

FIGURE 4

FORMAT OF 'HAIKU'

Character's Name,
Verb, verb, (-ing ending)
Adverb, adverb, adverb,
Adjective, adjective,
Character's name

Interactive Writing

Interactive writing takes many forms – essentially the pupils write to someone – each other, the pupils in another school, or to me as their teacher. 'Pen-palling' is a very worthwhile activity which encourages pupils to engage in writing.

I usually undertook this on a class-to-class basis in co-operation with the other teacher. This was so as to ensure that each pupil had someone to write to and was assured of a reply. I also engaged the pupils in writing to me. A full account of this writing project is detailed in 'Dear Mr O'Shea, What is a Reply Anyway?' (O'Shea, 1995). The correspondence was maintained by use of notebooks. The pupils wrote to me and I replied – we never discussed the content other than through writing. It was a time-consuming exercise but one which was really worth while. In both cases the pupils were communicating through writing and interacting with another person. An interesting starting point can be to encourage the pupils to carry on a conversation with each other using writing.

Conclusion

The project stretched over two terms and yielded a wealth of interesting written work by the children. This written account of the project does not provide a forum for sharing the wonderful texts and illustrations created by the children. These written texts became the most sought-after reading material in the class library. A wonderful literacy-cycle was engaged in – reading-writing-reading-revising-reading-writing. This process allowed the children to engage in meaningful literacy by creating texts for a real audience. As the children grew more confident as writers and as readers, their sense of themselves as successful learners gradually improved.

REFERENCES

Department of Education. (An Roinn Oideachas). (1971). *Curaclam na Bunscoile – Lámhleabhar an Oide – Cuid a hAon.* Dublin: Foilseacháin an Rialtais.

O'Shea, F. (1995). 'Dear Mr O'Shea, What is a reply anyway?' In G. Shiel, U. Ní Dhálaigh and B. O'Reilly (Eds.). *Reading development to age 15: Overcoming difficulties* (pp. 86-99). Dublin: Reading Association of Ireland.

Write Out of This World – The Process and the Product[*]

Mary Meaney
Irish Department of Education and Science

Write out of this World is a collection of fifty samples of creative writing by the pupils in a combined Second and Third class in an all-boys school in a provincial Irish town. Every pupil's work is included in the book. The selected samples were chosen by the children themselves. Publication was not an outset aim; rather it was a by-product of an ongoing process intended to facilitate independent writing among the young pupils. The activities described were not undertaken as a research project; instead they reflect regular classroom activities engaged in from September to December 1997. The book was launched on February 13, 1998. This paper presents a brief description of the participants, outlines the process approach used, and considers the children's writings in terms of genre, language, literary conventions, content and commonalities across texts. The final section addresses some links between the project and the literature on the teaching of writing.

The Participants

The participants were 23 boys in a combined class – 13 in Second and 10 in Third. Chronological ages, as of January 1998,

[*]Paper presented at the 23rd Annual Conference of the Reading Association of Ireland, Limerick, September 17-19, 1998.

ranged from 7 to 9 years. Standardised test results indicated a wide spread of ability in the class, including some very good readers and some fair readers. Leisure reading was encouraged in the school and in many of the homes. The class library included an extensive and graded selection of high-quality books. All the boys owned *some* books personally while 13 had impressive home libraries. A significant amount of oral work in class centred on discussing texts and recommending favourites to peers.

The pupils came from backgrounds that were supportive of education and positive home-school links were fostered. All children had one parent in employment and more than half came from double-income homes. During the publishing process, parents undertook diverse roles and responsibilities including collating and binding the book, writing press releases, co-ordinating the launch, organising shop-window displays and acting as treasurers. A shared sense of purpose characterised the endeavour, with all associated parties showing great interest in and appreciation of each other's work.

The Process of Writing

The topics for the children's writing were selected by the teacher, following suggestions from the class. Each theme was developed over the course of a week according to a threefold approach of planning, drafting and reviewing work. The reciprocity of author and audience was emphasised as pupils were reminded that their work was that which they wished to communicate and that which others wanted to hear and/or to read. The planning activities concentrated on: (i) the content; and (ii) its expression through language and via a particular genre. Reference was also made to the importance of sequencing and the accurate use of writing conventions. These skills were taught at other functional writing sessions.

When the topic of writing was announced, the pupils were assigned three home tasks: (i) to reflect on their own content; (ii) to record 5 examples of appropriate vocabulary; and (iii) to consider possible titles. On the following day, during an oral language class, the pupils shared their selected words and phrases and the teacher complemented these with further options and with relevant readings. The homework assignment was repeated and on the third day the boys worked in 5 mixed-ability groups pooling individual wordlists to compile a group inventory. Each group chose a representative to report to the class and finally the five compilations were combined to form a class Word Bank.

Content ideas were also discussed in general terms. Specific content was often carefully guarded! Titles were presented but they remained the 'copyright' of the author.

The write-up was scheduled for day four and took place between the morning and lunchtime breaks. The children were free to write for approximately one hour. Each pupil had an individual copy of the word bank, and access to a dictionary and a variety of additional resources. The boys often initiated conversations about their writing with the teacher, who responded using a set of rhetorical prompts.

The follow-up, reading texts aloud, was one of the favourite periods of the entire week. Peers listened enthusiastically and were held spellbound by each other's work. They were invited to comment and the responses were positive and complimentary. Editorial suggestions, from the teacher or from classmates, were generally accepted and incorporated into re-drafts. At this stage the pupils and/or the teacher restated the importance of a coherent text and of presentation to help the audience enjoy and interpret the work. Pupils re-drafted the scripts the following day and the final versions were read aloud. These were then corrected by me and word-processed. Printed texts were displayed on the bulletin boards and copies were filed in folders which were available in class. As the scripts filled folder after folder, it was decided to investigate the possibility of publishing a selection. Pupils, parents and school authorities were unanimous in their support and the publishing process began.

The Educational Approach in the Classroom

The classroom was characterised by a highly interactive teaching and learning dynamic. Much of the work, across the range of subjects, was grounded in a constructivist approach and influenced by the theories of Bruner and Vygotsky, particularly their ideas on 'scaffolding' and providing learning experiences that are within a pupil's 'zone of proximal development.' Both theorists stress the dialogic nature of the teaching and learning process, and each discusses the guidance/direction provided for the child by a more informed other. Vygotsky (1978) described the 'zone of proximal development' as being 'the distance between the actual developmental level as determined by independent problem-solving and the level of potential development as determined through problem-solving under adult guidance or in collaboration with more capable peers' (p. 86). Bruner considers scaffolding as the means whereby a teacher assists a pupil to achieve that which without help s/he would be unable to achieve. He also explores the process of transfer where the children come to take control of their leaning for themselves. A further dimension is his emphasis on the social nature of learning:

'I have come increasingly to recognise that most learning in most settings is a communal activity, a sharing of culture. It is not just that the child must make his knowledge [sic] his own, but that he must make it his own in a community of those who share his sense of belonging to a culture. It is this that leads me to emphasise not only discovery and intervention, but the importance of negotiating and sharing – in a word, of joint culture creating as an object of schooling and as an appropriate step en route to becoming a member of the adult society in which one lives out one's life' (Bruner, 1986, p. 127; quoted in Berne, 1998).

These perspectives contributed to shaping the classroom practices.

The Content of the Written Texts

The writings were based on the following topics: 'Autumn', 'The Sea', 'Halloween', 'Winter', 'Christmas', 'An Imaginary Land Made of Bubbles', and 'People, Familiar or Famous'. The texts were distinctly individual and focused on specific attributes of the topic, imagined, desired or observed. The variety of titles provides an indication of the diversity of response. While an initial reading of the anthology suggests variety and dissimilarity, closer scrutiny reveals remarkably similar trends and concerns among the young authors.

One predominant issue which emerged is the centrality of the self. The writer himself is involved in 47 of the 50 scripts and appears in three broad and sometimes overlapping contexts which characterise the exploration of the self:

(i)   the child as positioned in the world of childhood with its specific rituals and its own cultural symbols

(ii) the child as a member of a social order and relating to significant other, family, peers and school community

(iii) the child and the world – part of the real world, protagonist in an imagined world, and observer of the natural world.

The writers fulfilled many roles from the realistic child as player to the surrealistic child as superhero. The sense of the author as child, as peer, as relative, as pupil, as gregarious altruistic individual, as heroic, as vulnerable and as fearful was explored tellingly and repeatedly.

The motif of power and the need for protection was another recurrent subject. Evil creatures from children's fiction, goblins, elves and Jack Frost among others, sought to attack and destroy aspects of the children's world. The boys were successful in outwitting them and after their frightening experiences they sought and found a welcome refuge in their homes. The dilemma of good versus evil was resolved with the good overcoming dark forces. The power to help was generously used: Santa Claus, Boyzone and peers were all benefactors of a caring impulse.

Negotiation of the overlap between the child's and the adult's worlds was another significant strand among the writings. These two worlds were treated as different and distinct, though intersecting. The children described many attempts to persuade adults using various modes. Parents caved in to pressure 'after me begging on my knees for an hour and a half.' A gift for the teacher resulted in a night free of homework for the pupil. A parent's frustration with a child who could not wait for Christmas was a source of victory for the boy who delighted in his parent's annoyance: 'Got ya that time, Mam!' While these vignettes portray a degree of conflict between adulthood and childhood, there are as many examples of harmonious co-existence. Help given by either group was recognised by the other. When members of Boyzone were welcomed as guests in a pupil's home, they gave tickets to shows and visited the host's school. The adult and the child's world converged where public figures were concerned; both enjoyed the Boyzone encounter and likewise appreciated the presidential inauguration. The security and comfort of the world created by the grown-ups in a place called home was recognised time after time. Many writings ended as the author went home to relive a pleasant day, find refuge from a frightening experience, or to have a party to crown a particular event.

The children also modelled mores of the adult lifestyle. The rituals and festivals of society were regular backdrops to the various stories. Parties were celebrations for celebration's sake, or sometimes a recognition of the resolution of some difficulty.

The children's world of friendship emerged as a happy comradeship with little conflict. Their friendships were mediated via the experience of play. The playscapes were visits to magic lands, meeting leaders, imaginary trips to far-flung places, building snowmen, kicking leaves in autumn, going on real trips with peers.

The scaffolds of their writing were part of the inherited cultural symbols of society. Archetypal characters such as Jack Frost, witches, ghosts and goblins shared the pages with family and peers. The places included the real and the imagined – under the sea, Bubbleland, Frostland, Santa's home and dinosaur habitats, and, of course, the familiar settings of home, school and neighbourhood.

The children's writings may be read as a metaphor for aspects of their lives. In their work they wrote about a world they chose to create, based largely on ideas with which they are familiar. They subscribed to the ideal of everything working out well and the fairytale plot of living happily ever after.

The Children's Writings – Selected Genres

The narrative genre was by far the most common. All the children chose this, some selectively and others exclusively. High levels of competence in this style were generally evident. Texts were highly organised, well sequenced and the conventions of writing were appropriately used. A small selection had minor gaps and required some inference on the part of the reader. Variety in proficiency, however, related to the degree of sophistication within the genre rather than to an ability (or inability) to employ the conventions of the narrative.

A group of pupils enjoyed writing poems and two nominated samples for inclusion in *Write Out of this World*. One of the boys composed in rhyming verse while the other produced blank verse. A strong sense of rhythm was a feature of their writing.

Descriptions of scenes and seasons, and character sketches formed another category. These texts tended to be highly subjective and the language used conjured vivid images as well as evoking atmosphere and mood. The writers exhibited a degree of reflection and an awareness and appreciation of the qualities they described.

A final group included some diary-style entries, dialogues/ mini-plays and fictional reports based on actual events. The writers working within these formats displayed competence and mastery in several genres. They were all from the Third Class cohort and were authored by children with good reading ability.

The Use of Language and Literary Conventions

The children's use of language was far richer than had been anticipated. The preparation focused on vocabulary extension and development but did not address, per se, the opportunity to experiment with words. Similarly, any use of the literary conventions was implicit rather than explicit. However, the general classroom practices included a concentration on enhancing oral language skills and provided a wide-ranging experience of children's literature. The boys' writings revealed a creativity in patterning words and a facility in using several literary conventions. These aspects were among the most serendipitous outcomes of the entire process.

Words were used as tools to be explored, pushed and pulled from familiar to novel contexts and moulded to the author's needs. The use of well-known phrases as titles and in text was a common feature of many works. 'Hubble, bubble, toil and trouble'; 'Spice up my Life' and 'Get out of There' are examples of the titles selected. Other everyday expressions served as finishing flourishes. 'They all lived happily ever after'; 'Oh no, here we go again' and 'Only time will tell' are typical phrases. There was some experimentation with puns, constructed words and the play of conversation between peers, as in:

'I wonder where the frostiest place is?'
'Frostland' said Rory.
'No' I said.
'Oh yes it is' said Rory. 'It was cool!'
'Get it cool, ha, ha, ha' I said. 'I'll have time to laugh at that next year'.

Homonyms were swopped, particularly 'see' and 'sea' in the writings based on 'Life under water'.

One of most notable aspects was the frequency of direct speech, used in thirty-six of the fifty texts. Reported speech featured in others. Conversations were between peers, family members, or between the child and some of the stereotypes of the world of childhood, for example, in encounters with Santa Claus or with a witch.

Alliteration was used extensively, for example in titles such as 'Bugs and Baddies', 'Fun with Frost' and 'Atlantic Adventure'. Alliteration appears regularly in the texts also. Examples include 'I come from the soft and smooth land,' 'Jack sparkled his spells like diamonds till dawn' and 'All I could see was a glimpse of glossy golden glittering gold'.

The apparent concern with the sound or musical quality of the language was further expressed through the regular use of partial internal rhymes in sentences like the following: 'I went outside to slide on the ice until I slipped through and landed in a place called the Paradise of Ice'. The children whose work included assonance had good reading ability and an impressive command of oral language. Alliteration, on the other hand, was widely used across the range of abilities.

Samples of onomatopoeia emerged in writings on the sea, autumn and winter. The motion of the water resounded in the titles 'Ocean Echo' and 'Underwater World' while the lapping of the waves can be heard in 'Here I am under the water as a zebra fish. I live in a castle made of shells, the balcony's made of floating seaweed . . . .' The crunching sounds of leaves and of ice were also resonant in relevant texts.

Examples of the Children's Writing

In this section, four of the texts authored by children in the Second and Third classes and included in *Write Out of this World* are discussed.

The Leaves of Autumn. The text 'Leaves of Autumn'(see Appendix) was authored by a writer in Second class with average reading ability. It is one of the shortest entries in the book. Nonetheless, it illustrates many of the points made in this paper. It has a coherent and logical structure. Metaphor and personification are used effectively. The work has a strong visual and aural quality. 'Sunburn' is used to serve the writer's needs and 'fire dresses' conveys the intensity of the autumnal colourscape. Sounds are captured by Dr. Wind's whistle. There is a descriptive objectivity about the opening lines which are followed by a reference to hibernating animals and here a gentler quieter atmosphere is conveyed. Finally, there is the author's voice in the closing line: 'Goodnight little animals', which gives a sense of completion and finality to the writing.

King Neptune's Day. This text was composed by a pupil in Second class with an advanced reading age. The writer uses language with enthusiasm, creating a magical/secret world down in the deep. He begins with an action-packed festival where all are happily enjoying a care-free day only to find their world shattered by 'Jaws'. The attack is repelled and the party continues. A reflection on the day's events is included in the narrative – this was atypical. The atmosphere changes to a quieter ambience where textures of underwater habitats are described. Finally, there is almost an appreciation of 'good qualities' – the altruism of the protectors and of the generous is recognised.

The 'types' of the world of childhood are included – kings, monsters, the general population, heroes, places of fear and refuge and the writer himself, as commentator and as the creator of the underwater world.

There is a cadence and a pace in the use of words from the active opening to the contrasting calm of 'in his secret cave there is a carpet made of seaweed'. The end is the resolution of the victory of good over evil and the sense that all works out well. The structure of this piece is less secure than is the use of language. The helterskelter of thoughts rushing into the author's mind appears to have been allowed flow uninterrupted to the page.

A Lucky Boy. This text was written by a pupil in Third class with average reading ability. This work shows a boy positioning himself among significant others in his life. He begins with his daily routine, then his granny's house, her friends, his birthday, remembered conversations and concludes with almost a statement of appreciation about his grandparents. The title anchors the writing and reminds us that it is autobiographical. Otherwise, it can appear a little disjointed at first reading. While many play a part in the story, it is about the writer, 'A Lucky Boy'.

King of the Colours. The writer of this story is a pupil in Third class with good reading ability. This story was selected by the class to be the first entry in the book.

The story has a strong and concise narrative structure. It features many of the 'types' of the child's world: the King, mayor, judge, assistant judge, competitors and audience. Titles abound here – an attribute that was particular to this writer. The self is integral to the plot and he is centre-stage throughout the story.

There is abundant use of personification, metaphor, alliteration and direct speech. The ending is the familiar 'they all lived happily ever after'. . . and then there is a postscript to remind us that this competition will take place again next year. The sense of finality becomes a matter of anticipation.

Links with the Literature

In this section, the processes and products of the project are interpreted with regard to the literature on learning in general, and the teaching and acquisition of writing in particular.

The teaching of writing in Irish schools. There exists a paucity of research on the teaching and learning of written expression in Ireland. However, that which has been undertaken indicates that the scope of the programme is limited and that the progressive mastery of the craft of writing receives insufficient attention. In *English in the Primary School* (Department of Education, 1982), inspectors suggested that the activities they had observed might not contribute substantially to the development of effective written communication. O'Shea (1989) found a concentration on content in some cases and on accuracy in others. Martin and Morgan (1994), Hall (1995) and Kavanagh (1995) report that revising and redrafting work is an infrequently used strategy, that pupils appear to be unaware of their audience and that the sharing of texts among peers is uncommon. The classroom described in this article seems atypical in these respects.

Parental interest and involvement. The assumption that parental interest promotes a child's learning is conveyed in the literature (e.g., Chavkin, 1993; Epstein, 1986; Kellaghan et al., 1993). The parents of the writers involved in the *Write Out of This World* project were highly supportive of the initiative and were instrumental in its completion. An environment in which literacy is valued as evidenced by the availability of books and the experience of seeing adults read has been associated with relatively high levels of literacy attainment (Wells, 1986; Martin & Morgan, 1994). The home and the school experiences of the authors of *Write Out of This World* privileged literacy greatly and are likely to have an ongoing enhancing effect on the authors' written expression.

The paradigm of process writing. The paradigm of a process-based approach has influenced pedagogical practices, particularly since the mid 1980's (see Smith, 1982; Graves, 1983). There have been challenges recently to the notion that a process approach alone enhances writing. Sperling (1996) and Gutierrez (1992) suggest that process-orientated classrooms varied widely and that only teachers following highly interactive and constructivist methods could support written work. The earlier sections of this article illustrate the process approach within a constructivist environment.

The influence of audience and peer interaction. These influences have been widely studied and centre on the premise that a writer's knowledge of his/her audience improves the writing and that peer interaction can support the outcome. Following Vygotksy and Brunner, the research regards readers, audience and peers to be in dynamic communication. These contacts have been likened to scaffolded events and have been compared to the writer's internal deliverative processes while composing. Analysis of the degree of influence of the classroom interactions is beyond the scope of this paper. However, redrafts and revisions were often undertaken following such conversations.

The consequences of being literate. Another recurring theme in the literature considers the outcomes of being able to write and the autonomy this confers on the learner. Donaldson (1978) treats the ability to write in relation to the development of disembedded thought. Flower (1994) and Dyson (1995) present writing as a construct for the exploration of the self and of one's place in the world. Central to this social cognitive view of writing is the relationship between writers, readers and texts. Consideration of texts in *Write Out of This World* supports the connection between learning to write and in Dyson's words 'learning to interpret – and potentially re-interpret – the social world and one's place in it' (1995, pp. 5-6).

The speaking-writing connection. A further dimension of the extant research is based on the oral language-written language interface. At one extreme, the view is that writing is different from speaking while the other perspective encourages the blurring of the writing-speaking boundaries (see Sperling, 1996). The children's widespread use of direct speech indicates some overlap between speaking and writing. Their unexpected facility in the use of several literary conventions suggests that they are aware of the differences between the spoken and written word. Purcell-Gates (1998) concluded that exposure to books makes children conversant with the features of written narrative discourse. This was reflected in classroom experiences.

The use of language and literary techniques. The unexpected use of metaphor, simile, alliteration, onomatopoeia and word associations have been outlined above. Similar findings have been reported by Daiute (1989), Daiute and Dalton (1989), and Dyson (1993).

Conclusion

This paper set out to focus on the writing experience in a particular Second and Third multi-grade class. A limitation of the paper is that a comparative analysis with the work of similar age groups could not be undertaken and the outcomes reported must be considered as 'stand alone' trends which may or may not be replicated in other settings. There is a shortage of material on the teaching and learning of written expression in Ireland. This is in sharp contrast to the availability of data on reading achievement. Much more work is needed.

REFERENCES

Bearne, E. (1998). *Use of language across the primary curriculum.* Routledge: London.

Bruner, J. (1986). *Actual minds, possible worlds.* Cambridge, MA: Harvard University Press.

Chavkin, N.F. (Ed.). (1993). *Families and schools in a pluralistic society.* Albany: State University of New York Press.

Daiute, C., & Dalton, B. (1989). 'Let's brighten it up a bit': Collaboration and cognition in writing. In B. Rafoth & D. Rubin (Eds.), *The social construction of written communication.* Norwood, N.J.: Ablex.

Daiute, C. (1989). Play as thought: Thinking strategies of young writers. *Harvard Educational Review, 59,* 1-23.

Department of Education. Curriculum Development Unit – Primary Branch. (1982). *English in the primary school: Survey report.* Dublin: Author.

Donaldson, M. (1978). *Children's minds.* London: Fontana.

Dyson, A.H. (1993). *Social worlds of children learning to write in an urban primary school.* New York: Teachers College Press.

Dyson, A.H. (1995). Writing children: Reinventing the development of childhood literacy. *Written Communication, 12*(1).

Epstein, J.L. (1986). Parents' reactions to teacher practices of parent involvement. *The Elementary School Journal, 86,* 227-294.

Flower, L. (1994). *The construction of negotiated meaning: A social cognitive theory of writing.* Carbondale, IL: Southern Illinois University Press.

Graves, D. (1983). *Writing: Teachers and children at work.* Portsmouth, NH: Heinemann.

Gutierrez, K.D. (1992). A comparison of instructional contexts in writing process classrooms with Latino children. *Education and Urban Society, 24,* 244-262.

Hall, K. (1995). Discovery learning and writing development. *Oideas, 43,* 5-21.

Kavanagh, J. (1995). A survey of writing instruction in Dublin primary schools. In G. Shiel, U. Ní Dhálaigh and B. O'Reilly (Eds.), *Reading development to age 15: Overcoming difficulties* (pp. 73-85). Dublin: Reading Association of Ireland.

Kellaghan, T., Sloane, K., Alvarez, B., & Bloom, B.S. (1993). *The home environment and school learning: Promoting parental involvement in the education of children.* San Francisco: Jossey-Bass.

Martin, M., & Morgan, M. (1994). Reading literacy in Irish schools: A comparative analysis. *Irish Journal of Education, 28,* 3-101.

O'Shea, M. (1989). *A study of the teaching of compositional writing in eight primary school classrooms in Cork city and county.* Unpublished M. Ed. Thesis, University College Cork.

Purcell-Gates, V. (1998). Lexical and syntactic knowledge of written narrative hold by well-read-to kindergarteners and second graders. *Research in the Teaching of English, 22,* 128-160.

Smith, F. (1982). *Writing and the writer.* Melbourne: Heinemann.

Sperling, M. (1996). Revisiting the writing-speaking connection: Challenges for research on writing and writing instruction. *Review of Educational Research, 66(1),* 53-86.

Wells, G. (1986). *The meaning makers: Children learning language and using language to learn.* Seven Oaks, Kent: Hodder & Stoughton.

Vygotsky, L.S. (1978). *Mind in society.* Cambridge, MA: Harvard University Press.

APPENDIX

Children's Writing Samples

1. *The Leaves of Autumn*

In autumn, the leaves turn to lots of beautiful colours like red, yellow, brown and sunburn. All the oaks and the sycamores have their fire dresses on for the autumn holiday. Dr. Wind is playing his whistle loud and quiet. The pond is a net of colour. All the little animals are going to sleep for autumn but in the spring they will come out again. Goodnight little animals.

2. *King Neptune's Day*

It was King Neptune's Day under the sea. Everybody was having a great time. The starfish were doing cartwheels. The octupuses were doing fancy dancing. The fish were doing summersaults. Everyone was invited except Jaws, the great white shark. Then he came. He bashed in through the window. But the hammerhead shark chased him away. The sea creatures were so happy that they celebrated even more. When King Neptune's day was over the sea creatures went home to bed. The next day when the fish got out of their frogspawn beds they had oysters for breakfast. When breakfast was all over, the fish talked about King Neptune's day and when Jaws burst in. Now Jaws lives in a hidden place under the sea-bed. All the seaweed is growing out of the entrance so you can't see it. Jaws is a mean shark, I can tell you. This is his diet crabs, clams, scubadivers, plankton and scallop tails. It seems like an unhealthy diet but it's true. In his secret cave there is a carpet made of seaweed. His bed is made of frogspawn and his quilt is made of octopus skin. It sounds awful but he let me sleep in it for a night and it felt lovely! It was lunchtime for the crabs and they ate baby octopus. The hammerhead sharks were good. They were the fish heroes because they chased Jaws away. The whale shark was the nicest fish because he gave all the sea creatures lots and lots of sweets and presents.

3. *A Lucky Boy*

Every day when I get up I go and dress. I go to school. After school, I go to my granny's house. It is very small but I still like it because it is so close to where my mother works. It is called the MacBride Home. It is for old people. My granny is old but she does not go to it because she lives very close to it. Sometimes one of my mam's friends comes to her. It is nearly always Lily. The priest comes to her every Sunday.

One day when I went to her on my birthday I got £20 and a pack of sweets. You know, not every boy gets that. I said 'Thank's a million'. My grandad is dead now. My mother said every time they went over the bridge he said 'Would you look at the bridge I built, doesn't it look nice?' Mum said, 'Yes it looks lovely.' My granny is about 83 years old and she has a rough face and hands and is very nice. Now my grandad was very old. He was about 93 years with very rough hands and a rough face. He was very nice.

4. *King of the Colours*
In autumn the trees had a competition to find out who was going to be the king. 'King of the colours', the big oak said to me. He added in a small voice, 'for a whole year too.'

Anyway, I went down on the day to be the judge. Everyone was there. I mean every tree was there! There was old Mr. Oak, Mr. and Mrs. Chestnut, little Miss Maple, and Mayor Sycamore. One thousand trees were there. All I could see was a glimpse of the glossy golden glittering gold! Mayor Sycamore won last year and it was his turn to help me choose the winner. Every tree was waiting for this fun-packed thrilling moment. All of a sudden I announced 'In third place, burst of brown, Miss Maple'. Everyone clapped. 'In second place, glossy Mrs. Chestnut and in first place, Mr. Oak!'

I said, 'Congratulations' to everyone and they all lived happily ever after.

P.S. Until next year.

ACKNOWLEDGEMENTS

Acknowledgement is due to the authors of the four writing samples:
The Leaves of Autumn – Mark Moody, Second Class
King Neptune's Day – Robert Browne, Second Class
A Lucky Boy – Keith Farrell, Third Class
King of the Colours – Shane O'Doherty, Third Class

Writing in the Revised English Language Curriculum for Primary Schools: Are Teachers Ready?*

. . . .

Fidelma Healy-Eames
Mary Immaculate College – University of Limerick

Theory and practice confirm that writing is a complex activity requiring complex teacher interventions. In recent times, the teaching of writing in Irish primary schools has been the subject of considerable scrutiny from both the curricular end, with the launch of a revised *English Language Primary School Curriculum* (Ireland, 1999a, 1999b), and from a research perspective, with the completion of several studies of the teaching of writing in primary schools (e.g., Kavanagh, 1997; Healy-Eames, 1999).

This paper reviews the development of the revised Primary School Curriculum and its relevance for the teaching of writing in primary schools. Firstly, it outlines the background to the recent revision of the curriculum. Secondly, it examines the main findings of a National study, conducted by this author in 1997, which reveals how teachers went about the teaching of writing

---

*An earlier version of this paper was presented at the 23rd Annual Conference of the Reading Association of Ireland, Mary Immaculate College, Limerick, September 17-19, 1998.

prior to implementation of the revised curriculum. Thirdly, it compares the current status of the teaching of writing with what is outlined (and intended) in the revised curriculum.

Revision of the English Language Curriculum

The launch of the revised *English Language Primary School Curriculum* and other curricular areas in September 1999 marked the end of a curriculum revision process that had lasted several years. The curriculum is viewed as 'revised' since it retains many of the core principles of its predecessor – *Curaclam na Bunscoile* (Department of Education, 1971). The series of reports and policy documents that preceded or were published during the curriculum revision process are outlined in Table 1.

The fundamental principle of language as the meaning-maker in learning and literacy development is advocated in the literature (see Tierney & Shanahan, 1991; Short, 1986b; Applebee, 1978; McGinley & Tierney, 1989; Hall, 1998). Two language principles underpin the revised *English Language Primary School Curriculum* – 'language learning' and 'learning through language'. They emphasise the teaching of writing as written language and as a form of communication whereby language is received by pupils in the first instance, and is subsequently used as a tool with which to learn. Examples of how it is planned to achieve this are evident in some of its key content objectives (e.g., by enabling pupils to write for a range of purposes to a variety of audiences, and so to empower pupils to become adept in a variety of written genres). The methodology advocated for the teaching of writing stresses that the approach to teaching writing (a process approach) is as important as the written products generated by pupils. Similar to *Curaclam na Bunscoile* it reiterates the importance of operating out of the real contexts and experiences of the pupil, underscoring, once again, the need for pupils to use writing for real practical purposes and the importance of shifting away from an over-focus on the manipulation of discrete segments of language in workbook exercises (Dept. of Education, 1982; 1990).

TABLE 1

REVISION OF THE ENGLISH LANGUAGE PRIMARY SCHOOL CURRICULUM: IMPORTANT MILESTONES

TITLE OF DOCUMENT/ REPORT	MAIN CONTENT RELEVANT TO THE TEACHING OF WRITING
Curaclam na Bunscoile (1971)	• A radical, new, idealistic document in the climate of the time, it acted as the catalyst for much subsequent change in the area of writing in the primary school (e.g., it placed a new emphasis on creative writing and environmentally-based learning)
English in the Primary School (1982)	• Report prepared in part by the Inspectorate of the Department of Education • Advocated a shift from written exercises in workbooks in favour of more purposeful forms of writing (i.e., the primary skills of writing) • Emphasised need for a greater emphasis on letter-writing and poetry • Useful guidance given in the area of writing correction and feedback
Report of the Review Body of the Primary Curriculum (1990)/ Quinlan Report	• Challenged educators to be more questioning and reflective about their practices and made specific recommendations for the future revision of the English language programme in *Curaclam na Bunscoile* (1971); • Underscored the communicative nature of writing by emphasising the need for active fostering of creativity and imagination, and the discouragement of excessive reliance on workbooks. • Recommendations included: Teaching strategies to be defined sequentially for the infant, middle and senior standards of the primary school; The application of broader criteria for evaluating writing; A national programme of in-service training for teachers
English Language Curriculum Draft Documents (1995-1997)	The formulation of an innovative curriculum framework comprising four major *Strands** within which there are *Strand Units* for Oral Language, Reading and Writing. The four *Strands* are as follows: • Receptiveness to Language • Competence and confidence in using language • Developing cognitive abilities through language • Emotional and imaginative development through language

TABLE 1 (Contd.)

English Language Curriculum (1999)	An emphasis on two language principles, namely '*language learning*' and '*learning through language*'. Teachers are reminded to bear in mind the following key concepts when teaching writing: The centrality of oral language The integration of oral language, reading and writing for language learning and teaching The process of writing is as important as the product. The need to assist pupils to write for different purposes and audiences and in a variety of genres to achieve their goals Flexibility in the way time is allocated to writing; Greater autonomy for children in choosing topics for writing Classroom planning: The advice for teachers is to 'teach to the four curriculum strands' Assessment-wise: A new emphasis on writing portfolios and curriculum profiles in writing.

*The four curriculum strands mentioned in relation to the draft curriculum comprise the organisational framework of the curriculum itself (Ireland, 1999a).

The *Content Statement* and *Teacher Guidelines* in the revised *English Language Primary School Curriculum* (Ireland, 1999a, 1999b) are in line with current international thinking on the teaching of writing (e.g., Czierniewska, 1992; Graves, 1994; Cox, 1991; Wray & Lewis, 1998). While well presented and easily accessible, and the content reflects some of the main recommendations set out in the *Quinlan Report* (1990), nevertheless, the analysis undertaken by this author highlights aspects which will require further clarification in order to be understood and implemented. Specifically, there is a need for tighter definitions for the four English curriculum strands; there is an absence of explicit aims for writing, reading and oral language; there is a need to match broad objectives to appropriate content objectives; and there is a need for specific content guidelines for home-school activities. Otherwise, some of these important aspects may be overlooked by teachers.

Similarly, the changes advocated for writing assessment in the revised *English Language Primary School Curriculum,* which include 'curriculum-based' assessment, are quite removed from current practice and are radical in the Irish context. Hence, there is a need to support teachers in implementing the new assessments. As a teaching support, the *Teacher Guidelines* document is an important and useful addition to the curriculum itself and is strong in the area of instructional advice for teachers. However, in the area of assessment in the classroom, more specific guidelines will need to follow.

Clearly, therefore, while not all of the content of the revised curriculum is new, its presentation is especially new and, in addition to the new emphasis on performance-based assessment, the process of planning instruction with reference to the four curriculum *Strands* is radically new in the Irish context. The implication of the cumulative effect of these changes is that the provision of quality in-service education and professional development support for teachers is a necessity.

A National Study of the Teaching of Writing in Irish Primary Schools

This study examined the instruction, curriculum and assessment of writing at fourth grade level through the use of a large national, stratified, random survey of teachers, which achieved a 77.5% response rate; and a case study in which instructional practices in two fourth classes were investigated in detail. Taken together, it is argued that survey and case study impart a comprehensive and detailed picture of how writing is taught to pupils in fourth grade in Irish primary schools.

The respondents to the survey comprised an experienced group of teachers, whose average teaching experience was almost 19 years, and who taught in more single fourth classes than in multi-class settings. Their grouping procedures for the teaching of English revealed that the use of 'two subgroups or more' is quite prevalent for the teaching of reading, that there is a split between 'whole class teaching' and the use of 'two subgroups or more' for the teaching of writing, and that there is a dominance of 'whole class teaching' for oral language. There is a tendency to find more 'subgroups' for writing in single fourth classes than in multi-class settings. Similarly, 'more experienced' teachers tend to use more 'subgroups' for the teaching of writing than 'less experienced' teachers. It is likely that where teachers already use a variety of grouping procedures, they may adopt a more flexible approach to implementing the process-based strategies for the teaching of writing outlined in the revised *English Language Primary School Curriculum.*

This study revealed findings in seven areas:

- Teachers' aims and practices for writing
- Teaching strategies implemented by teachers: process-based and traditional
- Links between oral language and writing
- Writing as a continuum of teaching stages
- Predominance of a 'traditional' approach to the teaching of writing
- Allocation of time during writing instruction
- Teachers' assessment practices.

Teachers' Aims for Writing Instruction

Teachers' aims for writing were examined in the survey. 85.4% of teachers selected 'developing effective expression and communication of ideas' as their 'most important' aim for the teaching of writing. Other aims selected, in order of importance, reveal a relatively favourable balance of primary and subordinate writing skills, consistent with the recommendations of the report, *English in the Primary School* (Department of Education, 1982). However, findings in relation to actual teaching strategies used in practice suggest that the frequency with which particular writing skills are taught does not match the relative importance attributed to them by teachers. Instead, they revealed a strong 'traditional' focus with the emphasis on the teaching of the secondary skills of writing such as punctuation and spelling. There is little awareness of activities being implemented to achieve such aims as 'helping children write for a variety of audiences'; 'developing writing skills in different areas of the curriculum'; and 'developing pupils' ownership of their texts' which ranked 7, 9, and 10 respectively out of ten possible aims. These low-ranked aims are strongly featured in the broad objectives and writing content objectives of the revised *English Language Primary School Curriculum*. When the 'development of pupils' ownership of their written texts' was investigated in the case study, it was concluded that a 'traditional' approach did not seem as supportive of this important principle as a 'process' approach. A 'process-based' approach, such as that implemented by the process-based teacher in the case study, emphasises pupil-teacher talk at many stages in the writing process and the management of peer talk with in-built class structures (e.g., reading-writing groups) (see Healy-Eames, 1995; 1999). A supportive teacher style and classroom environment, it was found, is more likely to support ownership of pupils' writing. Largely, it seems that Irish teachers are not conscious of implementing this type of flexible teaching approach.

Strategies Implemented by Teachers

A combination of writing theories and language links (e.g., oral language – writing [see Britton, 1970; Bakhtin, 1973; Johnson, 1991; Czerniewska, 1992; Reece & Cumming, 1996; Sharples, 1996] and reading-writing [see Tierney & Shanahan, 1991; Raphael, Kirschner & Englert, 1988; Graves, 1994; Protherough et al, 1989]) can be usefully incorporated into comprehensive 'process' and 'strategy-based' approaches to the teaching of writing. The literature recommends that the type of classroom environment found in 'process' writing classrooms/'Writer's Workshops' facilitates the development of these concepts and principles (see Graham & Harris, 1996). My case study described a 'process-based' teacher putting a workshop-style approach into action. With regard to Irish primary teachers generally, only 9% present as 'strong' users of 'process' strategies (Healy-Eames, 1999). Consequently, the type of writing classroom environment, in which teachers implement process-based strategies appears to be a relatively rare occurrence in Irish primary schools.

Establishing Links between Oral Language and Writing

The development of links connecting the teaching of writing with oral language is recommended in the literature on teaching writing and in the Teacher Guidelines accompanying the revised *English Language Primary School Curriculum* (Ireland, 1999b). It is difficult to determine the real extent to which the oral language-writing link is capitalised on by Irish primary teachers. On the one hand, teachers' priorities for the teaching of English, their aims for writing, and the factors they report as influencing pupils' ideas when writing suggest that they accord a primary importance to oral language. Yet, on the other hand, selection of teaching strategies, use of class time, and choice of writing genres/content areas suggest otherwise. Quite simply, practice is not congruent with reported principles. However, some teachers report favourable satisfaction outcomes when they employ oral language-writing based teaching strategies. Satisfactory achievement outcomes in writing were reported when teachers used such strategies as 'assisting pupils to select their own topics for writing', 'discussing audience for the proposed text', and 'using media as a stimulus to writing'. Table 2 provides a summary of the writing outcomes on which the application of these strategies had a favourable impact, according to teachers.

Writing as a Continuum of Stages

Theories of writing propose an appropriate combination of cognitive (e.g., Flower & Hayes, 1981; Bereiter & Scardamalia, 1987), affective (e.g., Wilkinson, 1986), social (e.g., Hayes, 1996) and creative (e.g., Sharples, 1996) conditions to effect broad, multi-dimensional writer development across a range of writing genres, including narrative. It appears that Irish primary teachers may not be conscious of implementing an explicit writing theory or combination of theories. On the whole, there does not seem to be an awareness of the teaching of writing as a cyclical continuum of stages: preparation/planning, involvement, and feedback/response. This is reflected in the level of emphasis that teachers place on various stages of the writing process in terms of levels of instructional interaction with pupils (see Table 3).

TABLE 2

STATISTICAL LINKS BETWEEN FREQUENCY OF IMPLEMENTATION OF ORAL LANGUAGE-BASED WRITING STRATEGIES AT DIFFERENT STAGES IN THE WRITING PROCESS AND TEACHERS' REPORTED SATISFACTION WITH PUPILS' WRITING

ORAL LANGUAGE-BASED TEACHING STRATEGY	TEACHER-PUPIL ENGAGEMENT		
	BEFORE WRITING	DURING WRITING	AFTER WRITING
1. Pupils' ability to write for a variety of different purposes is related to: assisting pupils to select their own topics for writing	*		
discussing the audience for whom text was written			*
2. Pupils' ability to *revise their own written texts using a range of revision strategies* is related to: assisting pupils to select their own topics for writing	*		
using media as a stimulus to guide writing	*		
drafting texts e.g., poetry, narrative	*	*	*
sharing pupils' writing with other classes in school		*	
3. Pupils' ability to *demonstrate awareness of and sensitivity to audience* is related to: discussing the audience for the proposed text	*		
4. Pupils' ability to *employ ideas from a variety of different sources* is related to: using media as a stimulus to guide writing	*	*	*
reading own written text aloud		*	*
discussing creative writing with teacher		*	*
discussing the audience for whom text was written		*	
5. Pupils' ability to *listen to writing of classmates and offer feedback* is related to: reading own written text aloud		*	*

*Asterisks refer to statistically significant correlations between frequency of strategy implementation and satisfaction with the quality of pupils' writing (see Healy-Eames, 1999).

TABLE 3

STAGES OF WRITING DURING WHICH TEACHERS PROVIDE MOST
ASSISTANCE TO PUPILS

WRITING STAGE	PREPARATION/ PLANNING	INVOLVEMENT IN WRITING TASK	WRITING FEEDBACK/ REVISION
Teaching Emphasis by Irish teachers	Medium	High	Low

Table 3 shows that Irish teachers place most emphasis on the transcription or involvement stage of writing. Some emphasis is placed on the preparation stage (planning), and least emphasis is placed on the feedback stage (response). Since the literature (e.g., Levy & Ransdell, 1996) suggests that the planning and revision stages are the most difficult for many pupils, one would expect teachers to place at least equal emphases on these stages as on actual writing.

Predominance of a Traditional Approach

Four findings emerged in this study which confirmed the existence and predominance of a 'traditional' approach to the teaching of writing.

With regard to teaching approaches for writing, Irish teachers are more product-oriented than process-oriented. A majority favour strategies such as 'assigning topics to pupils before writing'; 'providing directions regarding layout of text'; 'learning spellings'; 'answering reading comprehension questions in writing'; and 'pointing out problems with language usage and sentence structure'. Meanwhile, the survey findings reveal that there was, at best, only an emerging awareness of 'process' approaches to the teaching of writing, since only 9% of Irish teachers were 'strong' users of 'process' approaches on a 'regular' basis, and of these, 'less experienced' teachers tended to use more 'process' strategies than 'more experienced' teachers. Notwithstanding these results, the findings of the case study showed that the 'process' class produced a higher quality of writing than the 'traditional' class. This conclusion was arrived at when 18 raters used a comprehensive writing scale to rate pupils' writing samples across six dimensions (i.e., writing as communication; attitudes to writing; writing content; writing organisation; writing conventions; and a holistic component).

With regard to teachers' satisfaction with their pupils' achievement, Irish primary teachers are more satisfied with writing outcomes when they employ 'traditional' strategies (e.g., 'produce neat legible handwriting' and 'use capital letters appropriately') than 'process' outcomes (e.g., 'listen to writing of classmates, offer feedback'; 'write for a variety of different purposes'; and 'demonstrate awareness of and sensitivity to audience'). This is not an unexpected finding since traditional writing strategies are widely practised and consequently pupils are strongest in areas where most teacher-time is invested.

Allocation of Time during Writing Instruction

Irish teachers spend an average of 15.2% of total weekly class time on 'creative/personal writing'; 'spelling', 'grammar, vocabulary and language usage', and 'functional writing'. Of these teachers, the 'less experienced' group actually spend significantly more time on the 'teaching of writing' overall and on the teaching of 'spelling' than 'more experienced' teachers. Moreover, the majority of Irish primary teachers (85.4%) spend most of this time on functional writing activities (i.e., 'completion type exercises in workbooks'). Additionally, when the cumulative time picture is taken into account, more time is spent on the subordinate/lower-level skills (e.g., handwriting, spelling, punctuation and functional writing skills) than on the primary/higher-level writing skills (e.g., development of writing as communication, narrative writing, creative/personal writing). The allocation of large amounts of time to these activities may indicate skill duplication in isolation, and point to the absence of a clear plan for writing – an issue discussed as far back as 1982 by the Department of Education.

Assessment of Writing in Classrooms

Findings on the state of writing assessment in fourth grade immediately in advance of the implementation of the revised *English Language Primary School Curriculum* showed that teachers were clearly entrenched in 'traditional' approaches to summative assessment (e.g., the *'end of year report card'* and the *'annual parent-teacher meeting'* are implemented 'almost always' by 81.3% and 76.4% of teachers respectively). Only 14.6% of teachers 'almost always/sometimes' used 'process' approaches to summative assessment (e.g., a combination of writing portfolios and use of informal parent-teacher meetings). Curriculum-based writing assessment procedures (e.g., *'writing portfolios'*) were rarely implemented. Formative assessment approaches were more difficult to quantify. In this regard, the analysis identified that more focused attention needs to be given in the course of instruction to 'assisting pupils to write for different purposes'; 'revising written texts'; 'developing a sense of audience'; and 'proofreading/editing texts'.

Synthesis and Recommendations

This study confirms that there is some distance between where Irish teachers are currently at and the recommendations on teaching writing in the revised *English Language Primary School Curriculum* (Ireland, 1999b). It is estimated that fewer than 10% of primary teachers are currently implementing the instructional and assessment approaches advocated in the revised writing curriculum. In addition the teaching and planning framework of the curriculum is new and the methodologies advocated require flexibility and are largely oral-based. Thus, the productive implementation of the revised *English Language Primary School Curriculum* requires a fresh understanding and an openness to new approaches by Irish teachers. The following section outlines four recommendations which would help to bridge the gap between current practice and recommended curriculum guidelines.

Recommendation 1

At this juncture it would seem wise that the Department of Education and Science would assess what is working well in the Irish context and validate these practices for Irish teachers. It is important that the Irish system learns from its own best practice as well as that of other countries. To achieve this, a system of regular built-in review needs to be arranged. Use of current resources (e.g., Inspectorate, regional Education Centres, current research) to achieve this end would be important.

Recommendation 2

It is important that instruction and assessment are seen as integral aspects of the teaching of writing. Teachers would benefit from an understanding of the use of more balanced approaches to writing assessment. Effective writing development emerges when there is a focus on both process and product. Therefore, while maintaining an emphasis on writing processes, it is also important that the quality of pupils' written products be comprehensively evaluated at regular intervals. To achieve this, teachers need to learn how objectives can be linked to instruction and assessment. Assessment tools should be broad enough to measure important aspects of both process and product.

Recommendation 3

Teachers will benefit from being reminded about the importance of operating out of real contexts, and the experiences of the child when teaching writing. Pupils' personal experiences, ideas generated during class discussion and gleaned from t.v./video, were cited by teachers as being the top influences on pupils' writing content and ideas (see Healy-Eames, 1999). Teachers will reap the benefits of implementing interactive, dialogue-based approaches where pupils have opportunities to write on both teacher-assigned topics and topics selected by themselves. Above all, it is vital that there is a concerted effort on the part of teachers to reduce the use of de-contextualised workbook exercises as a tool for teaching writing.

Recommendation 4

The consolidation of old advice and the integration of new practices can only be achieved through an extensive, and focused in-service programme. Such a programme was lacking following the launch of *Curaclam na Bunscoile* in 1971. There is a need to implement a range of suitable in-service education/training initiatives and adequate follow-up professional support for teachers in order to support implementation of the revised *English Language Primary School Curriculum*. This points to the importance of a serious investment in teacher-training programmes so that on the ground in-service provision for teachers is of a very high standard. Certainly, in this regard the current situation will not suffice – this study's findings revealed that attendance at in-service education on writing is inconsistent and dependent entirely on teacher interest. 32.5% of Irish teachers did not attend any writing courses since their initial teacher qualification. There is, however, one interesting finding which may help with curriculum implementation, namely that almost 50% of the sample reported that they 'read articles on the teaching of reading and writing' at least monthly. Articles and web-based texts should be capitalised on in the provision of further support for teachers.

Like pupils, teachers too have different learning styles and a comprehensive programme of teacher support needs to broadly reflect this so as to influence a wide range of teaching styles.

REFERENCES

Applebee, A. N. (1978). *The child's concept of story: Ages two to seventeen*. The University of Chicago Press.

Bakhtin, M.M. (1973). Marxism and the philosophy of language. In Tierney, R.J., & Shanahan, T. (1991). *Handbook of reading research* (Vol. 2, pp. 246-280). New York: Longman.

Bereiter, C., & Scardamalia, M. (1987). *The psychology of written composition*. New Jersey: Lawrence Erlbaum.

Britton, J. (1970). *Language and learning*. Penguin: Middlesex.

Calkins, L. (1986). *The art of teaching writing*. Portsmouth, NH: Heinemann.

Cox, B. (1991). *Cox on Cox*. (pp.140-154). Seven Oaks: Hodder & Stoughton.

Cox, B. (January, 1998). *In conference: The teaching and usage of English.* Dublin: University College Dublin..

Czweniewska, P. (1992). *Learning about writing: The early years.* Oxford: Blackwell.

Department of Education (1971). *Curaclam na bunscoile (Primary school curriculum): Teacher's handbook, Part 1.* Oifig Díolta Foilseacháin an Rialtais.

Department of Education, Curriculum Development Unit (1982). *English in the primary school: Survey report.* Dublin: Author.

Flower, L., and Hayes, J. (1980). The dynamics of composing: Making plans and juggling constraints. In L. Gregg and E. Steinberg (Eds.), *Cognitive Processes in Writing.* Hillsdale, NJ: Erlbaum.

Flower, L. & Hayes, J. R. (1981). A cognitive process theory of writing. *College Composition and Communication, 32(4),* 365-387.

Graham, S. & Harris, K. (1996). Self-regulation and strategy instruction for students who find writing and learning challenging. In C.M. Levy and S. Ransdell, (Eds.), *The science of writing: Theories, methods, individual differences, and applications* (pp. 347-360). New Jersey: Erlbaum.

Graves, D. H. (1983). *Writing: Teachers and children at work.* Exeter, NH: Heinemann Educational Books.

Graves, D.H. (1994). *A fresh look at writing.* Heinemann, NH

Hall, K. (1998). 'Our nets are what we shall catch: Issues in English Assessment in England'. In G. Shiel and U. Ní Dhálaigh (Eds.), *Developing language and literacy* (pp. 153-167). Dublin: Reading Association of Ireland.

Hayes, J.R. (1996). A new framework for understanding cognition and affect in writing. In C.M. Levy and S. Ransdell (Eds.), *The science of writing: Theories, methods, individual differences, and applications.* Mahwah, NJ: Lawrence Erlbaum.

Healy-Eames, F. (1995). Teachers and children talk about writing: The story of two third classes. In G. Shiel, U. Ní Dhálaigh and B. O'Reilly (Eds.), *Reading development to Age 15: Overcoming difficulties* (pp. 73-85). Dublin: Reading Association of Ireland.

Healy-Eames, F. (1999). *Teaching writing in primary schools.* Unpublished Ph.D. dissertation. NUI-Galway.

Ireland. (1999a). *English language primary school curriculum – Content statement.* Dublin: Stationery Office.

Ireland. (1999b). *English language primary school curriculum – Teacher guidelines.* Dublin: Stationery Office.

Johnson, D.J. (1991). Written language. In J.F. Kavanagh (Ed.), *The language continuum: From infancy to literacy.* York Press.

Kavanagh, J. (1997). *A survey of the approaches to the teaching of English compositional writing in a sample of Irish primary schools.* Unpublished Ph.D. dissertation, National University of Ireland, Dublin.

Levy, C. M., & Ransdell, S. (1996). *The science of writing: Theories, methods, individual differences, and applications.* New Jersey: Erlbaum.

McGinley, W. & Tierney, R.J.(1991). Traversing the topical landscape: Reading and writing as ways of knowing. In R.J. Tierney and T. Shanahan, (Eds.), *Handbook of reading research* (Vol. 2, pp. 246-280). New York: Longman.

National Council for Curriculum and Assessment. [NCCA]. (1995). *English language curriculum. Content statement. Draft.* Dublin: Government Publications.

National Council for Curriculum and Assessment. [NCCA]. (1996). *Curriculum for Primary Schools: English. Draft.* Dublin: Author.

National Council for Curriculum and Assessment.[NCCA].(1997a). *English language curriculum. Content statement. Draft.* Dublin: Author

National Council for Curriculum and Assessment. [NCCA]. (1997b). *English language curriculum. Teacher guidelines. Draft.* Dublin: Author.

Protherough, R., Atkinson, J., & Fawcett, J. (1989). *The effective teaching of English.* London and New York: Longman.

Raphael, T.E., Kirschner, B.W., & Englert, C.S. (1988). Expository writing programs: Making connections between reading and writing. In Tierney, R.J., & Shanahan, T. (1991), *Handbook of reading research* (Vol. 2, pp. 246-280). New York: Longman.

Reece, J. & Cumming, G. (1996). Evaluating speech-based composition methods:Planning, dictation, and the listening word processor. In C.M. Levy and S. Ransdell (Eds.), *The science of writing: Theories, methods, individual differences, and applications* (pp. 361- 380). New Jersey: Erlbaum.

Review Body on the Primary Curriculum (1990). *Report.* Dublin: Stationery Office.

Rosen, H. (1986). *Stories and Meanings.* London: National Association of teachers of English.

Sharples, M. (1996). Writing as creative design. In C.M. Levy and S. Ransdell (Eds.), *The science of writing: Theories, methods, individual differences, and applications* (pp.127-148). *New Jersey: Erlbaum.*

Short, K.G. (1986b). Literacy as a collaborative experience. In Tierney, R.J., & Shanahan, T. (1991), *Handbook of reading research* (Vol. 2, pp. 246-280). New York: Longman.

Tierney, R.J., & Shanahan, T. (1991). Research on the reading-writing relationship: Interactions, transactions, and outcomes. In R.Barr, M.L. Kamil, P. Mosenthal, and P.D. Pearson, (Eds.). *Handbook of reading research* (Vol. 2, pp. 246-280). NewYork: Longman.

Wilkinson, A. (1986). *The writing of writing.* Buckingham: Open University Press.

Wray, D. & Lewis, M. (1998). An approach to scaffolding children's non-fiction writing: The use of writing frames. In G. Shiel and U. Ní Dhálaigh (Eds.), *Developing language and literacy: The role of the teacher* (pp. 101-110). Dublin: Reading Association of Ireland.

SECTION 4

Assessment

Measuring Reading in the New Millennium: The Pennsylvania Reading Assessment*

. . . .

Jeanne S. Cranks
Duquesne University, Pittsburgh
United States

Moving into the new millennium means many things to many people. We will see significant changes in the way things are done. Old rules will no longer apply. The field of education is no exception. Already many changes in instructional practices have taken place. As we gain new knowledge and information about how students learn and what they need to know to carry them well into the twenty-first century, we will continue to see many significant changes.

One significant change within the field of education, particularly in reading, is the way students are assessed on their understanding of text. In the United States, Pennsylvania is one state where major changes have already taken place. This paper will describe the new look of large scale reading assessment as it has been designed, developed and implemented in Pennsylvania.

For Pennsylvania, measuring reading in the new millennium is grounded in and revolves around standards. The inter-relatedness of assessment, curriculum and instruction is the foundation upon which the measurement of reading is based.

*Paper presented at the 23rd Annual Conference of the Reading Association of Ireland, Limerick, September 17-19, 1998.

Pennsylvania has developed and implemented a large-scale assessment known as PSSA (Pennsylvania System of School Assessment). This assessment includes assessments in reading and mathematics for all students in the state who are in grades five, eight and eleven as well as a writing assessment for all students in grades six and nine. In 1998, the total number of students assessed in reading/mathematics was 388,787. There are several purposes for these assessments. One purpose is to determine the proficiency levels of Pennsylvania students in the basic skills of reading, mathematics, and writing. Another purpose is to provide results to school districts for consideration in developing strategic plans and curricula. A third purpose is to provide information to the state and general public about student achievement and how schools in Pennsylvania are doing. Yet another purpose is to focus the direction of educators in the field by sharing assessment results. A final purpose of the assessment is to provide widespread in-service training to teachers' on the assessment techniques used in the Pennsylvania System of School Assessment.

The focus of this paper is on the measurement of reading in the PSSA. In the next section, a brief description of academic standards in Pennsylvania, and definitions of related assessment terms are given. Assessment will then be discussed in the context of its development in Pennsylvania, including the role of the Pennsylvania Reading Assessment Advisory Committee. Following this, the components of this reading assessment will be described, as will their implications for instruction. Finally, a brief discussion of accommodations for students with special needs will be presented.

Standards in Reading

What are standards? Standards are defined as statements about what is valued in a given field such as language arts, and/or descriptions of what is considered quality work. Pennsylvania Academic Standards have four features. First, they have *rigour*. Each standard will challenge the learner. Second, they have measurability. Each standard reflects learning which can be measured. Third, they have application. The knowledge and skills reflected in the standards have applications throughout one's lifetime. Fourth, they have clarity. Each standard clearly states for parents, students, teachers, employers and others what is to be learned.

An *academic standard* is defined as what a student should know and be able to do at a specified grade level. In Pennsylvania, five major categories of academic standards for reading have been established. They are:

1.1 Learning to Read Independently
1.2 Reading Critically in All Content Areas
1.3 Reading, Analysing, and Interpreting Literature
1.4 Characteristics and Functions of the English Language
1.5 Research

For each category, descriptors have been developed for grades three, five, eight and eleven.

Assessment is defined as a valid and reliable measurement of student performance on a set of academic standards in a subject area and answers the question, 'What does achievement of specific content standards at the proficient or advanced levels look like?' at specified grade levels.

For Pennsylvania, this assessment has a life cycle that undergoes several phases. First, each test item in the assessment is aligned to a reading standard at specific grade level. Next, each test is piloted and then field-tested. Following field testing, the reading assessments are administered to all students attending Pennsylvania public schools in grades 5, 8 and 11. These assessments use a combination of census testing and matrix sampling procedures. Census testing requires all students to complete the same set of items while matrix sampling is accomplished by dividing a large set of items into several test forms with an equal number of items in each form. Matrix sampling helps to limit the time required for the assessment, provides for consistent administration procedures and reflects a broad curriculum content. A passage, along with its items, is first used in matrix sampling, and then moves into the census testing, where it becomes a common item. After a few years, the passage, along with its items, is released to the general public and is no longer used in the reading assessment.

Curriculum answers the question, 'What should students know and be able to do as a result of their schooling?' It is described as a series of planned instructions that is coordinated, articulated, and implemented in a manner designed to result in the achievement by all students of specific knowledge as well as the application of that knowledge.

Instruction refers to the delivery of academic and vocational content by teachers that enable students to achieve the academic standards. *Planned instruction*, then, is instruction that is based upon a written plan which consists of at least the following elements. First, it includes objectives to be achieved by all students. Second, it includes content, materials and activities, as well as estimated instructional time to be devoted to achieving the standards. Third, the relationship between the objectives and academic standards is identified. Finally, procedures for measurement of the objectives are included.

In Pennsylvania, the *academic standards* describe the knowledge and skills that students will be expected to demonstrate before graduating from a public school. Appropriate *instruction* is provided through the *curriculum* so that students may develop knowledge and skills in reading, writing, speaking, and listening and attain pre-defined academic standards. In addition, the *curriculum* is designed to provide students with instruction needed to attain these academic standards.

Assessment in Pennsylvania

The concepts on which the Pennsylvania Reading Assessment is based were chosen by the Reading Assessment Advisory Committee, a committee of over 60 Pennsylvania educators. This committee is comprised of teachers from all levels, reading specialists, supervisors, curriculum co-ordinators, administrators, college professors, and policy makers from all parts of Pennsylvania. Among their defined responsibilities are to:

- develop test items, performance tasks, and statements
- make recommendations to strengthen and expand the Pennsylvania System of School Assessment
- articulate long-term goals and objectives of the Pennsylvania System of School Assessment to parents, employers and the community
- provide in-service training to local school districts
- provide training and staff development for classroom and large-scale assessment

Changes in assessment reflect a new definition of reading. The Reading Assessment Advisory Committee examined reading research results from recent years and investigated revised reading assessments from several other states as well as the U.S. National Assessment of Educational Progress (NAEP). Based on their investigations, a new definition of reading that reflects what is now known about the reading process was recommended. This definition states that reading *is a dynamic process in which the reader interacts with text to construct meaning. Inherent in constructing meaning is the reader's ability to activate prior/background knowledge, use reading strategies and adapt to the reading situation.*

A good reader is no longer one who demonstrates mastery of isolated skills, but rather one who applies appropriate strategies, interacts with texts, and constructs meaning.

In order for assessment to reflect this new view of reading, many changes were necessary. No longer is assessment in reading limited to reading several short paragraphs and answering four or five multiple-choice questions about each one. Rather, students are given two or three longer selections and are asked to respond to twenty to twenty-five selected response items, and to construct a text-based written response for each selection.

The Pennsylvania Reading Assessment is based on current thinking about teaching reading as a holistic, reflective literary process. Its purpose is to:

- assess students' progress in transacting with text as they construct meaning from a variety of texts
- activate prior/background knowledge in order to relate the new to the known
- respond to information and ideas gained by reading texts from varied sources
- analyse and make critical judgments about what is read

Based on the premise that readers think and use text differently depending on the types of text they read and their purposes for reading, three broad purposes for reading have been identified: (i) reading for the literary experience, (ii) reading for information, and (iii) reading to perform a task.

In addition to the purposes for reading, there are differing responses or stances that readers may adopt as they read text. These stances are not hierarchical, nor are they mutually exclusive. Rather, they are distinguished by the complexity and thoroughness of a reader's response coupled with the difficulty of the text. They are used by all readers, regardless of age or ability. These stances are as follows:

- *Initial Understanding.* This is the first impression or gist of a text.
- *Developing Interpretation.* This involves the extension of ideas and may involve linking information across various

parts of the text as well as focusing on specific information. It also includes inferential responses such as drawing conclusions, inferring cause and effect, and interpreting actions of a character.

- *Responding Personally.* This involves connecting information from the text with personal background knowledge and experience.
- *Responding Critically.* This involves forming critical judgments about the text. It requires standing apart from the text, reflecting upon it, and judging it.

All assessments in Pennsylvania are based on the Pennsylvania Academic Standards, are criterion-referenced, and include some constructed responses that are open-ended.

In Pennsylvania, assessments in reading are administered in grades 5, 8, and 11 while the Pennsylvania Writing Assessment is administered in grades 6 and 9. Performance on the Pennsylvania reading assessments is demonstrated through selected responses to comprehension questions as well as written responses to in-depth comprehension questions about the passages. Performance on the Pennsylvania writing assessment is demonstrated by the quality of written compositions linked to a variety of prompts in various modes.

Two types of passages are used in the Pennsylvania Reading Assessment. *Narrative* passages include complete works drawn from authentic (primary) sources and may include illustrations relevant to the text. *Informational* passages are drawn from content materials such as news articles and magazines that are age and interest appropriate. They may include structural aids such as headings, subheadings, bold or italic typefaces as well as other interpretive aids such as maps, charts and graphs. In addition, the informational category may include materials from practical sources such as manuals and directions that assess document literacy.

Performance assessment tasks require the students to perform, create, produce, or do something. These tasks tap into higher-level thinking skills as well as problem-solving skills. Performance assessment tasks answer the question, 'What counts as evidence that students understand specific concepts?'

In addition to performance tasks, the Pennsylvania reading assessment includes multiple-choice/selected-response items. Single response multiple-choice/selected-response items appear on the assessments in grades 5 and 8 and follow the 'four answer, one correct response' format in which the distracters appeal to some kind of misinterpretation, predisposition, unsound reasoning, or casual reading. The grade 11 Pennsylvania reading assessment, however, uses a multiple-response multiple-choice/selected-response item format which includes five response choices where one, two, or three of them may be correct. These multiple-response multiple-choice/selected-response items are identical in format to the traditional selected response items in that they contain a stem, one to three correct answer choices, and two to four distracters. The rationale for using this format in eleventh grade is that it communicates to the students that there is often more than one correct answer to a question.

Constructed responses are responses that are opened-ended and require students to construct or produce a response rather than select a response from a set of alternatives. These responses enable students to demonstrate their comprehension about what they have read in ways that cannot be addressed through traditional multiple-choice/selected-response items. This kind of response allows students to reflect on what then have read, integrate prior/ background knowledge with text-based information, extend meaning and express their ideas. Each task is constructed so that it is text-dependent and reflects the Pennsylvania Reading Assessment Scoring Rubric. In contrast, a writing prompt is used in the Pennsylvania Writing Assessment. A writing prompt is defined as a statement designed to elicit a student response about a particular topic and differs from a constructed response in that a prompt is not text-dependent.

The format for the constructed response consists of a purpose statement, reading passage, performance task, reminder statements, and the space for the written constructed response.

The *Purpose Statement* gives students a preview of the text, motivates students to read, hints at what will be expected in the performance, and may define an unfamiliar term.

The *Performance Task* is open-ended, grade-level appropriate, and text-dependent. It allows students to respond critically as well as connect prior knowledge and experiences to the text. It does not ask for a specified number of items since this would then become a counting task, and therefore be a quantitative rather than qualitative measurement.

The *Reminder Statement* correlates with the task and gives more specific information about the task. It appears after the performance task and before the designated answer space. In Pennsylvania, the reminder statement contains five bulleted items. The first three refer to the specific task and the last two remind the student to write neatly and clearly and use only the space provided.

In developing constructed response items, it is important to note that the performance task is always written first. In this way, the purpose statement and reminder statements are built around the performance task.

Constructed responses, because of their open-ended nature, allow students to respond at different levels. The sole consideration when evaluating a student-constructed response, then, addresses the question, 'Did the student read and understand the passage, and at what level?'

Constructed responses are scored by using a scoring rubric. A rubric is a scoring guide that is used to score a single piece of work. Scoring rubrics have several characteristics. Each rubric includes a set of criteria that are used to evaluate a performance. In addition, each rubric contains a fixed scale and includes a list of characteristics that describe a level of performance for each point on that scale.

The Pennsylvania Reading Assessment rubric contains three sets of criteria. *Understanding the text* is demonstrated through a response that is both text-based and factual. *Level of comprehension* of the text is demonstrated through levels of thinking, from literal to personal, critical, or evaluative responses. *Connection to the text* is demonstrated through responses that make connections to and go beyond the text. The Pennsylvania Reading Assessment rubric is a four-point scale that includes the characteristics of each criterion for each point on that scale.

The Pennsylvania Reading Assessment rubric is an example of a *holistic rubric*. Holistic rubrics view a performance or product as a whole and yield a single score, providing an overall judgment. They are descriptive in nature in that they describe the characteristics of different levels of performance, and generally have four to six levels. They require that a single score be assigned that is based on the overall quality of the student's work. Features and dimensions for each score level are described in summary and do not provide information linked to specific tasks. Therefore, holistic rubrics are not appropriate for diagnosing specific student strengths and weaknesses. Holistic rubrics are summative assessments that communicate a general level of progress to outside evaluators; hence they are appropriate for large scale assessments such as those done in Pennsylvania.

On the other hand, *analytic rubrics* distinguish specific skills, concepts, and/or knowledge from which separate scores can be derived. They are very useful for revealing individual strengths and weaknesses and help improve individual learning in terms of what aspects of the performance are acceptable and where specific problems exist.

Implications for Instruction

Since assessment informs instruction, there are many instructional activities that teachers can offer as they link assessment with instruction. These are applicable to all classrooms and in all subjects across the curriculum.

First, reading materials should include many types of authentic texts drawn from a variety of sources. Fiction and non-fiction selections related to the areas of study should be drawn from primary sources and read in their entirety.

Second, rather that a classroom where teachers talk in questions and students talk in answers, teachers should engage the students with opened-ended questions and performance tasks that provide many opportunities for them to construct responses that are text-dependent.

Third, teachers should provide direct strategy instruction by explaining, modelling, and providing guided reading instruction that actively engages students with text before, during, and after reading.

Accommodations for Students with Disabilities

In Pennsylvania, all students enrolled in the public schools are to be included in the assessment process. There are some students, however, who because of a specific disability, have difficulty. Therefore, accommodations that allow students to participate in this assessment are appropriate. The intent of providing an accommodation is to ensure that a student with a disability is not put at a disadvantage in a testing situation. The accommodation, however, should not provide the student with an unfair advantage.

Accommodations must not change what is being tested. For example, it is not appropriate to read a reading test to a student if the test is designed to measure how well the student reads. If, however, the test is designed to measure whether a student can draw meaning from text, then this would be appropriate. The accommodations that are used depend upon the type of test and the purpose for testing.

There are a number of areas in which accommodations that are appropriate for a reading assessment can be made. In the area of presentation, for example, directions can be quietly repeated, or a student may be cued to remain on task. Regarding responses, a student may respond orally on an audio-tape, point to a response, or mark responses in the test booklet rather than on an answer sheet. Examples of test modifications include Braille or large-print versions, highlighting key words or phrases in the directions, and masking portions of the test to direct the child's attention to specific areas. Settings can be altered by allowing the student to use adaptive or special furniture (e.g. a study carrel), testing in a separate room or in small groups, and securing papers to a work area with tapes. Timing and scheduling adaptations include increasing or decreasing opportunities for movement, permitting additional breaks during testing, and increasing the testing time. Assistive devices such as a magnifier and the use of assistive technology such as portable writing devices and computers are also acceptable. Other options include the use of chubby or thin pencils depending upon the student's needs. By making appropriate accommodations, students with disabilities can be successful with a reading assessment.

Conclusion

Pennsylvania has transformed large scale reading assessment from one that focused on skills to one that is standards-based, informs instruction and curriculum, and provides opportunities for all students to demonstrate their comprehension of a variety of texts in several ways.

REFERENCES

Lytle, S. L., & Botel, M. (1990). *The Pennsylvania framework for reading, writing, and talking across the curriculum.* Harrisburg, PA: Pennsylvania Department of Education.

Pennsylvania Department of Education. (1998). *The Pennsylvania assessment system reading instructional handbook* . Harrisburg, PA: Author.

Pennsylvania Department of Education. (1998). *Reading assessment handbook.* Harrisburg, PA: Author.

Pennsylvania Department of Education. (1998). *Writing assessment handbook* Harrisburg, PA: Author.

Assessing Children's Oral Language[*]

. . . .

Gerry Shiel
Educational Research Centre,
St Patrick's College, Dublin

The prominence given to the development of oral language in the revised *English Language Primary School Curriculum* (Ireland, 1999) inevitably gives rise to the question of how oral language can be taught and assessed. This paper describes some of the elements of oral language that teachers may wish to assess, discusses why these elements are sometimes difficult to assess, and provides strategies for engaging in the assessment of oral language and the recording of assessment outcomes.

The Content of Oral Language

There are several reasons why curriculum developers and teachers are beginning to place a stronger emphasis on the development of oral language in the first language. First, there is a recognition that proficiency in oral language is related to proficiency in reading and writing. Second, there is the belief, which underpins the framework for oral language in the revised *English Language Primary School Curriculum*, that oral language is implicated in children's general cognitive development (i.e., the development of thinking and reasoning skills). Third, there is a

[*]Paper presented at the Annual Spring Seminar of the Reading Association of Ireland, Church of Ireland College of Education, Rathmines, March 20th, 1999.

recognition that oral language is important for progress in a range of subjects. Fourth, there is an understanding that oral language contributes to other important areas of development such as personal, social, emotional and imaginative development. Finally, it is recognised that there are elements of oral language that should be developed for their own sake – such as ability to deliver an oral report or present a persuasive argument.

Oral language proficiency contributes to the development of reading and writing, not only in the initial stages of acquisiton, but at all points in the developmental sequence. Learning to read and write depends on a child's unconscious expectation that written language, like oral language, contains meaning, follows a particular structure, and comprises sentences, words and parts of words. Therefore, it is important for the teacher to focus on and assess children's understanding of:

- the structure of written texts including (a) the structural elements of stories (narratives) such as setting, characters, problems, attempts to solve the problem, and resolutions; and (b) the structural elements of informational texts such as the chronological sequence of events, explanations of cause and effect, comparison and contrast, and summary statement/ main idea.
- the structure of sentences – children benefit from an opportunity to reflect on and discuss the sentences they encounter in oral and written texts, and to use particular structures as they recall or compose text; children need to meet more complex syntax and more elaborate use of tense in oral contexts (for example, in listening to and discussing texts read aloud by the teacher) before they encounter them on their own in written texts;
- vocabulary knowledge or knowledge of word meanings – children's understanding of word meanings can be expanded through discussion of words encountered in oral and written contexts, and by gathering and rehearsing words that are

relevant to their needs; reading comprehension and writing quality are both dependent on a wide and varied vocabulary;
• knowledge of word parts, including prefixes, suffixes, inflectional endings and root words and a knowledge of how these elements combine to contribute to meaning.

Oral language is also important in that it can promote *cognitive development* by providing children with a tool for making connections between the new and what is already known, for making sense of new experiences and for making new discoveries. Abilities that are fundamental to cognitive development – questioning, reasoning, formulating hypotheses, exchanging ideas with others and solving problems – can be developed by engaging children in *purposeful* oral language activities.

Competence in oral language is also important for progress in a range of subjects. The development of oral language draws on the content of other subjects, and is cross-curricular in its application, while understanding of other subjects draws heavily on oral language. This implies that oral language can be taught and assessed in a range of curricular areas.

Oral language can contribute to other areas of pupils' growth in a range of non-cognitive areas. According to Cregan (1998), it contributes to:

• *personal development*, by enabling the development of self-awareness, personal identity, a sense of confidence, and feelings of competence
• *social development,* by enabling children to interact with one another, and to communicate more effectively with others, thereby allowing them to develop relationships
• *emotional development,* by enabling children to label their feelings, recognise that others have similar feelings, and allow them to cope with feelings; and
• *imaginative development* enabling children to enter magical and mystical worlds and give expression to their innermost feelings.

Many of these skills are embodied in the strands underpinning the revised *English Language Primary School Curriculum* (Ireland, 1999), which focuses on the development (and assessment) of four inter-related aspects of language at *all* class levels:

- Developing receptiveness to oral language – including an awareness of the context in which oral communication occurs;
- Developing competence and confidence in using oral language – including ability to use language in a variety of circumstances, and to initiate and sustain conversations;
- Developing cognitive abilities through language – including the development of vocabulary and the ability to ask questions to gain information, to seek and give explanations, to argue a point of view, and to persuade others;
- Emotional and imaginative development through language – including development of the ability to respond to story and poetry.

Finally, it is almost stating the obvious to assert that children should become effective language users because language is important for everyday life. The ability to greet others, inteact socially with them, and, later, present a logical argument or report on a project, are important in school contexts and for life in general.

The Challenge of Assessing Oral Language

The increased emphasis on developing oral language in the first language in the revised Primary School Curriculum is likely to give rise to increased interest in assessing oral language, not only in the Infant classes but at all class levels. However, unlike reading and writing, where decontextualised tasks (standardised reading tests or timed writing tasks) can be administered and scored in a systematic manner, the assessment of competence in oral language involves observing children interacting with one another in real language situations, for authentic purposes. Such purposes might include explaining a problem, asking or answering a question, contributing to a class discussion, retelling a story, responding to a persuasive talk, or delivering a speech.

A second difficulty in assessing oral language is that growth in this area is less obvious than in reading or writing. According to Cregan (1998), 'Though not impossible, it is a remarkably slow, difficult, painstaking and cumbersome process to assess a child's oral language development, and to determine the level of competence reached. This makes it remarkably difficult to see what has been achieved and to plan for future development' (p. 5). This, perhaps, reflects the recursive, non-linear nature of growth in oral language, particularly after the initial stage of acquisition. Pupils may return repeatedly to an aspect or stage of competence that had been achieved earlier, to experiment with language or to reinforce their skills. Hence, it may not always be obvious that growth has occurred.

A third difficulty associated with assessing oral language (particularly when it is assessed in interactive situations) is that a range of factors can affect performance on a particular occasion. These factors include, but are not limited to:

- The type of task that has been set to stimulate the use of talk; ·
- The nature of the audience and the listener (e.g., participating in a group situation, conferencing with the teacher on a one-to-one basis, or reporting to the class as a member of a group);
- The pupil's interest in and ownership of the task;
- The pupil's previous experience in using speaking and listening during this type of task;
- The pupil's gender and that of other group members;
- The composition of the group in which the pupil works.

Notwithstanding these difficulties, there have been several attempts to assess oral language, both in the context of large-scale assessments, and in classroom situations.

Assessemnt of Oral Language: The APU Experience

National assessments of oral language have been conducted in several countries, including England and Scotland. Indeed, Brooks (1994) reminds us that the Certificate of Secondary Education (CSE) in England between 1965 and 1987 represented the largest system of oracy assessment seen anywhere, with over 90% of each cohort of 500,000 students entered for the exam from 1980 onwards. However, he argues that the assessment was limited to the extent that it adhered to a 'social accomplishment' view of language rooted in the English 'public speaking' tradition, rather than the more modern 'communicative competence' or 'language for learning' views, which stress the value of talk both as a tool for learning in school, and as the most important means of communication in the world generally.

The Assessment Performance Unit (APU) of the National Foundation for Educational Research in England and Wales conducted national assessments of oral language, at ages 11 and 15 in its 1982, 1983 and 1988 language surveys (Gorman et al., 1988, 1991). Among the principles that underpinned the assessment of oracy were the following:

1. *Listening should not be artificially separated from speaking.* Though there are some frequent and important non-reciprocal speaking-listening situations (e.g., listening to the radio), listening is best assessed implicitly, from students' responses in some following-speaking task, or by their involvement in interactive talk.
2. *Different purposes require different types of talk.* The appropriateness of talk used in a given situation is an important criterion of assessment.
3. *Pupils should interact with a real and meaningful audience during assessment.* Because one of the main functions of talk is to communicate tasks which require pupils to repeat information to someone who already possesses it should be avoided.

4. *Assessment of oral language should include dialogue as well as monologue.* Despite the greater difficulty of assessing interaction, interactive talk should be assessed since interaction is the most important form of talk.

5. *The content of oral language assessment should include subject matter in such areas as geography, mathematics and science.* The content of oracy should not be confined to the literary, personal growth or social issues – content typical of many first-langauge syllabuses, or to designated 'language' lessons. Rather, it should extend into other subject areas.

6. *Pupils should be assessed on several oral language tasks.* Since a fair method of assessing oral language must give pupils a chance to show what they can do across a range of purposes for language use, no pupil should be assessed on one task on a single occasion.

These principles support the communicative competence and language for learning views of oral language. All of the tasks developed by the APU were interactive, either involving two or four pupils, and represented a wide range of purposes for which talk is used inside and outside of school, including planning and telling a story, speculating, predicting and problem solving, evaluating, informing, explaining, instructing and reporting, and arguing and persuading. The following are examples of assessment tasks that were administered to 11-year olds in 1988, the last year of the APU oracy assessments. ·

- *The Bridge.* One pupil in a pair was given two pictures of metal-span bridges; the other was given six pictures of bridges, including the two his/her partner had. The pupil with the two pictures described each of them in turn, and the other pupl was then asked to identify both bridges from the full set. The pupil describing the bridges was assessed separately on ability to describe each bridge. The identifications made by the second pupil (the listener) were recorded only for statistical purposes. Listeners were not assessed.

- *Spiders.* Two pupils listened to a tape-recording of how a garden spider builds her web, and were asked to arrange six diagrams to correspond to the six stages in the process. Next, they listened to the recording again. Then, using the diagrams, one pupil explained the process to two other pupils who had not heard the tape. This pupil's description of the process was assessed.

- *Motorways.* Four pupils were invited to participate in a simulated meeting precipitated by plans to build a motorway through the viliage of 'Greenvalley'. Pupils were presented with a picture representing the village and sites threatened by the motorway plans: an electronics factory, a village school and a nature reserve. Three of the pupils were given a card with information relating to one of the three sites, while the fourth, selected to 'chair' the meeting, was given a card with information on what was expected of such a position. The task comprised three distinct phases: presentation of information relating to each of the three sites, group discussion, and summing up. Pupils were assessed on their contributions to these different stages.

- *Can-openers.* Two pupils were asked to consider the problems old people might encounter with can-openers and (were asked) to think of ways can-openers might be improved to make them easier for the elderly to use. First, the pupils had to speculate on the difficulties elderly people might have with can-openers. Then, the pupils were given two actual can-openers to evaluate. Finally, they reported on their findings. Pupils were assessed on each of the three phases.

Pupils' responses to these tasks were scored in a variety of ways, including a holistic, 'on-the-spot' assessment by a trained assessor, involving the application of a 7-point overall impression scale, and a 5-point 'orientation to listener' scale. Subsequently, tape-recordings of some tasks were assessed by trained raters who applied an analytic scoring scheme that evaluated performance in such areas as propositional/semantic content, sequential structure, lexico-grammatical features (syntax, lexis) and performance features (self-correction/hesitation, tempo etc.). One difficulty with the overall approach was that outcomes were not aggregated statistically across tasks. This meant that statistical data for each task were reported separately. For example, in relation to the Motorway task, it was found that:

> . . . the less familiar opening stage of the task proved to be problematic for a high proportion of pupils who found it difficult to exploit the information with which they had been provided (mean 3.5 for factory, 3.6 for school, 3.7 for nature reserve). Only a minority of pupils felt confident enough to elaborate on the information they had been given in presenting the case for preservation. . . Pupils demonstrated their confidence with argumentative and persuasive talk and their ability to take account of opposing points of view. . . The final stage of this task, the village representative's summing up (mean 3.4) proved less difficult than the earlier presentation stage, although pupils tended to give either incomplete or unfocused summations . . . Eleven-year old chairpersons tended to adopt a highly subjective view, frequently assuming control over the final decision. . . . (Gorman et al., 1991, p. 42).

Among the conclusions reached by the APU (based on a consideration of the outcomes across all oral language tasks for pupils at ages 11 and 15) were the following:

- Teachers should provide opportunities for pupils to develop skills in a wide range of types and purposes of talk . . . Certain types of talk [are] which are important for education and for life generally are under-represented in the curriculum. When opportunities for various kinds of talk are presented, opportunities for assessment also arise.

- The development of oracy implies providing opportunities for a good deal of small-group work, but also for occasions when individual pupils have the opportunity to address a larger group, perhaps the whole class, uninterruptedly and at some length.
- Effective assessment of oral language implies an understanding of the features which constitute effective talk in different circumstances. For all types of talk, appropriate content is the principal feature attracting high marks.
- In all forms of talk, organisation of ideas is also a significant correlate of high scores. Pupils who organise their ideas well do better than pupils who are less proficient in this area. In the case of a monologue, such as the description of an objective, a clear structure principally consists of a simple, general opening statement, followed by a list of important features, supplemented as needs be by a catalogue of details.
- For interactive talk, organisation takes the form of discourse strategies such as respecting other people's turns, not interrupting, not holding the floor too long, building on others' ideas, repairing breakdowns in understanding, putting ideas forward and testing them against others' opinions.
- A review stage might be built into some oral language activities to allow for pupil self- and peer-assessment. For example, pupils might be asked whether (in a task that demanded it) they had planned properly, allowed every member of the group to contribute, spoken up when they had something to say, and learnt how they might do a similar activity better another time. Such reflective, formative self-assessments, suitably moderated by teachers, can form a good basis for teacher's own summative assessments.

Unfortunately, the APU surveys were discontinued with the advent of National Curriculum Assessment in England and Wales in the late 1980's. Now, teachers of pupils at Key Stages 1 and 2 (ages 7 and 11) in those countries, are required to assess their pupils against specific level statements (learning targets). Unlike reading and writing, the assessment tasks that teachers administer are informal (non-standardised).

Assessment of Oral Language in the Classroom

As suggested above, classroom-based assessment of oral language needs to generate two types of assessment information: formative information, which is essentially diagnostic in nature, and can be used to plan teaching and learning activities, and summative information, such as an overall score, which can be used to record overall achievement in oral language on class records or on reports to parents. Assessment of oral language should occur at every class level. In the junior primary classes, assessment will often occur in conjunction with specific oral language activities that are organised during English classes. From third class onwards, assessment may also occur in the context of other subjects such as mathematics, history, geography, social, personal and health education, or science, where pupils will continue to listen and respond to texts or content presented by the teacher, describe objects, make arguments, or report on activities and events.

Among the main tools that can be used to assess oral language and record assessment outcomes are anecdotal notes, checklists, rating scales and scoring rubrics, and curriculum profiles. Before describing these instruments, it should be noted that children's difficulties with oral language may, in some cases, be attributed to factors such as hearing problems (which affect how well children process or understand information) and speech difficulties (which may impede effective communication). Where observation of a pupil suggests difficulties in either of these areas, it may be necessary to arrange an appropriate assessment by a specialist.

Anecdotal notes. Anecdotal notes are short notes made by the teacher about a pupil's achievement. In using anecdotal notes to record information about proficiency in oral language, it is recommended that the teacher record three or four observations about each pupil each month. In planning and presenting an oral language activity (for example, listening to a story, newstelling, presenting short reports etc.), it is useful to focus on one or two dimensions of the task that can be assessed, and to observe particularly carefully how pupils perform on those dimensions. For example, if pupils are telling the news, assessment might focus on ability to use descriptive language in presenting an object or describing an event, ability to sustain a conversation about a topic, or use of appropriate non-verbal behaviours such as facial expression or gesture. Figure 1 gives an example of the anecdotal notes made by one one teacher during newstelling.

FIGURE 1

EXCERPT FROM TEACHER'S ANECDOTAL NOTES ON TELLING THE NEWS

Date	Pupil	Observation
20/3	Paul	Described what he had done during the weekend, though few details were provided. Was not prepared to answer questions posed by other pupils. Couldn't remember St Patrick's Day parade.
20/3	Anne	Spoke confidently about her weekend trip. Described in detail a street carnival which she had attended and speculated on how some of the props might have been developed.
27/3	Paul	Described a new computer game he had been given. Was unable to explain the objective of the game or how to play it. Said he would bring the manual to school.
27/3	Anne	Described a courtcase she had seen on television from two different perspectives – those of the plaintiff and the defendant, indicating some sensitivity to point of view.
28/3	Paul	Explained the pictures in the manual for the computer game. Spoke enthusiastically about various 'cheats' he had used to advance to a higher level.

Notes such as these can be drawn on by the teacher when planning lessons, or at the end of the school year, when an overall score for a pupil's language proficiency is generated. A key point to bear in mind when developing a note-taking system is whether or not one wants to be able to share the notes with other teachers and/or parents at some later time. Notes that are likely to be shared in this manner may need to be more objective than those that are developed for the teacher's own exclusive use.

Checklists. Checklists offer a convenient and flexible approach to assessing oral language. Checklists can be developed by teachers to include the particular skills and strategies reflected in their teaching plans, or checklists developed by others can be to adapted fit particular teaching/learning contexts. Figure 2 gives an example of a checklist that might be used to assess pupils' presentation of oral reports. The teacher's role is to appraise the performance of pupils on the task, and to indicate whether, or to what extent, each element in the checklist was addressed. The checklist also provides for the possibility of observing development over time, as provision is made for recording outcomes on three different occasions.

FIGURE 2

CHECKLIST FOR ASSESSING THE EFFECTIVENESS OF PUPILS' ORAL REPORTS

The pupil. . .	First Observation Date: Topic:	Second Observation Date: Topic:	Third Observation Date: Topic:
Appears interested in the topic			
Is knowledgeable about the topic			
States main points clearly			
Uses examples or reasons to make a point clearly			
Summarises main points at end of talk			
Selects words that express ideas clearly			
Keeps attention of audience during talk			
Uses appropriate visual aids (diagrams, charts etc.)			
Appears to be at ease			
Uses appropriate non-verbal signals and gestures			

Teachers can make an on-the-spot evaluation of whether the pupil achieved the skill in question by recording a simple 'yes/no' (+/-) quite clearly. There is no absolute standard where judging the achievement of skills on a checklist such as this is concerned. Rather, the teacher must identify a standard that is appropriate to the class level of the pupils and apply that standard when making a judgement.

Rating Scales. Rating scales are similar in many ways to checklists – a list of indicators is provided, and the teacher must evaluate a pupil's achievement against the indicator. In the case of rating scales, there is the possibility of indicating varying degrees of achievement. For example, a 3 might be awarded if an indicator has been clearly demonstrated by the pupil; a 2 might be assigned if some evidence of achievement has been demonstrated. Finally, a 1 might be assigned if no evidence of achieving the indicator has been demonstrated. Teachers may wish to develop their own scales, using some of the moderating activities described below.

Standardised rating scales which have undergone rigorous development and have known psychometric properties, are useful when the accuracy of assessment data is more important than their formative value. Standardised rating scales, such as the *Bury Infant Check* (Pearson & Quinn, 1986) or the *Belfield Infant Assessment Profile* (BIAP, Spelman & McHugh, 1994), for example, may be used to identify children who have or are likely to develop learning difficulties. Though not focusing exclusively on oral language, these instruments typically include subscales for assessing various aspects of oral language. In the BIAP, for example, five of the 25 items deal with 'language and communication', highligting the importance of oral language in early learning. Indeed, Spelman and MacHugh (1994), found that the five communication items accounted for 40% of the variance in children's total scores on the BIAP and has a higher combind reliability than any of the other constructs underpinning the assessment.

Scoring Rubrics. Scoring rubrics are used to assess performance on specific language tasks – such as a retelling of a story that has been read aloud by the teacher, or a talk that seeks to persuade the principal to change a school rule. Figure 3 provides a scoring rubric for assessing telling (or retelling) of a story and attempts to incorporate some of the structural elements of story referred to earlier in this article:

FIGURE 3

RUBRIC FOR ASSESSING A STORY RETELLING

Score	Description
5.	A very-well developed narrative. Includes focus, organisation, and support/elaboration. There is a unifying event and theme. Major episodes are clear and coherently developed throughout the retelling.
4.	A well-formed narrative, but all the elements are not equally developed throughout the retelling. The purpose of the story is apparent.
3.	An adequately-formed narrative. The narrative is simple and clear, presenting nothing more than the essentials. Some inferences on the part of the listener are required.
2.	A partially-developed story. The narrative attempts to address the assignment, but only the rudiments of techniques for forming focus, organisation, and support can be detected. There is often some confusion or disjointedness.
1.	Does not resemble a story. Consists of a set of unrelated events. No organisation present.

Teachers wishing to assess pupils' retellings using a rubric such as this, will need to develop a shared understanding of the meaning of each score description in the rubric. One approach to accomplishing this would be for the teachers at adjacent class levels in the school to assemble a range of retellings of a particular story (for example, tape-recordings of pupils' retellings), and to apply the scoring rubric to each story in order to develop a shared understanding of the meaning of each score point. Scoring rubrics such as this would also be relevant for the assessment of structure or organisation in children's writing.

Curriculum Profiles. Curriculum profiles in English have been developed in a number of countries, including Ireland, in recent years. Typically, profiles allow for the assessment of pupils against specific curricular outcomes (objectives) that are represented by indicators. The set of indicators in Figure 4, which is from the *Drumcondra English Profiles* (Shiel & Murphy, 2000), illustrates the range of oral language outcomes against which teachers might assess pupils.

FIGURE 4

PROFILE INDICATORS FOR ORAL LANGUAGE (FOURTH CLASS)

	When rating a pupil's achievement, begin at the top of the set (the indicator regarded by teachers as being the most difficult) and continue downwards until you reach the highest indicator that has been achieved by the pupil independently, on more than one occasion.
8.	Listens to and compares two poems on the same theme or by the same author, and supports a personal interpretation (See Note)
7.	Delivers a prepared report to the class on a project topic, using appropriate vocabulary and giving relevant, organised information
6.	Talks clearly and audibly to different audiences (e.g., groups, own class, other classes), varying pace of as appropriate delivery
5.	Prepares for and conducts an interview with another pupil or adult to obtain information about a topic
4.	Predicts and justifies future events and likely outcomes at appropriate points in book-length stories read aloud
3.	Presents a point of view to the class, offering some reasons or arguments
2.	Identifies and comments on humour in stories and poems read aloud by other pupils or by the teacher
1.	Participates in class discussions by sharing relevant background (prior) knowledge about a topic

Note: In interpreting poems, puils may refer to content, format, mood, and language.

The indicators in this set are arranged in order of difficulty, with those indicators deemed by teachers to be most difficult for pupils towards the end of fourth class appearing at the top of the list, and those deemed to be easiest appearing near the bottom. In assessing a pupil on an indicator set, teachers are asked to begin at the top of the list, and proceed downwards until they reach the first indicator that has been achieved independently by the pupil more than once. The number corresponding to this indicator is then converted to a scale score (between 0 and 10) using a table of norms. In applying the profiles, teachers are encouraged to draw upon the assessment data they have assembled throughout the school year to inform their judgements. Inevitably, measurement error will be associated with the scores that teachers assign to their pupils. Such error can, however, be minimised if teachers in a school work towards achieving a shared understanding of the meanings of particular indicators and the specific criteria needed to achieve them. As with scoring rubrics and ratings scales, it is advisable that teachers within schools work towards establishing standards or criteria by which they can judge pupils' proficiency.

Profiles are useful to the extent that they allow for a comparison between different elements of English – oral language, reading and writing, at a particular class level. Such an exercise can highlight links between oral langauge and other aspects of English.

Conclusion

The revised *English Language Primary School Curriculum* indicates a stronger emphasis on oral language, not only in English language classes, but throughout the curriculum. One implication of the increased emphasis on oral language is the need for class teachers to assess their pupils while they are engaged in language activities, and to record and communicate the outcomes of their assessments.

A key principle underpinning the teaching of oral language is that children (from an early age) must be given opportunities to use language constructively – not just everyday conversational language, but the vocabulary, syntax and discourse that is found in printed materials as well. In addition, oral language activities must be structured in a way that allows pupils to engage in various forms of higher-order thinking, including questioning, reasoning, generating hypotheses, and solving problems. Pupils also need to engage in oral language activities such as delivering a report, making an argument, summarising a text, or evaluating a story or poem.

Procedures for the assessment of oral language are not nearly as well developed as those for reading or writing. Much depends on the appropriateness and accuracy of the judgements and conclusions that teachers (or raters) draw. Often, the context in which an oral language activity occurs (for example, a small-group discussion on a particular topic) will impact on the quality of pupils' responses, and, by implication, on assessment outcomes. Not surprisingly, it is recommended that pupils should be assessed on a variety of tasks and in a range of contexts before firm conclusions about their overall performance in oral language, are drawn.

A range of assessment tools are available to teachers wishing to assess their pupils' oral language. These include anecdotal notes, checklists, rating scales, scoring rubrics, and curriculum profiles. Typically, these tools focus on the processes of gathering assessment information, interpreting that information, and recording assessment outcomes. Teachers assessing oral language for the first time may find that most can be gained from assessing a particular task in detail (for example, newstelling, delivering a report, recalling a narrative or informational text), and gradually expanding their assessments to incorporate a broader range of learning outcomes.

A persistent problem in the assessment of oral language is the variation in the interpretations that teachers attribute to checklist items, points on a scoring rubric, or profile indicators. This problem can be addressed, in part, if teachers work together to arrive at shared understandings of the meanings of these learning outcomes. A useful beginning in this regard is for teachers to dicusss how different pupils perform on a particular (designated) task, and how the resulting assessment information can be used to plan teaching and learning activities. This, after all, is the essence of classroom-based assessment.

REFERENCES

Brooks, G. (1994). The assessment of oral language. In D. Wray & J. Medwell (Eds.), *Teaching primary English: The state of the art* (pp. 37-44). London: Routledge.

Cregan, A. (1998). Oral language development: An eye on the revised curriculum. In G. Shiel and U. Ní Dhálaigh (Eds.), *Developing language and literacy: The role of the teacher* (pp. 3-15). Dublin: Reading Association of Ireland.

Gorman, T.P., Purves, A.C., & Degenhart, R.E. (1988). *The IEA study of written composition I: The international writing tasks and scoring scales.* Oxford: Pergamon Press.

Gorman, T.P., White, J., Brooks, G., Maclure, M., & Kispal, A. (1988). *Language performance in schools: A review of the APU Language Monitoring 1979-1983.* London: Department of Education and Science.

Gorman, T.P., White, J., Brooks, G., & English, F. (1991). *Language for learning: A summary report on the 1988 APU survey of language performance.* London: HMSO for SEAC.

Ireland. (1999). *English language primary school curriculum. Content statement.* Dublin: Stationery Office.

Pearson, L., & Quinn, J. (1986). *The Bury Infant Check.* Windsor: NFER-Nelson.

Shiel, G., & Murphy, R. (2000). *Drumcondra English profiles: A framework for assessing oral language, reading and writing in primary schools.* Dublin: Educational Research Centre.

Spelman, B.J., & McHugh, B.A. (1994). *Belfield Infant Assessment Profile: Teacher's handbook and resource manual.* Dublin: Folens.